THE NEW Complete
POODLE

by LYDIA HOPKINS

revised by MACKEY J. IRICK, Jr.

ILLUSTRATED

FIFTH EDITION

SIXTH PRINTING—1976

HOWELL BOOK HOUSE, INC.

730 FIFTH AVENUE · NEW YORK, N.Y. · 10019

Leila

DEDICATION

I dedicate this book to Mrs. Tyndall's beloved Leila, who has played so great a part in the pedigrees of winning Miniature Poodles, and to my own dear Ch. Marcourt Sabot, Leila's worthy descendant and my faithful little friend for so many years.

Library of Congress Catalog Card Number: 68–56175
Printed in the U.S.A.   ISBN 0-87605-255-3

Publisher's Note

THE COMPLETE POODLE by Miss Lydia Hopkins stands as a classic in dog books. Since its first publication in 1951, more copies of it have been sold than of any other breed book published in America.

Miss Hopkins owned and loved dogs all her life, and bred and showed champions in a number of breeds. Her excellent articles were featured in dog magazines for over fifty years—from 1909 until her death in 1965.

Her first kennel included all the Toy breeds, among them many champions. The Sherwood prefix was granted her in 1910. The early Sherwood Pekingese champions were among the first of all English breeding in America, and were so famous that they are included in all the text books on the breed. Miss Hopkins at one time bred Cocker Spaniels, and her chapter in Ella B. Moffit's book on that breed is well-known. Sherwood Hall also played a strong hand in the development of the Cairn Terrier in this country.

Miss Hopkins won early recognition as a judge, too, and in 1915 judged the Pekingese Club of America's Specialty Show, the first American to have this honor.

One of the first to start breeding Miniature Poodles in America, she also had Standards and Toys, the latter from early days. Her Poodles established enviable records both in the show rings and as producers. After ten years of selective breeding, she achieved the so-called impossible, and actually produced several black Toy champions of all Miniature breeding.

Thus few people had as firm a grasp on the subject of Poodles, or as long an experience in breeding, judging, or writing of show dogs. In this book are comprehensive and clear instructions on all the fundamental care of

Poodles, with practical and detailed accounts of rearing, breeding, clipping and show care as well as training.

The book does not stop there, but goes on to give the foundations of the winning strains of Poodles in America. There are interesting tabulations of the male lines in all three varieties that have produced our foremost American champions. There is also an informative chapter on the Poodle in France, written by Princesse Amedee de Broglie of Lamorlaye Kennels fame.

Included in this edition is a new chapter on "Clipping Your Poodle for the Show Ring" by Anne Rogers Clark. Now a highly respected judge, Mrs. Clark was for many years one of the most successful of professional handlers, and along with many other legendary wins three times guided Poodles to Best in Show at Westminster Kennel Club show in Madison Square Garden.

Mackey J. Irick, Jr. brings to his revision of the book a deep reverence for the original work, and a well-qualified background as Poodle breeder and journalist. His interest in purebred dogs started early with Cocker Spaniels, and by high school he was already submitting thoroughly-researched articles on breeding and bloodlines to *Popular Dogs* and *Dog World*. After college and military service, his interest centered on Poodles. His High Heritage kennels has bred or owned 18 Toy Poodle champions to date, and these include a Best in Show and four other Group First winners. In 1955, he founded *The Poodle Review*, and continues as its editor and publisher. In this capacity he came to know Miss Hopkins, and worked together with her on many articles for the magazine.

Chapters 1 through 7, 9 through 13, 16, 19, 26 through 29, 50, 58, and 62 through 68 are by Lydia Hopkins.

Chapters 14, 15, 18, 20 through 23, 25, 30 through 33, 48, 49, 51 through 53, 55 through 57, and 69 are by Miss Hopkins, as revised by Mackey J. Irick, Jr.

Chapters 24, 34 through 36, 38 through 47, 54, and 59 through 61 are by Mr. Irick.

Miss Lydia Hopkins
with her Toy Poodle,
Champion Sherwood Petite Mademoiselle

Foreword

THIS book is intended as a practical guide for those who love the Poodle. In it I have made no effort to treat general theories of breeding, general care of dogs, or illnesses. Such subjects are ably treated elsewhere and do not come within the scope of this book unless they have a definite application to the care and rearing of Poodles.

In regard to the tabulations of the Male Tail Lines which you find here, in an effort to let the known facts speak for themselves, I make no pretense that they are complete. Not only are new champions crowned almost every month, but the older dogs, in some cases, were not connected with line or family up to the time of publication of this book. Such tabulations are, fortunately, growing things to be added to year after year. These data must, therefore, be considered just as a nucleus for future work by persons who may be sufficiently interested.

As far as my knowledge goes, the names of dogs set forth in these tabulations are correct. I have included current English dogs wherever I have known them, but my knowledge of dogs later than those used in the founding of the respective strains is of necessity limited.

My dearest hope is that the facts presented, the methods advanced, and the photographs published here will give my readers as much pleasure as gathering them together has given me.

LYDIA HOPKINS

Foreword to the Fifth Edition

WHEN I first read *The Complete Poodle,* I thought it the best breed book ever published. As my interest in Poodles grew, I continued to study the book, and—at a time when little information on the Poodle was available—found it invaluable.

I started a correspondence with Miss Hopkins, and found her extremely knowledgeable and helpful. When I asked her opinion on starting a monthly Poodle magazine, she was most enthusiastic. She contributed an article for the very first issue of *The Poodle Review,* and followed with many more through the years for as long as her health permitted. I never ceased to be impressed with her brilliance of mind and great knowledge of the breed.

The time has come when it is necessary to bring her book up-to-date, and I am honored to have been asked to do this.

In the foreword to the Fourth Edition in 1964, Miss Hopkins had written:

> "In approaching the revision of this book, I have had several definite goals. First, to bring it up-to-date; second, to correct anything in it that time has proved impractical—or incorrect from today's point of view; third, to add any new discovery of value; fourth, to answer as many of the questions I've been asked since first publication of the book as is possible. In short, to 'round it out,' filling what gaps there are, and to make it as complete as possible. At the same time, I have felt it unwise to change those chapters which have satisfactorily served their purpose, and which have conveyed wanted information clearly.
>
> "The immense amount of work involved has been a labor of love on my part, and my sincere hope is that it will be of value to the breed, and of interest to the readers, to the end that Poodles and those who love them may best be served by this book."

These words have been my guide in this revision. I have made every effort to follow in the spirit of Miss Hopkins' writing throughout the book. Wherever possible, I have used her own words, for they could not be improved upon. I would like to feel that she would be pleased with the results.

MACKEY J. IRICK, JR.

Acknowledgments

I am indebted to Mrs. Sherman Hoyt, whose patient answers to my many queries cover a period of years and whose advice and aid are always ready for those interested in the Poodle; to Mrs. Audrey Tyndall, whose efforts to gather together old records, photographs and other materials in England are invaluable; and to those excellent kennel magazines, *Western Kennel World* and *Popular Dogs,* for their permission to include here parts of articles written by me and previously published by them.

LYDIA HOPKINS

I am indebted to many Poodle owners, breeders and handlers who have so enthusiastically contributed to this revision. I would like to add an especial appreciation to Evelyn Shafer for many of the lovely photographs included in this volume, to Ab Sidewater for his excellent ideas in presentation, and to Nelson Garringer for his invaluable aid and encouragement.

MACKEY J. IRICK, JR.

Contents

"The Traveling Mountebank"—(From a painting by Antonio Rotta).

1

Origin and History

THERE can be no doubt that the Poodle, one of the most intelligent and devoted of all breeds of dogs, is also one of the oldest. Perhaps the most ancient of its varieties is the small white Toy, always a separate branch of the family, called for many hundreds of years the "Petit Barbet." One imagines these little creatures were pet dogs in the breed's beginning, as they are now, and were even more closely associated with family life than their larger brothers.

The first illustrations of Poodles were carved on Roman tombs and other monuments of about A.D. 40, but the first known printed mention of them was made by Conrad Gessner in 1555. Clipped Poodles appear in French, Dutch and Italian paintings as early as 1454, and even earlier in illuminated manuscripts, notably those of the Burgundian House, preserved in the British Museum. The Hon. Mrs. Lytton in her interesting book, *Toy Dogs and Their Ancestors,* included several illustrations of very early Barbets, among them a particularly fine example in a picture by Jacob Da Empoli (1575), and another in a picture by Cima (1470).

The larger Poodles were called by various names, in France and elsewhere, Canis aviarius aquaricus, Grand Barbet, Caniche, Mouton and Moufflon; while the name in the German language is very nearly the same as in English —"Pudel," and there is little doubt that the early English "Water Dog" (not to be confused with the Water Spaniel) was also another branch of the family. Early writers treated the woolly coated Poodles as separate from the corded varieties; Herr von Schmeideberg, an early canine authority, called the woolly coated dogs the Schaaf Pudel (mouton) and the pedigreed

13

Poodle with corded coat, Der Schoner Pudel. While many persons credit Russia with the origin of the corded Poodle, Dr. Friz Inger, another German authority, in his *Hunde und Seine Racen,* states his belief that the Poodle originated in Africa, either in Morocco or in Algiers, and that the corded varieties had a Spanish, Portuguese or Greek origin. In the light of knowledge concerning other African breeds, such as the Saluki and Afghan Hound, which have been bred and preserved practically unchanged in Africa for centuries, it seems unlikely that the Poodle originated in Africa, since no trace of such an indigenous breed exists there today.

Several great authorities, one of whom is Mr. Crouch, whose English kennel of Poodles was famous, do not believe that the corded Poodle is a separate variety. Mr. Crouch states that any Poodle's hair can be corded if handled with enough care. We know that neglected Poodles develop mats of felt which show a cording tendency.

All authorities agree, however, that there were three Continental varieties: the German, the Russian, and the French, and that all three were to be found in small (but not Toy), medium, and large sizes. And certainly the early English "Water Dog" was also a Poodle. With one accord the authorities concur that white, parti-colored, or brown were common colors for ordinary, unpedigreed dogs, but that the aristocrats were black. That the blacks must have been crossed with other colors is evidenced by earlier difficulty in breeding blacks without white on chest or feet. Earlier writers classify the Poodle among the Spaniels.

In *The Museum of Animated Nature,* a book published in London in 1708, the following appears: "The French Poodle may be referred to the Spaniels; it appears to be very closely allied to the rough Water Dog figured by Bewick, the 'Grand Barbet of Buffon.' The rough Water Dog is a most intelligent animal, robustly made in cover and size and strength, but has the same aquatic habits and docility and is much used as a retriever by shooters of water fowl." Dr. Caius, in one of the earliest existing books about dogs, written in 1570 and entitled *Of Englishe Dogges,* describes the Water Dog. Nicholas Cox in his book entitled *The Gentleman's Recreation,* published in the early nineteenth century, devotes much space to the Water Dog and its training, and says of him, "To proceed then, your dog may be of any color yet excellent, but choose him of long hair and curled, not loose or shagged, his head must be round, his ears broad and hanging, his eyes lively and quick, his forelegs straight, his buttocks round and his hindquarters strong, his thighs brawny." William Taplin, in *The Sportsman's Cabinet* published in 1803, says, "The head is round, the ears long, broad and pendulous, his eyes lively and solicitously attracting, his hindquarters round and firm, his pasterns strong and his hair adhering to his body in natural elastic curls, neither loose nor shaggy." John Scott in *The Sports-*

14

man's Repository says, "On the opposite and more Northern parts of the Continent they have Water Dogs like ours, which in truth have a foreign appearance." Youatt in 1845, ". . . laying stress upon his compactness of form, his head is long, his face smooth, his carcass round and his hair long and closely curled." Youatt, like Scott, believed the Water Dog to be imported.

I have quoted these authorities at length to show that it is quite probable that Poodles were imported into England as working and hunting dogs long before they were recognized as a distinct breed and assigned a name. The Irish Water Spaniel, which even today shows a strong resemblance to the Poodle, was undoubtedly descended from it. No official mention of the importation of Poodles, as such, into England is recognized until the Napoleonic Wars in the early part of the nineteenth century.

The difference between the Poodles from the three countries, France, Germany and Russia, is mentioned in many of the earlier books.

In France, where the larger Poodles, or Moutons, were used for draught dogs, as well as for retrievers, truffle hunters, and circus actors, the earlier dogs were sturdy, thick-set animals, with wide skulls, light, round eyes, rather short necks, fairly high set ears, and thick, woolly coats. In comparison with the German dogs, the Caniche (or French Poodles) were, however, slighter in build. Mr. Furness, in his monograph on the breed published in the *American Book of the Dog,* edited by G. O. Shields and published in 1891, describes them as follows: "The skull should show a well defined stop, very broad across the ears and a pronounced dome; the neck should be rather long, the shoulder upright, the barrel well ribbed up, with strong arched loins. The feet should be round and webbed down to the nails. The legs should be long and muscular, the hind ones are usually straighter than those of the German Poodle, thereby giving the dog a proud but stilt action when walking. The coat tightly curled and somewhat woolly in texture." Of course, this description is preposterous as it pertains to the modern Poodle.

The same Mr. Furness evidently prefers the German Poodle for he says he "is really the type of the family and is a powerful, compactly built dog, with deep narrow brisket, in shape not unlike the greyhound, a strong loin, slightly arched, with a good square back, powerful hindquarters to propel him through the water; round compact feet with toes webbed to the nail. The head is wedge shaped; is very broad, and flat between the ears." He is, no doubt, describing the Schoner Pudel of which von Schmeideberg writes, for he goes on to say that the coat cords in long strands.

The Russian Poodle was most like the Greyhound in body type, but with a wiry, springy, curly coat and was higher on the leg, a much slighter dog in bone though larger in size than the French and German dogs. The

"Au Prise Avec Un Butor."

webs between the toes extend only half way. Vero Shaw much prefers the Russian to the other two varieties, saying, "The Russian Poodle proper should be lithe and agile; while coming more into Central Germany the black Poodles seem to be thicker in the legs and have short, slight muzzles, assuming more staid, sturdy and aldermanic proportions." He describes a prize-winning Russian dog named "Posen" as weighing 31 pounds and being 20½ inches high.

We have, then, the three main sources of our modern dogs, differing from each other mainly in coat and in thickness of bone, but there is no doubt that in all three varieties were to be found smaller dogs used more for pets than for sporting purposes.

The foundation of the Miniature Poodles in America and England was laid in the nineties of the last century with importations from France, whether intermixed in their native land or not is unknown. Miss Millie Brunker, one of the greatest and oldest among the English breeders, in an article which appeared in the (English) *Dog World,* stated that the earliest importations of white Miniatures came from France in the nineties, many of them being brought into England on trading vessels and offered for sale.

16

She also states, however, that many of the present-day white Miniatures are of German extraction. There is no doubt that the white Miniatures, at least, are connected with the ancient Petit Barbet breed, and the majority of them still possess the old faults of too round eyes and flying ears. The blacks, blues, and Miniatures of brown breeding are different, for, although they, too, came originally from France, the early dogs were, as I remember them, much larger than those of today and obviously but a slightly smaller edition of the Caniche of the day. And as the little chaps seem to have existed in all three of their native lands, France, Germany and Russia, side by side with the larger Poodles, it took but the cleverness of the English fanciers to fix size, color, and type, which now tend to breed true.

No doubt, remnants of all the various types of bygone Poodles are to be found in our modern show dogs, which still vary as to stature, texture of coat and other items of conformation. And it is interesting to classify them in our minds, but with these differences: modern methods of breeding and the clear and definite printed Standards laid down in England and America, have unified and refined the type to such an extent that show dogs now are comparatively uniform in their structure, and variation is largely confined to size and color.

Ch. Lady Margaret of Belle Glen (by Am. & Can. Ch. Wycliffe Thomas ex Ch. Bridget of Belle Glen), Standard, bred by Isabelle McMullen, owned by Helen Cosden. Best in Show winner.

Ch. Jocelyene Marjorie (by Ch. Wycliffe Virgil ex Mogene's Beauzeaux), Standard, shown going Best of Breed at the 1968 Poodle Club of America Specialty under judge Miss Frances Angela (at left). Mrs. Harold Ringrose, club president, is at right. Owned by Joan S. Wicklander and Freeman Dickey, and shown by Mr. Dickey.

2

Description of the Ideal Poodle

Written for the Author in the Early 1900's
By Miss Millie Brunker

He (the Poodle) is chic from tip to toe. His expression is usually a supercilious and a haughty one—at least for the world in general. The tender, speaking look I know so well is for his mistress only.

His coat is long and so crisply curly that, when combed out (and of course his daily toilet is an affair of grave importance), his head and shoulders are grotesquely large in proportion to his slender, shaven flanks, which are garnished with rosettes to accentuate their grace. His straight, elegant legs are encircled with the neatest of frills around the wrist and ankles.

His ears are long and wide and give him a strangely dignified and judge-like aspect. When he opens his long and narrow jaw, strong white teeth shine within like ivory set in coral. His perky tail is short and ends in a pompon that spells defiance to his enemies. As a rule he is gentleness itself and polite to all men, if a little indifferent to those outside his circle; but he allows no liberties and can hold his own with any dog. His proportions are just right, short in the back but not in the leg, and he moves as freely as a Greyhound. His intelligence is quoted as a proverb, and his reputation is no more than his due, for he can learn a trick as soon as other puppies can walk. He is game, too, and many keepers have been forced to confess that a Poodle may put a trained gun-dog to shame.

But it is at home that my ideal Poodle is known at his best, and in my eyes he has but one fault—he cannot live forever.

As a sportsman the Poodle's keen abilities are unsuspected; as a performing dog he is pre-eminent; as a personal pet, perfection.

(Note: Miss Brunker, long dean of the Poodle fancy of England, owned the famous Whippendell Kennels, the foundation of almost every strain of English Standards or Miniatures, which were of many colors.)

EARS set low: hanging close to head: leather long, wide, heavily feathered

NECK well-proportioned, strong: length to allow head carried high with dignity; skin snug at throat

SHOULDERS strong, muscular: should slope back from point of angulation at upper foreleg to withers. Back short, strong, slightly hollowed (bitches may be slightly longer than dogs); loins short, broad, muscular

TAIL straight: rather high set: length sufficient to insure balance: carriage up-gay

THIGHS well-developed, muscular: width in stifle region

STIFLES well-bent

HINDLEGS very muscular: turning neither in nor out

HOCKS well-let-down

CLIPS: "Puppy Clip" for Poodles under one year of age. "Continental" or "English Saddle" for dogs over one year of age

COAT dense throughout: profuse: texture harsh

SIZE determines 3 varieties: STANDARD. over 15" at withers: MINIATURE. over 10" (to 15") at withers. TOY. 10" or under at withers

SKULL moderately rounded

STOP slight but definite

EYES set far apart: very dark: oval appearance

NOSE sharp: nostrils well-defined: color (see COLOR)

MUZZLE long, straight, fine; slight chiseling under eyes: strong without lippiness; chin definite enough to preclude snippiness. Teeth white, strong: scissors bite

CHEEKS: Bones, muscles flat

CHEST deep, moderately wide

FORELEGS straight from shoulder: parallel: bone and muscle in proportion to size

COLOR even, solid at skin: in blues, grays, silvers, browns, cafe-au-laits, apricots, creams, coats may show varying shades of same color (ears, ruff, etc.): clear colors preferred. Browns, cafe-au-laits—liver-colored noses, eye rims, lips, dark toenails, dark amber eyes. Black, blue, gray, silver, apricot, cream, white Poodles—black noses, eye rims, lips, black or self-colored toenails, very dark eyes. Apricots—black preferred: liver-colored noses, eye rims, lips, self-colored toenails, amber eyes permitted

DISQUALIFICATIONS: Parti-colors where coat is not even solid color at skin but variegated in patches of two or more colors. Only specified clips allowed in show ring: only specified sizes for each variety permitted

RIBS well-sprung: braced up

PASTERNS strong

FEET rather small: oval: turning neither in nor out: toes arched, close: pads hard, thick, well-cushioned

Visualization of the Poodle standard. (Courtesy, *Popular Dogs*.)

3

The Poodle Standard

General Appearance, Carriage and Condition—That of a very active, intelligent and elegant-appearing dog, squarely built, well proportioned, moving soundly and carrying himself proudly. Properly clipped in the traditional fashion and carefully groomed, the Poodle has about him an air of distinction and dignity peculiar to himself.

Head and Expression—(a) *Skull*—Moderately rounded, with a slight but definite stop. Cheekbones and muscles flat. (b) *Muzzle*—Long, straight and fine, with slight chiseling under the eyes. Strong without lippiness. The chin definite enough to preclude snipiness. Teeth white, strong and with a scissors bite (c) *Eyes*—Set far apart, very dark, oval in appearance and showing alert intelligence. (d) *Ears*—Hanging close to the head, set at or slightly below eye level. The ear leather is long, wide, and thickly feathered, but the ear fringe should not be of excessive length.

Neck and Shoulders—Neck well proportioned, strong and long enough to permit the head to be carried high and with dignity. Skin snug at throat. The neck rises from strong, smoothly muscled shoulders. The shoulder blade is well laid back and approximately the same length as the upper foreleg.

Body—The chest deep and moderately wide with well-sprung ribs. The back short, strong and slightly hollowed; the loins short, broad and muscular. Length of body and height at shoulder are in such proportion as to insure the desirable squarely built appearance.

Tail—Straight, set on high and carried up, docked, but sufficient in length to insure a balanced outline.

Legs—The forelegs are straight and parallel when viewed from the front. When viewed from the side with a leg vertical, the elbow is directly below the highest point of the shoulder blade. The hind legs are muscular with width in the region of the stifles. The pasterns are strong and the stifles well bent. The length of the leg from the stifle joint to the hock joint is considerably greater than the length from the hock joint to the foot.

Feet—The feet are rather small, oval in shape with toes well arched and cushioned on thick firm pads. Nails short but not excessively shortened. The feet turn neither in nor out. Dewclaws may be removed.

Coat—*Quality*—Of naturally harsh texture, profuse and dense throughout.

Clip—A Poodle may be shown in the "Puppy" clip or the "English Saddle" clip or the traditional "Continental" clip. A Poodle shown in any other type of clip shall be disqualified.

A Poodle under a year old may be shown in the "Puppy" clip with the coat long. The face, throat, feet and base of the tail are shaved. The entire shaven foot is visible. There is a pompon on the end of the tail. In order to give a neat appearance, a slight shaping of the coat is permissible; however, a Poodle in "Puppy" clip that is excessively scissored shall be dismissed.

Dogs one year old or older must be shown in either the "English Saddle" clip or the "Continental" clip.

In the "English Saddle" clip the face, throat, feet, forelegs and base of the tail are shaved, leaving puffs on the forelegs and a pompon on the end of the tail. The hindquarters are covered with a short blanket of hair except for a curved shaved area on each flank and two shaved bands on each hind leg. The entire shaven foot and a portion of the shaven leg above the puff are visible. The rest of the body is left in full coat but may be shaped in order to insure over-all balance.

In the "Continental" clip the face, throat, feet and base of the tail are shaved. The hindquarters are shaved with pompons (optional) on the hips. The legs are shaved, leaving bracelets on the hind legs and puffs on the forelegs. There is a pompon on the end of the tail. The entire shaven foot and portion of the shaven foreleg above the puff are visible. The rest of the body is left in full coat but may be shaped in order to insure over-all balance.

In all clips the hair of the topknot may be held in place by an elastic band or barrette. The hair is only of sufficient length to present a smooth outline.

Color—The coat is an even and solid color at the skin. In blues, grays, silvers, browns, cafe-au-laits, apricots, and creams the coat may show varying shades of the same color. This is frequently present in the somewhat darker feathering of the ears and in the tipping of the ruff. While clear colors are definitely preferred, such natural variation in the shading of the coat is not to be considered a fault. Brown and cafe-au-lait Poodles have liver-colored noses, eye rims and lips, dark toenails and dark amber eyes. Black, blue, gray, silver, cream and white Poodles have black noses, eye rims and lips, black or self-colored toenails and very dark eyes. In the apricots while the foregoing coloring is preferred, liver-colored noses, eye rims and lips, and amber eyes are permitted but are not desirable.

22

Parti-colored dogs shall be disqualified. The coat of a parti-colored dog is not an even solid color at the skin but is of two or more colors.

Gait—A straightforward trot with light springy action and strong hindquarter drive. Head and tail carried high. Forelegs and hind legs move parallel turning neither in nor out. Sound movement is essential.

SIZE

Standard—The Standard Poodle is over 15 inches at the highest point of the shoulders. Any Poodle which is 15 inches or less in height shall be disqualified from competition as a Standard Poodle.

Miniature—The Miniature Poodle is 15 inches or under at the highest point of the shoulders, with a minimum height in excess of 10 inches. Any Poodle which is over 15 inches or 10 inches or less at the highest point of the shoulders shall be disqualified from competition as a Miniature Poodle.

Toy—The Toy Poodle is 10 inches or under at the highest point of the shoulders. Any Poodle which is more than 10 inches at the highest point of the shoulders shall be disqualified from competition as a Toy Poodle.

VALUE OF POINTS

General appearance, temperament, carriage and condition 30	Body, neck, legs, feet and tail .. 20
	Gait 20
Head, expression, ears, eyes, and teeth 20	Coat, color and texture 10

MAJOR FAULTS

Eyes—Round in appearance, protruding, large or very light.
Jaws—Undershot, overshot or wry mouth.
Feet—Flat or spread.
Tail—Set low, curled or carried over the back.
Hindquarters—Cowhocks.
Temperament—Shyness or sharpness.

DISQUALIFICATIONS

Clip—*A dog in any type of clip other than those listed under "Coat" shall be disqualified.*

Parti-colors— *The coat of a parti-colored dog is not an even solid color at the skin but is of two or more colors. Parti-colored dogs shall be disqualified.*

Size—*A dog over or under the height limits specified under "Size" shall be disqualified.*

Approved November 10, 1970

Good front.

Poor front —
too narrow.

Poor front —
out at elbow.

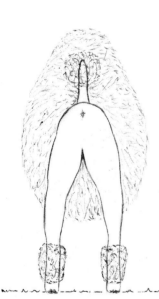

Good rear.

Poor rear —
cowhocked.

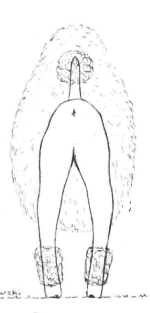

Poor rear —
bandy-legged.

4

Blueprint of the Poodle

HEAD

IN many cases too little attention is paid by both our judges and breeders to refinement of head in all three varieties of Poodles. There seems to be some difference of opinion among judges as to just what is the best type of head.

Perhaps the best single word to use in describing the head and the general impression of it is "lean." This is sometimes mistakenly interpreted to mean snipey and too pointed. There should be a reasonable width of skull, described in the Standard as "moderately rounded," and it should by no means be flat but should have a "moderate peak." The eyes should not be too close together either, and the foreface should be in proportion to the topskull and both as long as possible, with a beautiful clean outline and enough underjaw to preclude any underbalanced, too snipey finish. There should be a slight molding under the rather wide set eyes, but the molding should never be too deep or accentuated. The length of head between ear and corner of eye is, in the best heads, usually almost as great as that from eye to end of muzzle. The ear leather should be more or less fan shaped and set on the head at the level of the eye or lower, but never higher. When drawn forward, the ear leather—not fringe—should be long enough to reach the tip of the nose or beyond.

Poodle eyes should be as dark as it is possible to breed them. They should range in color from very dark hazel to black in black dogs and be definitely several shades darker than the dog's coat in the dilute colors of brown, apricot, or cream. There is room for improvement in eye color all along the line. The shape of the eyes is very important, also, as dark oval eyes have a great deal to do with correct Poodle expression. The two most common incorrect eye shapes are round (found in Toys and some Miniatures), and a rarer but much more unpleasant formation, the slit or buttonhole shape of the eyes. The latter occurs most often in the white Miniatures or in the Toys that are of mixed Toy and Miniature breeding. Usually the Toy breeders struggling with the too round Toy eyes regard these too small, slit-shaped eyes as an improvement, but they are, to my mind, worse and more untypical than the original fault of roundness.

There are three kinds of incorrect heads in Poodles. One, the commonest, is undoubtedly ancestral. In it the skull is very broad and flat, with the ears set on a level with the skull and very short of leather, sometimes described as "flying." The eyes are very round and sometimes very light in color. The modeling under the eyes is deep and accented. The muzzle is short and pointed with weak underjaw. The whole head in such a dog presents a wedge-shaped appearance. This was undoubtedly the head of the earlier dogs, and every now and then it crops up again.

The second incorrect type is a head that is too narrow throughout, snipey and needle-like in general appearance. In this type of head the eyes are often slitty and there is no modeling under the eyes whatever. The whole head, and usually the dog that goes with it, lacks substance and balance and has a sly, ferrety appearance. It is to be found in some silver strains and at times in the third and fourth generations of Toy and Miniature breeding.

The third, but fortunately not too common, incorrect head type is one of general thickness and coarseness all over. Its most prominent feature is a too thick muzzle inclined toward lippiness and, in some cases, the upper lips hang over like those of the sporting dogs, such as Cockers or Setters. With this type usually appear too large a nose and wide round nostrils.

There is nothing more beautiful in all dogdom than a beautiful Poodle head, with its clean-cut, lovely outline. And there is nothing lovelier than the soft, intelligent expression of a Poodle's eyes. But in order to achieve this beauty the head must be correctly constructed. A thick, flat skull or snipey muzzle is not beautiful. Light eyes give the dog either a shallow, vapid expression, or, if they are orange tinted, a hard, hawk-like look that is most unpleasant and unattractive.

The time to catch such faults is when they first appear, perhaps merely as a tendency. And, of course, the real fancier must develop an accurate and critical eye in order to see these faults before they become stamped on a strain, and he must set himself on guard to avoid them in his breeding. Line MA is unquestionably the best headed line in Miniatures, and Standards have lines equally as good in head type.

SIZE

All things being equal, size should not be stressed if the dog is definitely within the prescribed limit of its variety. That is, 10 inches or under for Toys, 15 inches or under for Miniatures, and over 15 inches for Standards. But it is not at all uncommon for judges frankly to state that they do not like a small dog or a large one—"Some like 'em hot, some like 'em cold"; but personal likes or dislikes have no place in the show ring, and those persons who express them in their awards have no right to be judging.

One thing and one thing only is what should count—Poodle type. If the largest dog in the ring (always granted that it is within the specified limit of height) is the best Poodle that day, it should win, and if its smallest competitor is a better Poodle, it should win.

It is time Poodle breeders and exhibitors stood by their guns and demanded from judges something more valid than a personal preference for size for the defeat of a good, honest, typical dog. As far as Miniatures and Toys are concerned, diminutiveness is a deciding factor only when all other points are equal. But suppose the smallest is also the best Poodle, point by point? Nothing in the Standard indicates that it should not win over a less perfect larger dog; nor should a good Poodle of Standard size go down to defeat to a less perfect Poodle of small or medium size. It is time that first things came first, and certainly Poodle type should have first consideration in the show ring.

STRUCTURAL SOUNDNESS

Structural soundness covers shoulders, legs, feet, hindquarters, back line, and chest, and without it no Poodle of whatever size can boast show quality and that sound, fluid beauty of movement that the printed Standard requires.

Neck and shoulders are covered up by the thickest and longest hair and therefore are often ignored by breeder and judge alike. But without sound, sloping shoulders the front is often faulty in placement and, therefore, in action. The neck should be long enough to insure that proud carriage of head so necessary in a show dog. It ought not to be forgotten that the Poodle was a retriever in the beginning and had to have a long neck and neck muscles strong enough to enable it to carry a heavy bird, like a goose or duck. I have said elsewhere that I thought the study of a really good Cocker trimmed for show would be of value to the average Poodle breeder in this respect, and, incidentally, for the shape and placement of ear leathers as well. Many Poodles have short, thick necks and a great many Miniatures have straight shoulders and wide fronts. These faults can be eliminated by the selection of soundly constructed Poodles as mates for dogs with such defects. Naturally, however, a fault must first be recognized before it can be corrected. A common Toy fault is for the front legs to turn incorrectly outward at the wrist or pastern joint.

Hindquarters, being clipped, are easier to see and ought therefore to be studied more often than they are. Straight hocks were a feature of some of the earlier Caniche. Also, in some strains of Miniatures there exist well bent hocks weak in the hock joint, and therefore unsound. The hindquarters should be extremely powerful, strong, well muscled, properly let down, and curved at the hock. Again, it ought to be remembered that all the early descriptions of the Poodle as a hunting dog stressed this as being very important in his activities in the water. All sorts of unsound actions behind are to be found, ranging from actual cowhocks to legs set too close together and interfering when the dog is in action, to legs that straddle too widely behind or are thrown forward too much. There is a formation quite common in Toys and in some strains of Miniatures that can aptly be described by the term "Chippendale," as the legs are exactly like the legs of a Chippendale chair, all of which makes for extremely awkward and unsound action. It goes without saying that no dog with any of these faults of construction, front or back, can move evenly or soundly with the feet following one another in unison like the wheels of a locomotive. The waddling front action of a Poodle with too wide a front throws its hindquarters out of gear as well. The unsound movement behind makes the front action peculiar. In short, to move correctly and soundly a Poodle must be soundly constructed both in shoulder and front as well as behind. It is correct structural conformation that makes a Poodle a good Poodle, while poor construction makes a Poodle a poor Poodle.

Feet are also important, and the spring of gait is, I believe, strongly affected by good, highly arched, tight feet with thick pads.

The straightness and strength of the back line is also of great importance in the general picture of soundness. Crooked or curved spines are due to weakness and dogs having such faults should not be bred from. The back should be as short as possible.

The chest is another important point, and depth of chest is often lacking. It should not, however, be overly wide, another fault often met with.

I cannot emphasize enough the importance of good structure, for our Poodle is no mere bundle of fur on just any kind of legs but is a sound, healthy sportsman and this should be exhibited in his action.

28

Ch. Montmartre Marlaine (by Montmartre Ring-Master ex Montmartre Mme. Pompadour), black Toy import, shown going Best of Variety at 1968 Poodle Club of America Specialty under Mrs. George Dow. Owned by Mr. and Mrs. A. C. Pearson, handled by Richard Bauer.

COAT

Coat, color and texture, count only 10 points in the Standard, but in general practice and under many judges, count almost one hundred percent. Thus, many Poodles of poor type and many with highly unsound structure have gained the title of champion on the strength of length of coat alone. This, of course, is of great detriment to the breed and to Poodle type. Also, if a Poodle must have an enormous jacket to win, then a sensational youngster teeming with type must automatically go down to older dogs of poorer type, because to be in full bloom (if not conditioned by injurious and artificial means) a dog must be at least three to four years old. It is rare that we find a voluminous coat on a young Poodle. A good coat alone does not make a good Poodle. On the contrary, it very often covers up a multitude of faults.

Of course, a Poodle on exhibition at a show should have plenty of glistening, stand-off coat, about six or more inches long. That comes rightfully under the head of "show condition." But as between a very typical Poodle in just such condition and another with serious structural defects and general lack of type but with a huge coat, no judge should hesitate to award the prize to the better type with moderate coat.

Also, much too little attention is given to coat texture, which should always come before mere length. A silky, woolly type of coat which is like thick plush is not a good coat no matter how long and profuse it may be. Coats of such texture are never to be encouraged.

29

In order to get thick, long coats of the proper curly, stiffish texture, Poodles must be bred from those strains that carry coats of this kind. Some strains are noted for coats that are profuse; others are not. Some strains have profuse coats of the wrong texture, others of fairly good texture, and still others have profuse coats of the correct texture. The proper coat is of great beauty and in some dogs has somewhat the look and feel of glistening spun glass. These are the characteristics of good texture: the coat, particularly in babyhood, is distinctly curly and always has a wave in it; the saddle curls tightly without any treatment except application of water, or a bath; the bracelets are thick and even and never look ragged or uneven. The ruff, when trimmed, is as even and as thick as a well grown hedge; it never parts. Another delightful thing about this sort of coat is that it seldom tangles, and whatever normal loose hair there is lies in the coat without making mats and is very easily brushed out so that the dog at maturity can be kept in perfect bloom with a minimum of work.

Coat color is another point, to my mind, of great importance. Blacks should be inky black, and the healthy coat should glisten. This is only accomplished by breeding black to black for many generations with no blue or silver blood whatever. Black dogs touched up by artificial means always have the dead appearance of charcoal without any of the natural highlights in their hair, whereas on a black that is naturally and soundly black, the coat has natural sparkle and life.

Ch. Edris Bet-A-Million (by Ch. Loramar's Banner ex Queens-court Sashay), black Miniature, owned by Priscilla Richardson. Group winner. Sire of many champions.

Ch. Round Table Loramar's Yeoman (by Ch. Round Table Cognac ex Loramar Quivala), white Miniature, shown going Best of Variety at 1968 Poodle Club of America Specialty under Mrs. Robert Sturm. Owned by Round Table Kennels, handled by John Brennan.

Blacks of unsound color are the result of too much intermixture of the colors and are very unattractive. Unsound blues with brown tinges, and dull, dark, unattractive steels and grizzled combinations are also the result of mixing black with silver. Another grave disadvantage is the fact that some dogs change colors at the most inconvenient time, and it takes six months or a year to clear properly. This is all very discouraging and gravely to be condemned.

There are few purebred silver strains in America and practically no lines that have been purely bred for such color as far as six generations. And the same statement applies to the blacks. The English breeders are even worse offenders along these lines than we Americans, as a glance at almost any English pedigree will show you if you have a knowledge of the dogs in it. Of course, there are a few exceptions, but they are very few and far between. French and German breeders breed much truer to color.

But, if this is the state of things at the time of writing, there is no reason why it should continue to be so. Ambitious breeders of today can start to remedy it by consistently sticking to color, and in time there will be invaluable color-bred strains. I know it can be done, as I started in like everybody else with a line of mixed silver and black. However, I bred black to black for generation after generation and eventually obtained Poodles with the soundest inky black coats. And they retained the sound color all their lives.

31

Ch. Alekai Marlaine (by Ch. Alekai Kila ex Ch. Davdon Captivation), Standard, shown going First in the Non-Sporting Group at 1967 Westminster Kennel Club show under Melbourne Downing, handled by Wendell J. Sammet. Owned by Alekai Kennels.

5

Grooming

GROOMING is such an important part of a Poodle's life that he should become accustomed to it in very early puppyhood, taught to lie on his side in the proper position and be brushed and combed for a minute or two every day just as soon as he begins to toddle. Poodle puppies are smart little beggars and very soon learn just what you want them to do.

If possible, older dogs should be groomed every day; if it is not possible every day, then just as often as it can be managed, for grooming not only removes the dead hair before it has a chance to mat, but it also stimulates the growth of new hair and is of general benefit to the dog's health and comfort. It must be remembered that Poodles do not shed their hair like other breeds but that dead hair remains in their coats and must be taken out.

The proper position for the dog being groomed is on its side, feet toward the workman. Groom the hair in layers from the stomach to the spine, then turn the dog, still with its feet toward you, and do the other side. The chest is done with the dog sitting up, as are the topknot and ears. Great care must be taken to part the hair with the brush clear down to the skin. I brush first the lower hair of the part, then the top hair in the opposite direction, and then I start another part about half an inch above the last parting, and so on up to the middle of the back, turn and start on the stomach on the opposite side.

Most experts are very much opposed to the use of the comb except for finishing after the hair is free of tangles and on the ears and the brow. The "tug and tear" methods of using the comb and brush, practiced by many rough-and-ready Poodle owners, is looked upon with horror by expert

Ch. Round Table Cognac (by Ch. Round Table Conte Blanc ex Surrey Dancer of Round Table), Miniature. Winner of many Bests in Show. Sire of champions. Bred and owned by Round Table Kennels.

groomers who will take an hour, if necessary, to get out one knot. The best way to avoid knots is to groom regularly, but when a dog is losing its coat it may tangle over night. With patience, tangles can be removed so that only the knot comes away without damage to the surrounding hair. To remove a tangle, start at the bottom and gently pull apart the hair until it is thoroughly separated, then brush out the loose hairs. Never start pulling tangles apart from the top, as this breaks the good hair and does not get to the bottom of the trouble. I may say right now that unless you are very gentle your Poodle will not lie dreamily and happily while you yank at his coat. No matter how well trained he may be, there is a limit to his patience, which is great. And just try to groom an uncooperative dog, wiggling and fussing, and see how far you get.

All creatures with hair, including ourselves, have just so many hair follicles, and a live hair and a dead one cannot exist in the same cell. So do not try to keep dead hair in. It is what my old hairdresser called "perished hair" and frequent gentle brushing will work it out before it makes trouble and will give the new hair a chance to grow. If, in this way, the shedding can be kept continuous and gradual, it will prevent the dog from suddenly getting rid of all his coat at once, which is disaster in a show dog.

There are several schools of thought regarding brushes. Some persons like the wire ones with a cushioned rubber base, but I have found that if these are too stiff they tear out the coat, and I prefer them for use in finishing off the surface only, after the coat has been well brushed. I prefer a brush designed for humans' hair, with rather long and pliable bristles and made on a curve so that one can, with a twist of the wrist, make a sweeping motion which penetrates right to the skin. These brushes used to be called "bristle combs" and were made of hog bristles, but they are now put out under various trade names and are made of nylon. A good brush that is stiffish but pliable is the best investment a Poodle owner can make, and, if easily washed without softening, goes a long way toward a good job of grooming.

Metal combs with a coarse to medium space between the teeth last longer, but great care must be taken to see that they are not too rough between the teeth or on the edges because this can do untold damage to a coat that is full. Lacking anything else, I use a good, smooth comb with wide teeth made for humans. Combs with bent teeth or with wide gaps in them should immediately be discarded, as they, too, can do a lot of tearing and damage.

Some Poodle groomers like to dampen the coat with lotions and what-not before working on it and have great faith in "this" or "that" tonic; if not too

Am. & Can. Ch. Loramar's I'm A Dandee (by Ch. Challendon Ivy League ex Loramar's Pixie), brown Toy. Winner of 85 Bests in Show. Sire of champions. Owned by Mr. and Mrs. Robert D. Levy.

drying, they do no harm. I have found plain soft water good, for, after all, there is no better tonic for the hair than old fashioned elbow grease. If you use a lotion, sponge it on with a washcloth, rub it briskly with a crash towel and brush the damp hair dry.

In the summer the hair sometimes appears very dry and the application of a very small quantity of cocoanut oil to the skin in the parts you make between the hair in grooming will lubricate the skin, and the spraying of some very light oil into the coat itself is of benefit, if it is brushed through the hair as you groom.

The final touch is to tie up the topknot. Many fanciers use an elastic band for this purpose, but I have found that unless this is put on very carefully it has a tendency to cut the hair and tangle with it and, if used at all, should be carefully cut out rather than untangled. I prefer a soft piece of cotton string or worsted, which is soft and does not injure the hair. If the hair is long enough, I divide it into strands, tying the cotton firmly at the base of the middle strand and using the ends in the two side ones. I then braid the hair like a Topsy pigtail and knot the two ends of cotton at the end of the braid. This pigtail must be unbraided and carefully brushed straight every time the dog is groomed; otherwise it, too, will tangle. If it does tangle, cut the cotton and do not attempt to tear the snarl out. I am old fashioned enough to like ribbons for dress occasions but always use barrettes for the shows. Something should always be used, since no dog can be at its best with hair in its face, which prevents its seeing the world and, even worse, weakens its eyes.

The care of the toenails is an important part of the dog's toilet, and nails should be cut regularly. This improves and neatens the appearance of the dog's feet and helps to tighten them up. Neglected nails may have a bad effect on the dog's posture and action. They should be cut just a trifle outside the curve. Take very little off at a time and be careful not to cut as far as the quick. If, by any chance, the quick is injured and the nail bleeds, apply saccrinate of iron, or any other of the remedies for bleeding, and press it into the cut firmly with your finger, holding it tightly for a minute or so, and no great damage will be done. The oftener you cut the nails, the further back the quick recedes, so that in the end it is possible to keep the nails quite short without reaching the quick at all or causing the dog any pain. Various clippers for dogs' nails are made; Spratt's puts out an excellent one which operates like a scissors, and the Resco Tool works like a small guillotine. Nail clipping is something most dogs detest, but a Poodle should be made accustomed to it early in life and should be made to understand that it is not punishment and that he will not be hurt in the process. Especial care should be used to maintain the dog's confidence, since a single injury to the sensitive quick of a nail may so terrify a dog that he will for the rest of his life resent, and even fight against, having his nails cut or his feet handled. From the first

36

manicure in the nest to keep a puppy from scratching his mother's breasts to a regular clipping all through puppyhood, so that he learns to accept the trimming of his nails, the Poodle should be shielded from indignity and injury.

A Poodle's teeth should be kept free from tartar. Use a small dental scaler and operate from under the gum downward, using your unfortunate thumb as a buffer between the sharp scaler and the lips and gums below. Boil or thoroughly disinfect the scaler before using it, and keep it oiled and free from rust. A damp rag wound around your finger and dipped in powdered pumice may be used to keep the teeth clean between scalings. After working in the dog's mouth in any way be sure to swab the gum thoroughly with cotton wrapped around a matchstick, or one of the swabs such as come already made up for babies, and dipped into tincture of iodine. The feeding of hard biscuits or the large, raw bones of beef will help to keep the teeth clean.

Carefully examine the insides of the Poodle's ears at every grooming and gently clean them out with a piece of absorbent cotton, dusting into the orifice a small amount of boracic acid powder afterwards. However, unless there is some definite trouble, do not poke around in the ears, and in the event of trouble it is best to consult your veterinarian.

Eng. Am. & Can. Ch. Tophill Orsino (by Am. & Can. Tophill Topflite ex Anngay Honeysuckle), Miniature. Best in Show winner in England and Canada. Owned by Mr. and Mrs. Robert Osborne.

Mr. Sherman Hoyt puts the finishing touches on Ch. Blakeen Jung Frau.

6

Bathing

A GREAT many Poodle fanciers and handlers believe that a Poodle's bath should be a semiannual event, and it is true that, for show dogs and pets that have daily grooming and care, not much bathing is necessary. However, in a kennel, the rank and file are different. It is a fact that a bath with soap temporarily softens the coat considerably and that, carelessly given, it can easily wreck a heavy coat. But there comes a time, even in the lives of well groomed dogs, when a bath is absolutely necessary.

First of all the preparation for a bath is essential. Your Poodle must be very carefully groomed and every tangle or knot teased out of his coat before bathing him. The brisk lathering and toweling—and it should be brisk—will increase mats a hundredfold and it is quite impossible thoroughly to rinse tangles. They remain sticky and make more trouble than ever. The bath will cause new tangles as rubbing loosens the dead hairs, but these newly freed hairs are easy to remove.

Soap is a most important item and should be of the best quality and mild, for it is wise always to remember that a dog's skin is much more delicate than our own. Any really good toilet soap will do, and I have used various kinds, from the soap I myself happen to be using at the time, to my old standby— Packer's Tar Soap—tincture of green soap, crown saddle soap and various shampoos used by humans, all of which, while they got the dog nice and clean, softened the coat somewhat. The best, I found, was one that had a sulphur preparation in it that had a harshening effect upon the hair. I have found most so-called flea soaps and others with disinfectants in them to be too irritating, and any good lather will get rid of fleas. Many dogs are allergic

Ch. Blakeen King Doodles, winner of thirty Best in Show awards, owned by Mrs. Robert D. Levy, Lime Crest Kennels.

to detergents, so I take no risks and now use only mild soap with a vinegar rinse. Before starting the bath, I always put a drop of castor oil or plain vaseline in both the dog's eyes so that if any soap gets in them by accident they are protected. First, the dog is wetted all over with tepid water and then soap is well rubbed into the coat and massaged for some minutes.

Rinsing is much more important than soaping, and at least five applications of clear water are required. In hard water I always use one vinegar rinse, afterwards giving the dog a final dousing with clear tepid water. Care must be taken not to have the water too hot or too cold. Special attention must be given the frills on the dog's legs, for if they stand in the rinse waters these do not get thoroughly attended to and remain full of soap and dirt. I often rinse them separately in a basin to be sure of getting them clean. Great care must be taken to avoid getting water in the dog's ears.

Now I let the dog shake out the extra water left in the coat and then I rub the dog rather roughly with a crash towel to start the circulation going. In summer the dog may go out in the hot sun until the hair has dried somewhat,

40

but I start to groom it while it is still rather damp, but not, of course, wet. In the winter I always use an electric hair dryer of the old fashioned goose neck type that used to be seen in hairdressing shops or, if the dog is a pet, one of the small hand dryers does very well. Be certain that the chest is perfectly dry. Now groom your dog as usual, and by doing this while the hair is still damp you can train it the way you want it to go.

After drying the ear flaps and inside the ear very gently with a towel, I use a cotton swab in all the corners and down the canal very gently and change the cotton until whatever moisture there may be in the ear is absorbed. Then I dust in dry boracic acid powder to further dry and disinfect the canal. Everything about the ear must be handled slowly and gently, of course, for carelessness in the manipulation of ears has caused many a bad canker, to which malady Poodles are, as a breed, somewhat disposed.

In cold weather a Poodle should be kept in a warm place for some twelve to twenty-four hours after a bath, gradually allowing the air to cool to the temperature he is accustomed to, but in the summer this precaution is not necessary.

Eng. & Am. Ch. Frederick of Rencroft (by Alistair of Eldonwood ex Ronlyn's Cassandra of Rencroft), black Miniature import. Top winning dog in America, all breeds, for 1966. Owned by Mr. Joe Glaser. Handled by Frank T. Sabella.

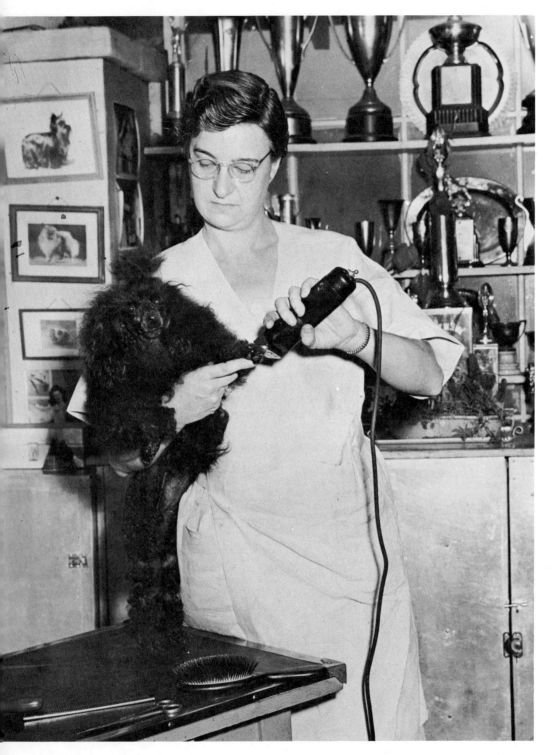

Miss Violet Boucher of Hollywood, California, noted Poodle clipper puts the finishing touches on Ch. Sherwood Vest Pocket Edition's tiny feet.

7

Clipping the Poodle

There are many different kinds of clips: three accepted by all Poodle clubs, including the Poodle Club of America, and many others that are not countenanced and that constitute a disqualification for the show ring.

Before I go into a description of the various clips and the correct way to produce them, let me explain why two of the unorthodox clips are frowned upon by those with the breed's best interests at heart. This disqualification of dogs unconventionally clipped is no arbitrary decision made without rhyme or reason, but one with a very definite purpose behind it. Both the so-called Dutch Clip and the Kerry Blue Clip destroy the line of face and neck and, if persisted in by breeders, would soon make the breeding of good Poodle heads a thing of the past. Naturally, those fanciers who have worked for generations to produce the lean skull, long foreface and other attributes of the correct Poodle head feel that the loss of these features to the breed would be so serious that they will not encourage anything which would ultimately lead to the neglect of head properties which are now deemed correct and essential to Poodle excellence.

There are only three clips that are acceptable for the show ring. The first of these is the "Puppy" Clip. A Poodle under a year of age may be shown in the Puppy Clip with the coat long except for the face, feet and base of tail, which should be shaved. To make the coat even, a slight amount of scissoring is allowed to cut off any straggly hairs. Dogs one year old or older must be shown in either the "English Saddle" Clip or "Continental" Clip.

In the "English Saddle" Clip the hindquarters are covered with a short blanket of hair except for a curved area on the flank and two shaved bands

43

English Saddle clip.

on each hindleg. The face, forelegs and tail are shaved, leaving puffs on the forelegs and a pompon at the end of the tail. The rest of the body must be left in full coat.

In the "Continental" Clip the hindquarters are shaved with pompons on hips (optional). The face, feet, legs and tail are shaved leaving bracelets

Continental clip.

Kennel clip.

on the hindlegs, puffs on the forelegs and a pompon at the end of the tail. The rest of the body must be left in full coat.

One of the most popular of the trims not allowed in the show ring is the "Kennel" or "Sporting" clip. This clip is similar to the "Puppy" Clip but the coat is clipped closer to the neck and body and the legs are left less full.

Dutch clip.

The shorter coat requires less attention and brushing and detracts nothing from a good Poodle's beauty. Actually, it is easier to study your Poodle's conformation in this clip.

Another popular trim with pet owners is the Dutch Clip. In it, the head is clipped, leaving a moustache on the end of the nose, and the ears are clipped, leaving only a fringe at the bottom. The topknot is rounded sometimes to a ball. The chest, stomach and back of the dog are clipped, leaving the long hair on all four legs either squared off about four inches above the elbows or coming to a point higher up like a raglan sleeve. Feet and tail are clipped.

General hints regarding clipping are these: never force the clippers, because to do so scrapes the skin and injures it, and do not attempt to stretch the skin too tight for the same reason. I always touch small cuts or scrapes with tincture of metaphen, if they show. It is sometimes impossible to avoid them with restless puppies. I have found that colored Poodles, whites, grays and browns, have more sensitive skins than do the blacks, and that a dog that is regularly clipped does not scrape as easily as one left unclipped for a long while. Sores made by scraping seem to develop a fungus, and so are best treated with a fungicide.

For puppies or dogs unused to clipping, the No. 10 or No. 15 Oster Clipper blade is best and safest. Older dogs can take a closer clip.

After clipping, all the clipped parts should be well rubbed with some soothing and antiseptic lubricant. This keeps the skin smooth and pliable.

Since all of us use the Oster Electric Animal Clipper and it is so much a part of the Poodle lover's equipment, a word about its care will perhaps be of value. After each dog clipped, I run my clippers in two cups of automobile motor oil to which I add two teaspoonfuls of Oil of Cresol (Merc.). This not only cleans the blades, removing most of the short hairs, but it also lubricates and preserves the clippers, and the disinfectant prevents the passing of any infection from dog to dog. If the blades still have hair between them, I clean them out with a razor blade. Clippers must be oiled and greased inside regularly and in using them care must be taken not to drop them. If you can afford it, it is a great convenience to have a number of heads for clippers. They can be changed in the midst of clipping if they get too hot, and whatever size blade you choose to use is always ready. The blades should be changed rather often, since a dull blade pulls the hair and tends to leave the coat ragged. The small carbon brushes and springs wear out quickly in an old clipper, making the machine rattle when it is run; as they are easily replaced by unscrewing the small knobs on the side of the machine, these extra parts should be always on hand.

8

Clipping the Poodle
for the Show Ring

By

Anne Rogers Clark

WITH your dog sitting securely on a firm, rubber-topped or towel-spread table, begin with the front feet. Clip up to where the dew claw is or was, using a #00 or #40 blade. Put a finger underneath each toe, one by one, to spread the foot for careful and meticulous clipping. When the feet are neat and clean, in between the pads, underneath as well as on top, use an electric buffer to shorten and round the nails. If the buffer is used between grooming sessions, the nails will be kept short and neat, without need for drastic measures. Attend to the hindfeet in the same manner, starting the clipped area just above the toes in front and just above the large back pad behind.

Next clip the front legs from just above the wrist to just below the elbow, using a #15 blade against the growth of the coat. Leave the elbow joint just-covered. The front puff should cover the wrist of the dog with just a little to spare.

Now clip the belly, also with the #15. Next do the base of the tail with the same blade, always clipping against the growth of the hair. Poodles clipped just after they are bathed will clip closer than if done before the bath. Leave as much tail bone as possible in the pompon to give it body and firmness.

Before beginning the pattern, get someone to set up the dog while you back off to get an overall picture and decide on the proper proportions for perfect balance. From now on, the individual interpretation of the Standard will apply.

There was a time when the mane started at the third rib, but I believe today this makes a dog look long in body. Try the mane beginning at the last

47

Am. & Can Ch. Wilber White Swan, white Toy, shown going Best in Show at 1956 Westminster Kennel Club show. Left to right: Mr. Paul Palmer, judge; Mr. William Rockefeller, club president; and Anne Rogers Clark, handler. Bred and owned by Mrs. Bertha Smith, Bermyth Kennels.

Ch. Fontclair Festoon, black Miniature import, shown going Best in Show at 1959 Westminster Kennel Club show. Left to right: Mr. William Rockefeller, club president; Anne Rogers Clark, handler; and Mr. Thomas Carruthers III, judge. Owned by Dunwalke Kennels.

rib. The line between the pack and rib on the dog's side is best done with scissors, and should be $\frac{1}{4}$ inch wide. Now, with a #30 clipper blade, place the straight edge on this line and make a half circle. Make a clean sweep on both sides before you comb and scissor and straighten out the future pack. A mistake on one side might just as well be made on the other, but keep your dog steady to avoid an error if possible.

On a long-backed dog, a short circle makes him look shorter. Squaring off the top of the pack will make the dog have greater continuity. The pack meets the mane on top without a line. This topline should be straight and level to give a put-together appearance. Let the judge discover whether or not the dog has a slightly hollowed topline as suggested by the Standard. This will also make the dog's tail look properly set, especially if the tail is not clipped precisely to the base.

If you are one-sided, do the most difficult side first.

Before beginning the bracelets, locate the sharp little bone on the outside of the dog's thigh. The top band should be centered on that bone in a medium-sized dog. On a short-legged dog, make the bone the top of the bracelet; on a long-legged dog, make the bone the bottom of the bracelet. Again use the scissors rather than the clippers to set the bracelets. The larger the dog, the bigger the band should be. On a Toy the scissors are sufficient, for you will have more hair left with which to work.

The bottom bracelet in a Miniature should be $\frac{1}{2}$ inch above the hock, sloping it regardless of the need for angulation. Correct the angulation by the trimming of the lower bracelet. Enhance the bend of stifle with careful sloping of the hair on the underside of the middle bracelet. Now before you do the finishing touches, put the dog in the run and watch him move.

Watch your dog carefully for a week or so before you begin again. Consider how he moves and carries himself. Your problem is to build the dog up to your ideal of the perfect Poodle. The dog should be put in pattern at least two or three, or better yet, even five or six weeks before the show to make him look as he should. Remember that fashions in grooming change with the times. What is acceptable today may look very odd tomorrow.

Many dogs are shown with their packs cut so high that their middle bracelet is too long, making the dog look awkward and out of balance. Comb the pack down, and comb the bracelets up and out. Let the hair set before you snip. Remember that you will need more pack on a thin dog than on a heavy one. When you comb the pack up and scissor, after the dog shakes the pack goes down and there are holes. So, comb it down to begin with!

A curly pack or one that gives a velvet plush look? Both have their admirers and they suit different dogs. For the plush pack, dry the coat under the dryer, brushing constantly with a carding comb, against the growth of the hair. For a curly pack, comb and brush the pack thoroughly before washing. Then do not dry, but comb through with a large tooth comb in the direction you wish it to lie when dry, and allow to dry naturally. Arrange the hair once more in the proper direction before scissoring.

The Continental with or without rosettes? This is to be decided by the shortness of your Poodle's back. The shorter the Poodle, the less room or reason for rosettes. Trim the shaved area with a #15 blade against the grain about three days before a show, and before bathing. By show time any clipper lines or very bare places will have darkened to the color of the dog's coat. Leave rosettes over the hip bones as follows: cut out the top and bottom of a tin can of the appropriate size, position the can on the hindquarter, hold or have held for you, and clip around area. Tidy up lines carefully after removing can. Improve the rosette to a plush or curly button on the hindquarter.

Make sure your dog is strictly clean, or your scissoring will be uneven. If you have time before setting your pattern, put your dog in a Continental clip and let the rear end grow in all in one piece. This will remedy thin or soft hair, and the new coat will trim better. Leave bottom bracelets on all four legs.

Allow six months for a Standard Poodle in Continental to grow out to an English Saddle. Toys and Miniatures grow out in less (but not much less) time.

Tails can be a problem. A longer tail is more graceful than a shorter one, but a long tail can have a snag in it, too—especially if it tends to curl over the back, which requires particular trimming.

The front bracelets should be fairly round. Taper them at the bottom, but not as much at the top. As your mane comes down in length, drop the front bracelets accordingly. It's best to have them fairly deep at the start.

The length of coat differs with the variety. Too much coat on a Standard makes them look cloddy and awkward, while a Miniature and Toy can carry more length of coat proportionately. Too much coat underneath any Poodle, or an overwhelming amount of length of side coat that gives the appearance of lumbering when he moves, detracts from the smart, elegant outline for which you are striving.

The bracelets should be fluffy, for the hair is of a different quality than the pack or the mane. Do not hold out the hair with your fingers while you scissor, else you will have holes when you are finished.

Wrapping the ears and topknots protects them against crate rubbing, food, etc. Waxed paper, Saran wrap, or light-weight plastic may be used. Take the ears down at least twice a week and re-wrap, or you will get mats where the waxed paper stops. Remember that a topknot that is too long looks awkward, and should be trimmed to frame the head.

For a Saturday or Sunday show, clip the face on a Wednesday or Thursday. Use a #15 blade on the face, and a #00 or #40 blade on the front of the face. A #00 blade is finer than a #30 and will not skin the Poodle or make it look pink, but a #000 blade is too fine. One inch to one and one-half inches below the Adam's apple on a Standard or Miniature is low enough to show off the neckline and length of neck. The tuft under the mouth in the pouch of the lower lip can best be done by stretching the mouth back with your thumb. The "V" between the eyes, at the stop, should be neither over or underdone. It should enhance the stop on a good-headed dog, and draw attention to the properly-placed and shaped eye. If clipped up too far, the dog may have a startled expression. If too low, a beetle-browed one. Start with it low, and work it back to the desired place.

The line on the side of the head runs from the corner of the eye to the ear opening. Do not clip above this line in the hope it will narrow a thick skull. It does not. It spotlights this fault.

"*Whip Stick,*" which is solidified beeswax, will coat the hair above the eyes to keep them up with the topknot when the dog is ready to enter the ring.

To roll the ear-feathers in paper, first comb out thoroughly. Take the feather in one hand, checking with your finger where the end of the leather is, so as not to catch the leather in the rubber band. Now roll the feather in paper, rolling along the length of the hair, not towards the ear. Then double up the paper roll and catch with a rubber band. Test with your comb to make sure the leather is free. Coat a bit of cotton with *capsicum,* which is liquid red pepper and procurable at any drugstore, and tuck it under the elastic to discourage chewing.

Ch. Cappoquin Little Sister, black Toy, pictured going Best in Show at 1961 Westminster Kennel Club show. Left to right: Mr. William Rockefeller, club president; Anne Rogers Clark, handler; and Dr. Joseph Redden, judge. Owned by Miss Florence Michelson, Tropicstar Kennels.

Ch. Puttencove Promise, white Standard, shown going Best in Show at 1958 Westminster Kennel Club show. Left to right: Mr. William Brainard, judge; Robert Gorman, handler; and Mr. William Rockefeller, club president. Bred and owned by Puttencove Kennels.

9

Showing the Poodle

THE conservatism of the Poodle's mind manifests itself in the show ring as elsewhere, and for this reason such a dog requires early and constant training to do his best while in the ring. At his best, there is no more perfect example of vanity, charm and showmanship. He is *THE SHOW DOG* par excellence. But to achieve this prodigy, many months of training and grooming are necessary.

As I have said before, start training your puppy to the lead early. Hold the lead straight and fairly tight in your left hand, and train your Poodle always to walk on your left side. Never allow him to walk on the right side, and teach him not to cross in front of you. If you start the puppy young enough, a soft slip lead is all that is necessary. If the dog is older and inclined to pull, a chain collar will prevent his tugging on the lead too much or bolting ahead at breakneck speed.

Start posing the future show dog on the table each time he is groomed. Teach him to allow you to place his four feet just the way you want them and to keep them that way. Then hold his head and his tail up and tell him to "Hold it," giving the command in a firm voice. If he does not obey and keeps moving, start all over from the beginning and keep at it until he understands just what you want; it will not take him too long. At first he should hold the pose for just a few seconds at a time, then gradually increase the time until he is standing still for five minutes and longer. Pet and praise him when he does this correctly or reward him with a tidbit. Sometimes counting helps, starting in with "one, two, three," said quickly, and allowing the dog to break his pose at three. Then gradually lengthen the time between the numbers, and still later add to them. In the end, the command to "Hold it" will be all that is needed. Then pose him on the floor, with people and other dogs moving around, and on the streets in traffic. Teach him to hold the pose anywhere at any time.

Open his lips and examine his front teeth and encourage members of the household to do so, then later, friends and strangers. Have people lift up his front feet, run their hands along his spine and handle his hindquarters and hocks. Soon he will take this all as a matter of course.

If you have other dogs—particularly well trained show dogs—stage a show ring of your own with, if possible, someone strange to the trainee acting as judge. Walk the dogs in a circle, all of them to your left, set them up, let the mock judge go over them carefully, move them toward him and away from him one by one. In short, reproduce the show ring procedure, complete in every detail. Do this as often as opportunity permits. And may I add, dogs are like children, you know, "Monkey see, monkey do."

Train your Poodle to play with a ball and other toys, as this keeps him gay and alert, and a plaything can be used to advantage to attract his attention in the ring.

Get your young Poodle out onto the streets and into traffic, into crowded stores, and into railway stations. Encourage strangers to pet and talk to him. Teach him to ride in automobiles and behave himself as a passenger. Teach him not to be afraid of loud noises. Get him accustomed to relieving himself on the lead in strange places. If possible, after he has learned to lead well, take along an older dog to show him the ropes. All of this will insure his arriving at his first show fresh and free from the strain of nervousness caused by his journey there and will give him a much better chance to show himself at his best.

A great many Poodles enter into the game of showing with zest and enjoyment and give of their very best. They seem to sense that the other dogs are rivals, and, with confidence in and affection for their handler, do their best to out-show their competitors. If they thoroughly understand the routine, they will snap right into it. But first they must know in detail just what you require of them; there must be no uncertainty or bewilderment.

Poodles can quite well be handled in the show ring by their owners, always provided the owners are calm and collected and have confidence in themselves and in the dog. If you plan to handle your own dog, go to a number of shows and watch very carefully the best handlers; see what they do and how they do it. Learn as much as possible of the technique of the ring, the maneuvers, how to keep your dog in the judge's eye in the most advantageous manner. Learn how not to permit too ambitious owners to push you and your dog into corners. If some other exhibitor allows his dog to annoy yours and put it off its stride, quietly drop out of line and fall in again next to

Eng. Am. & Can. Ch. Bibelot's Tall Dark and Handsome (by Ch. Wycliffe Virgil ex Ch. Lady Joan of Lowmont), black Standard, England's Dog of the Year 1966. Reserve Best in Show at Crufts (England) 1967. Bred and owned by Susan Radley Fraser.

some more considerate handler. Handling is not learned over night, but takes many years of patience and experience.

The ring is no place to train or discipline your dog; all of that should have been done at home. The judge can see at a glance whether or not your dog knows the ropes. Do not try to show off how well trained he is, either, or give loud commands. Just go quietly along, doing what is required in a pleasant way and without trying to call attention to yourself or the dog in any undue manner.

If you are fortunate enough to have your dog go Best of Variety and you, yourself, are not an experienced handler, my advice is to place your dog in the hands of a professional handler for the competition in the respective Group. This is no amateur performance; it brings together not only the cream of the Non-Sporting dogs in the show, but also the best professional handlers, and it is difficult for amateurs to compete on an even footing with

Ch. Carlima's J.D. (by Ch. Fieldstreams Valentine ex Chrisward Tambourine), black Toy, multiple Best in Show winner and Top Producer. Owned by Carruth Maguire, Carlima Kennels.

handlers who have had years of experience in getting out of a dog all that is in it. Your dog will have a much better chance in such company if it is handled by an expert.

Before you show your Poodle, make up your mind that you will meet other very good dogs in the ring. A knowledge of your dog's faults and virtues helps you to keep a balanced point of view. Study him against others in your own mind, study the printed Standard, study pictures of the best. Know just where your dog stands. Be fair enough to realize that, although your Poodle is a friend, and your affections are involved and you are justly proud of him, all the other exhibitors feel exactly the same way about their respective dogs. These natural sentiments, while giving everybody pleasure, have nothing to do with your Poodle's points as a show dog. The judge, expertly trained to see faults and virtues and weigh one against the other, is on this occasion invited to give his considered opinion about the dogs brought before him as they appear at that moment in the ring. He sees them but a brief time, and it is no part of his job to consider what they have won before and what they may win again, but only what he can see of them at the moment. He has but a short time to weigh every point as fairly as he can. No two of us see exactly alike, and all you can ask of the judge is that he give you his honest and expert opinion. Most judges try to be fair. They make mistakes, and who does not?

You may be sure, if you keep on showing, your Poodle will find his rightful level in the end; if he is really good, nothing can keep him down; if not, nothing can bring him up. And in the course of a long show career, you will be knocked down at times unjustly, and, on the other hand, you may win unjustly also. So unless you can cheerfully take whatever comes, make up your mind not to show. Be a modest winner and a good loser. It pays.

While in the ring, pay strict attention to the matter at hand. Concentrate your mind on your own dog and on the judge. Obey the judge's commands, gestures, and even glances, promptly, and be alert for them. The ring is no place for conversation or dreaming, either for you or for your dog.

I have said nothing about conditioning your dog for the show ring, for the simple reason that if the directions for clipping and grooming are followed, and if the Poodle is in perfect health, it should always be in show condition, more or less. But it goes without saying that for the day of the show he must be expertly barbered and in full bloom. Never show a good dog out of coat, thin, or not in the pink of condition. A puppy may go to several shows in puppy classes for experience, but do not expect to go to the top with him until he is in full bloom and has a mature finish of body. The better the youngster is the more it pays to wait until he is just right before bringing him out.

Ch. Estid Ballet Dancer, top winning Poodle of all varieties in 1961; top Miniature Poodle, 1960; top Non-Sporting dog in America, 1961; No. 3 for all breeds in America, 1961; winner of Quaker Oats Award, Western Division, 1961; Best Non-Sporting at Westminster, 1961; 30 Bests in Show. Owned by Mr. and Mrs. Richard Beard, and handled by Frank T. Sabella.

Ch. Blakeen Snow Flurry and three of her six puppies by Ch. Adastra Magic Fame. Snow Flurry was sired by Ch. Snow Boy of Fircot ex Ch. Blakeen Flurry, bred by Blakeen Kennels, owned by Silhou Jette Kennels.

10

The Brood Bitch

IN Poodles, as in other breeds, the selection of the mother of coming winners is of the utmost importance. Not only should she be from a family noted for the production of winners, but her pedigree on both sides should be well balanced and she should be line-bred, if possible. Make up your mind which virtues are most important to you, for you cannot have them all, and which faults you find most objectionable, and choose your bitch's family accordingly, for the foundation of your breeding operations should be anything but haphazard. Your matron should have no glaring faults. In fact, the better show dog she is, the better puppies she is likely to have. This is not always so, and there are cases in which the plainest one of a brilliant family turned out to be the best producer; but that cannot be known ahead of time, and to choose for good points is a wiser general rule. A bitch from a fine litter whose brothers and sisters, sire and dam, and grand-parents were not only good themselves but also noted for production, is the wisest choice.

Disposition in a brood bitch is as important as show points, for a shy mother seems to infect her brood with alarms from which they seldom recover, having been taught, both by inheritance and example, to be distrust-ful. A very nervous and fidgety mother or one that is over-anxious is seldom a good one, and she is prone to neglect or trample her puppies or to carry them around in her mouth so that they grow up undernourished and nervous, too. A calm, sensible, and intelligent mother is the best start any puppy can have in life. Puppies learn about living from their mother, and a level-headed mother can give them sense as well as health.

Ch. Summercourt Square Dancer of Fircot, Miniature, shown winning the Stud Dog class at the 1958 Washington Poodle Club Specialty under the late Col. E. E. Ferguson, with two of his get: Tedwin's Two Step (left, with John Paluga handling) and Tedwin's Top Billing (right with breeder Ted Young, Jr.). Square Dancer shown by Anne Rogers Clark. Two Step finished and became a Group winner. Top Billing developed into one of the top winners in the breed.

By no means the least important requisite is robust health. No bitch that is thin, harboring worms, or in any way out of sorts can do justice to a bouncing family; and unless a bitch is in the pink of condition she should not be bred. Bitches that come from a long line of show dogs, well fed and well cared for and not over-bred for many generations, inherit stamina; those that come from a line of puppy factories, with backyard care, without proper food for several generations, inherit deficiencies which they hand on to their puppies and which no amount of feeding and care can wholly cure. As Poodles have big families as a rule, one litter a year or, at most, two litters with six months rest before a third, should be the rule. Personally, I have found that one good, healthy litter a year, preferably in the spring, pays much better dividends in the end.

Poodle bitches are usually very good, patient and intelligent mothers. The pointed heads of the puppies at birth make their delivery easy; and, as a breed, Poodles are prolific.

11

The Stud Dog

IN Poodles, it has been my experience that to be a super successful stud dog a male must, in addition to excellent breeding, show quality, and abounding health, have real vigor of personality and be aggressively masculine. It seems to take an exaggeration of every Poodle characteristic successfully to stamp Poodle character on the progeny. A jaunty action and a cocky carriage, as well as a fine head and expression, and good legs and feet are so much a part of Poodle character that the stud dog should possess these attributes in abundance. Also, a stud dog should be bold and friendly.

The stud dog, of course, should have no really serious fault and, above all, no serious inherited fault; but a well balanced dog with a fault is better than one with a single outstanding virtue but lacking in proper balance. I would say that structural soundness, sloping shoulders, strong hindquarters with well let down hocks, a long neck, good tight feet, a well ribbed body, and a straight back are the most important requirements for a stud dog. Texture and profuseness of coat are also essential, and for the warmer climates this must be especially excellent to be stamped on the progeny at all. We all want lovely lean heads with dark, oval eyes and low-set, long ear leathers.

Aside from the stud dog's pronounced individual virtues of type and balance, his pedigree should also be well balanced and, in my opinion, it should show line breeding to a strain produced with a definite purpose in mind. No dog has every virtue, and no strain can have every wanted quality either; but certain strains can be depended upon to produce certain definite good points just as other strains stamp other important virtues. But a dog

61

Fircot Garcon de Neige (white Miniature) by Ch. Snow Boy of Fircot ex Cream Puff of Fircot, breeder-owner, Fircot Kennels, England.

Fircot Garcon de Neige and his little son, Fircot Flacon de Neige of Fircot Kennels.

Ch. Sherwood Cream Cracker (by Victor of Fircot ex Sherwood White Pique), bred by Sherwood Hall Kennels, and his son, Broughton Another Eric (ex Sherwood Sundance) both owned by Broughton Kennels.

with a pedigree that is a hodgepodge of many unrelated strains bred together haphazardly and without any predetermined intention will usually produce mediocre or even inferior stock.

There are two ways to stamp a virtue or virtues on stock. One of the most common methods is to breed together two related (cousins or closer) members of the same strain, both exemplifying that virtue. Even here to be successful the most rigid selection must be practiced. The second method is by pure selection to mate together unrelated dogs possessing the same virtue in a pronounced form for a number of generations. For instance, I once owned a Pekingese stud dog with no line breeding at all behind him but whose ancestors for some five generations had been chosen for fine heads; he was the one stud dog of my experience that, without line breeding, had the ability to stamp beautiful heads upon his puppies even when he was mated to poor headed bitches. This was logical enough, as he had no bad heads behind him. Such a pedigree is, of course, extremely rare; for such intelligent selection over a long period of years is very rarely practiced. The quicker way is through the mating together of related dogs who are themselves alike in the wanted quality to begin with and whose pedigrees indicate its inheritance.

The Poodle stud dog selected for your bitch should be as much like her as possible. If the two are related they probably have many of the same genes in common. At any rate, they should exhibit just as many virtues in common as possible, and none of the same faults. The mating of opposite types is almost never successful.

The father of your coming family need not necessarily be a famous champion, though puppies sired by a well and favorably known dog bring better prices and find a readier sale. Often, a lesser known stud dog that is thoroughly suited to your bitch in pedigree and appearance will produce better puppies. A great dog that makes the show circuit, full of fatigue, suffering from nervous strain and lack of exercise, is often not in the pink of productive health and may be exhausted from over-use even when he is at home.

The health and vigor of a sire depend upon the care and handling given him by his owner. That he shall have a complete diet high in its protein content, ample sunshine, exercise, and happy contentment, are all important.

I have known of stud dogs whose productivity of superior progeny was exhausted when they were four or five years old, while others have lasted well into old age. I have owned two champions, one a tiny three pound Pom and the other a small Miniature Poodle, that sired vigorous, outstanding champions at eleven years of age. Much depends upon the care and consideration given a dog during his breeding years.

Chriscrest Jubilee and Chriscrest Jamboree, black Miniature puppies at 10 weeks of age, by Duncount's Dauphin ex Ch. Chriscrest Franchonette. Bred by Christobel Wakefield. Both became champions and Top Producers.

White Miniature puppies by Ch. Summercourt Square Dancer of Fircot, bred by Maurice Lamb.

12

Poodle Puppies

POODLE puppies are sturdy little things needing only the sensible care required by any other canine infants.

For the first weeks of their lives they may be safely left to their mother. When they are three weeks old I try to teach them to lap milk, but very often, well fed babies are not interested. However, since Poodle families, as a rule, are large, it is a good plan to begin feeding the puppies a little extra to take some of the burden of suckling them from their mother as soon as they can be taught to eat. I press their small muzzles into milk to induce them to lap when they are three weeks old. When they are about four weeks of age, I add meat to their diet in the form of carefully scraped top round of beef, at first in very small portions—about the size of a large pea for Toys, a little more for Miniatures, and as big as a large marble for Standards. These amounts are gradually increased as the puppies grow. I give them four meals a day until they are three months old, after which I feed them three meals a day until they are six months, then two meals a day up until they reach one year.

The foundation of these meals is warm (not hot) milk—for preference, pure, undiluted goat milk. Canned irradiated milk, in the proportion of one part hot water to three parts milk as it comes from the can, is almost as good as goat milk, if the latter is not obtainable. To this, at weaning time, I add two teaspoonfuls of white Karo Syrup for each Standard puppy, one teaspoonful for each Miniature, and one-half teaspoonful for each Toy. I also add the same amount of D.C.P.340 (Di-Calcium Phosphate, as put up by Parke-Davis and Company), for each of the three sizes of Poodle puppies. Of

Perkamorph Liver Oil, put out by Abbott Company, I include six drops for each Standard puppy, three for each Miniature and from one to two drops for each Toy. The amount of milk should be all that the puppies will clean up comfortably, roughly two cups for a Standard puppy, one cup for a Miniature, and one-half cup or less for a Toy; but this amount must be regulated by the puppies' appetites, and they should have all they will drink.

At first and up until weaning the puppies, the milk is given to them plain and without any additions. At weaning time, or at five or six weeks of the puppies' age, the Karo Syrup, the D.C.P., and the Perkamorph Liver Oil are included in the formula, as I have stated above.

A little later, at six to eight weeks of the puppies' age, I begin to sprinkle Pablum on top of the milk, and as the puppies grow used to Pablum I gradually increase its proportion until the ration attains the consistency of a rather thick gruel. When the puppies are two and one-half months old, I add to the mixture the yolk of one raw egg for each two Miniatures, or a whole yolk for each Standard. Toys do not always digest eggs well. Use only the yolk of the egg. This is breakfast, and the only change in the formula is to substitute shredded wheat for Pablum when the puppies are six months old.

Luncheon is top round of beef, the portions gradually increased as the puppies grow. It should be scraped for easier digestion up until the puppies are weaned, after which time it may be finely chopped or ground. It should be fed raw at approximately body temperature.

The tea-time meal is of warm milk with a small amount of shredded wheat or other ready-to-eat wheat cereal added.

Dinner is of chopped, cooked beef together with its broth, which is thickened with shredded wheat. When the puppies are four to five months old, a good grade of kibbled dog biscuit may be substituted for the shredded wheat if it is desired.

I usually give weanlings a night meal of warm milk the last thing before I go to bed.

Meat is the staple food for all dogs, and without ample meat in its ration no Poodle can develop and grow as it should. A Standard puppy from five months onward needs approximately three-quarters of a pound of meat each day, a Miniature needs about one-half pound, and a Toy even less. Beef is probably the best meat for dogs, but other meats, such as lamb, beef and lamb hearts, beef liver, thoroughly boned or canned fish, may be fed to puppies after they are six months old. I do not feed vegetables to a dog until he is thoroughly mature, and even then only sparingly.

Now comes something that must be done long before weaning time, in fact before the puppies are five days old. This is the trying moment which

66

comes to all breeders of Poodles when the puppy tails must be cut off and the dew-claws removed. The operations are not nearly as bad as they seem.

First, get together everything that may be needed—a sturdy scissors, not too sharp, boiled and ready to use, some strong but soft cotton twine, an antiseptic, and the courage of your convictions. Suggested antiseptics are saccrinated iron, permanganate of potash crystals moistened with 10% nitrate of silver, or ordinary ground black pepper. Cut the twine into pieces about six inches in length, one piece for each puppy. Tie these strings tightly around the bases of the tails; this is the only really painful thing about the operation, but it numbs the tails and prevents excessive bleeding.

Next, decide how much of the tail to remove; some breeders take off one-fourth of the tail, others take off more. I try to gauge the proportion of tail to be left on the puppy to the size and length of its back. There is no cast-iron rule about the matter; but it is always to be remembered that more can be removed later, if necessary, whereas no part once removed can be put back. If at the dog's maturity his tail is too long, the veterinarian can amputate another section of it, but if it is too short nothing can be done to restore its length. Too short a stump of a tail destroys the balance of a heavy coated dog. This fact counsels moderation in its original amputation.

Now put the puppy on a table covered by a newspaper. Push the skin firmly toward the root of the tail so that there will be skin to cover the end afterwards, and with the scissors quickly snip the tail at the point previously determined. Then apply the antiseptic.

The dewclaws, always found on the front legs and often on the rear legs, must now be removed. If permitted to remain on the dog, they will be a trial and a hazard for the rest of his life. The ones on the front legs particularly are prone to catch on the clippers while the feet are being clipped.

The removal of the dewclaws is a more complicated business than docking tails and may be described as a gouging out rather than a mere cutting off. The best instrument for the purpose is a sturdy pair of nail scissors, not too sharp. They should, of course, be sterilized by boiling.

The tiny bone of the dewclaw must be dug right out, down to the joint by which it is affixed to the leg bone; if even a splinter of it is left, it will grow again. It requires considerable care to dig all of it out. The wound should be deep, the cut being toward the leg bone and not mere slicing in the direction the leg bone runs. This incision should be as small as is possible and yet remove the bone of the dewclaw.

As soon as the dewclaw is off, wipe away any accumulation of blood with absorbent cotton and firmly press into the wound with the finger tips the same kind of antiseptic used on the tails. If bleeding continues, apply more of the antiseptic and hold it firmly in the wound until the hemorrhage has subsided, several minutes if necessary.

One hour after the amputation of the tails, if all bleeding has stopped, the strings may be cut from their bases, and the operations are finished.

While all of this may sound gory, and most of us are reluctant to cause pain to our precious puppies, in reality the pain is trifling and momentary. After they have been docked, the rascals are soon sucking away under their mother's comforting care, and seem unaware that anything amiss has happened to them.

Poodle puppies, like all canine infants, need a lot of sunshine and healthy play. As they grow older, they are so lively and energetic that they are likely to overdo their activities and it is difficult to keep them in adequate flesh. I have found that a quiet rest in bed for an hour or so at noon, on the order of childrens' naps, is an excellent regimen for puppies.

Care and training of the Poodle's disposition and character are just as important as his physical development. The breed is rather set in its ways—in other words, stubborn—and the Poodle's education should begin early. When they are six weeks old, teach puppies to lie on their sides for brushing and the clipping of their little faces. First, I take them to the grooming table and run the clippers beside them without touching them at all. The following day I clip a little of their faces with a No. 10 or No. 15 blade, and the third day I clip the whole face, feet and tail, talking to them the while and encouraging their confidence. I do not grab them and hold them tightly nor permit anybody else to do so, but I just let them sit on the table while I work quietly with them, making their grooming a matter of course and not a frightening event. I have seldom had a puppy develop a fear of clippers or even grow worried about them. I also make my puppies stand in show position each time they are groomed, teaching them to hold their pose for a minute or two, gradually lengthening the time until they learn to stand still as long as may be required. This lesson requires but a few minutes and is of great value later on.

When puppies reach three months, I begin to teach them to accompany me on the lead. I do this gently without hauling or yanking, and the puppies enjoy the instruction as much as I enjoy giving it to them.

Much has rightly been said about Poodles' intelligence and quickness of perception. Since they are not fawning dogs by nature, they must be inculcated with perfect trust in their master before they can develop the self-assurance that every show dog needs. Poodles crave human companionship and understanding with the full depths of their nature, and they must be loved, played with, sensibly talked to, and handled from their earliest age. They soon learn that they can depend upon one, not as a severe critic but as a friend. Once confidence is established, with patience a Poodle can be taught almost anything a dog can learn. Although they are stubborn, Poodles never forget a lesson, once it is mastered.

68

When choosing a Poodle puppy, first choose its grandmother and be sure that both she and the puppy's mother have abundant good health and have been properly nourished as well as that they have the points that you would like in the puppy himself. Bitches from show stock in reputable kennels have had excellent care for generations, while those of ignorant backyard breeders often have been neglected. No amount of care and good food for a puppy will entirely overcome the ills caused by the neglect and malnutrition of its dam and granddam.

See to it that the little fellow you are about to buy is thoroughly healthy, with bright eyes, a damp, cool nose, and plenty of enterprise. It is well to sit quietly for some time, watching puppies play, before deciding which of them is to be yours. Of course, if the litter belongs to you, you will know them by heart before the time comes to decide which ones to keep for your own.

In choosing a show puppy, remember that a quality must be exaggerated at three months to remain fixed in maturity. To have a lean skull and a long head when older, a puppy's head must be almost too long and fine when about four months old, as heads tend to thicken and coarsen with age. Eyes never change in shape and rarely in color. Light eyes may even get lighter. Poodle puppies that are going to be very short backed are absurdly so in babyhood. A puppy that has the same measurement of height and length of back from shoulder to tail will not be too long of back, as a rule, but unless there are at least two inches difference, he will not be very short either. Feet seldom change; tight ones come that way in the beginning and will remain so unless through being kept on too hard surfaced yards they are spoiled. Hindquarters should be good, well let down, and strong from the beginning. Structural defects increase rather than disappear. Puppy coats should be thick and curly to develop into the proper texture later, though of course they are always rather silky in babyhood. In the warmer climates there must be a super coat inheritance for the jackets to be thick, stiff and bushy and keep so generation after generation. Choosing puppies is always a gamble, but they can usually be depended upon to be like their immediate family. Size is difficult to gauge. Miniatures very seldom grow much in height after six months, seldom over two inches at most, though sometimes a puppy that is outsized may keep right on growing, to its owner's dismay.

In breeding Toys by selection from Miniatures, one of the most disheartening things is the fact that a puppy may remain quite small to even ten or twelve months of age and then suddenly sprout a disconcerting inch or more. Just why this should be so nobody knows, but everybody who has tried to breed Toys from Miniatures knows that this sometimes occurs.

Undershot jaws are the horror of most breeders, but unless a puppy has undershot parents or near relations, and if it is only slightly undershot—and

American, Canadian & Bermudian Ch. Harmo Gay
Prospector, Miniature Poodle, Best in Show winner in
all three countries. Owned by Mrs. Anna H. Mosher,
Harmo Kennels. Handled by William J. Trainor.

I mean slightly—its mouth will in nine cases out of ten straighten out when the second teeth come in. So do not discard a youngster, otherwise good, until after the second teeth come through. Many amateur breeders have disposed of good puppies in the belief that they would remain undershot, only to be dismayed later to find that they have let a real winner slip through their hands.

Carriage and stylish action are born in some puppies; but, if not born in them, those traits can, to some extent, be trained into puppies with praise, wise handling, and encouragement on the lead.

In conclusion, your puppy must be well fed, groomed as often as possible, kept immaculately clean, taught with firmness and patience those things he must know in life. Above all, he must be quite sure of your love and understanding if he is to develop into the delightful companion he was meant to be.

70

13

Poodle Characteristics

OUR Poodle is a gentleman with all the reserve, dignity, and delicacy of feeling the word implies. Although he is of the Spaniel family, there is nothing fawning about him. He makes up his mind about you with deliberation, and, after due consideration, he places you in his world and very seldom changes his idea about your worth. If you and he are to be friends or better, he gives you his full, undivided devotion, and, from that time on, your moods and your commands are his sole concern in life. But this is on a friend to friend basis of perfect equality; he expects from you the same loving understanding that he gives you. If you fail him, he will still love you but his admiration will slip a little and he will let you know it in no uncertain terms. His full devotion is usually for one person only, after which he includes the immediate family in various gradations of affectionate regard. But, as Miss Brunker said of him so long ago, "The tender, speaking glance I know so well is for his owner only."

Poodles are polite to friends they know, but as a rule without enthusiasm. As a breed this distrust of strangers is quite marked, and makes of them guardians and watch dogs of the highest ability, both for the owner's possessions and for his person. There is a famous story of Moustache, the Poodle that went to war with his master who was killed in battle. The faithful dog refused to let the enemy soldiers touch his master's body and was killed defending it. When the French again took the field of battle, Moustache was buried with highest military honors with a grave marked *"Ce gît le brave Moustache."* A more recent incident of a similar sort occurred not very long ago with a small Miniature son of my Ch. Marcourt Sabot. Mrs. O'Brien, his

Eng. & Am. Ch. Moensfarm Marcelle of Montfleuri (by Eng. Ch. Rudolph of Piperscroft ex Moensfarm Mimi), black Miniature Best in Show winner. Sire of champions. Owned by Mrs. Nathan Allen, Alltrin Kennels.

owner, who was devoted to "Blackie," started out for a walk with him one evening and apparently dropped by the wayside, dying instantly. As she lived alone, she was not missed, and it wasn't until her body was found early the next morning that anyone realized what had happened. Blackie was faithfully on guard, and it was not until her own doctor came that Blackie was willing to leave the body of his beloved mistress or permit anyone to touch her.

We flatter ourselves when we say that Poodles are the most intelligent of all breeds. It is very true that those who watch them work out difficult problems by themselves believe that their reasoning faculties are sometimes uncanny, but I have owned other breeds that could think, too. The real difference in Poodle intelligence is, I believe, this: whereas other dogs think in a doggy way, Poodles' brains react in a much more human fashion and one that we humans can better understand. Perhaps their three hundred or more years of earnest effort to understand us has given them this quality of mind.

For all their independence, Poodles as a breed are pathetically dependent upon human companionship and understanding. Without it they become distrustful, morose and dull. They must be sure of their masters before they can be sure of themselves. All dogs need affectionate understanding, but

72

some other breeds can be happy in their own doggy sphere of life without much human companionship; Poodles cannot be even reasonably happy or smart without it.

It is their extreme sensitiveness that makes them such delightful companions, quick to respond to even unspoken thoughts; but this same quality makes them all the more sensitive to unkindness and severity. They seldom need correction other than the spoken word. A merited scolding—and it must be merited and perfectly just—will reduce them to the depths of woe, and it is only when the voice changes from grave disapproval to the all-clear signal of a brighter, approving tone that they regain their normal gaiety.

Their curiosity, like that of most intelligent creatures, is great, and they will share with you the pleasure of unwrapping a package—if done up with ribbons, so much the more intriguing. They always want to see just what is afoot, what's behind the closed door, or beyond the turn of the road. Although they will sometimes chase other little animals, domestic or wild, they seem to do it from a sense of fun rather than a desire to kill. Most of them enjoy playing with balls and other toys and have a lively sense of possession about such things. I have a Miniature Poodle who gathers together his treasured little hoard of playthings and carefully puts away all but one before he goes to bed, carrying his favorite to bed with him every night. And he will stand at the head of the stairs and bounce his ball down the steps, retrieve it and bounce it again for hours on end.

Poodles, perhaps because of the attention their toilets always have received, show great pride in their appearance. When groomed and clipped

Eng. Ch. Moensfarm Mascot of Montfleuri, black Miniature, winner of 7 Challenge Certificates. Sire of 18 champions. Full brother of Int. Ch. Moensfarm Marcelle of Montfleuri (p. 72). Owned by Mr. and Mrs. P. Howard Price, Montfleuri Kennels, England.

and "in their best bib and tucker," they enjoy it keenly and the praise people give them. They are very fastidious and do not like to be dirty, tangled or unkempt. Unlike other types of dogs, they avoid mud puddles and dirty places and will not plow through muck of any sort.

As to food, Poodles are gourmets. Although they are never greedy, they will eat sensible kennel fare; but they can tell the difference between stew meat and prime rib roast, between top round and filet mignon; and they very much appreciate tidbits of the more sophisticated sort, such as cheese, pretzels, smoked fish, and so on.

As a breed, Poodles are rather old-maidish and set in their ways. They like regular hours, their particular chair always in the same spot, their own dish to eat out of and their own belongings just so. With this in mind, it is wise to make their routine what you want it to be from the very beginning, for this trait does not make them adaptable and they do not take readily to changes.

No other dog has so great a sense of humor. It is a mistake, however, to think of the Poodle as a circus clown merely because of the early childish association we have for him in this role, for his humor is very often quite subtle. He unbends from the burden of his dignity to amuse you and himself in a bit of waggish fun, deliberately putting on an act, with an eye out for your reaction. This he doesn't take seriously nor does he expect you to, either. He simply feels he can relax among friends without permanent loss of dignity.

The teachability of Poodles is proverbial, and the only limit to what they can learn is that of your patience in teaching them. This applies to tricks, obedience work, hunting, or any other activity you may choose for them. They do not learn quickly as a rule and are sometimes rather stubborn; but with firmness, infinite repetition, kindness and patience, they can be taught almost anything a dog is capable of learning. Once a trick is mastered, they never forget it and even after years will remember what you wish of them, and respond with a finished performance to the same old command in the same voice. Inasmuch as many excellent books have been published upon obedience training of dogs, I shall not discuss the subject here except to say that the scores established by Poodles in obedience trials, Standards, Miniatures, and even Toys, are indicative of the intelligence and trainability of the breed.

As a friend of children the Poodle is unique, and many an old lady and gentleman look back to a Poodle of Victorian and Edwardian days with deep and sentimental attachment, and to shared pranks and confidences exchanged with a patient and sympathetic companion. Poodles seem to understand children, are infinitely gentle with them, and will play for hours without becoming impatient. Poodles have for children a tenderness and protective instinct which is extremely deep. In addition, their resourcefulness in inventing childish entertainment is unlimited.

Many noted people have been Poodle enthusiasts—Gertrude Stein, Helen Hayes, Booth Tarkington, Mignon Eberhardt, Greer Garson, Ben Hecht, Cardinal O'Connell of Boston, Chancellor Hutchins of the University of Chicago, Mr. Gosden of the Amos and Andy team, Winston Churchill, the Nobel prizewinner John Steinbeck, whose "Travels with Charlie (a Standard Poodle) in Search of America" won the Dog Writers' Association award in 1962, and many others including Alexander Woollcott, who says in his book, *Long, Long Ago,* "I belong—and for many years have belonged—to the brotherhood of the Poodle. This brotherhood is far-flung and wildly miscellaneous. We all have one thing in common—perhaps only one. We all believe that man as he walks on this earth, can find no more engaging companion than that golden hearted clown, the Poodle."

Three Piperscroft puppies: Cushla of Piperscroft, Piquant of Piperscroft, and Grisel of Piperscroft (dam of Ch. Busby of Piperscroft).

Eng. Ch. Montfleuri Sarah of Longnor, black Miniature, England's greatest post-war winning Miniature with 19 Challenge Certificates, with her son Tarka of Montfleuri at 7½ weeks of age. Owned by Mr. and Mrs. P. Howard Price, Montfleuri Kennels, England.

The Miniature Poodle

Two famous dogs from the Monarch line, Ch. The Laird of Mannerhead, and his litter brother, Ch. Limelight of Mannerhead, by Am. Ch. Sparkling Jet of Misty Isles, owned by Mrs. Campbell Inglis, Mannerhead Kennels, England.

14

Foreword to
Miniature Male Line Charts

THE word *line* as used here identifies the male descent from father to son.

In the last ten years, 1,012 Miniature Poodles have completed American Kennel Club championships. It is interesting to note that virtually all of the winners and producers of the variety today trace back to either one, or both, of two great male lines—the "Monarch" and the "Chieveley." It is even more surprising that these two lines, in spite of time and dilution, still breed fairly true.

Two other Miniature lines, the "Dancing Boy" and the "Blue Boy" have gained some importance, but even of these the "Blue Boy" is an offshoot of the Monarch line.

To some degree, the Monarch and the Chieveley lines represent the two opposite types in nature. These types exist in all animals: the long-headed, long-bodied, light-boned type (Monarch), and the chubby, heavy-boned, short thick-headed type (Chieveley). Of course, in both cases these types have been modified to a great extent, depending on the skill of various breeders in using them, on the bitches brought to them, and on the amount of interweaving between the two lines. In Poodles, we go directly against Nature when we try to breed long, lean heads on short, cobby bodies. For this reason, it is the combination of the two lines that has been the classic recipe for success.

The Monarch line brings to the combination the beautiful heads and true Poodle expression. The Chieveley line contributes the short-back body type, tight feet and sound hindquarters. Here and in England, some fanciers have

Eng. Ch. Angelica (by The Aide de Camp ex Eng. Ch. Arc Angel), bred by Mrs. Jack Taylor.

made the mistake of completely discarding one line in favor of the other. Most breeders, however, have combined them to great advantage to produce the in-between type embracing the virtues of both lines, although even now, many years later, families and individuals still tend to resemble one line more than the other.

There even appear to be periodic swings in popularity from one type to the other. A particularly prepotent stud will appear on the scene and win a large and enthusiastic following, with result that almost everyone rushes in that direction, doubling and redoubling the line and type until it is carried to excess. This emphasis continues until it is so exaggerated that the followers begin to have doubts. Eventually the virtues of the opposite type become more attractive, and the pendulum swings in the other direction. Actually, all of this helps keep the variety in better balance, as it is the combined type that has proven the most desirable.

English Miniature imports have been an important source of supply for American Miniature breeders since the very beginning, and continue to be. Many of the top English winners or producers, or their sons, have been brought to this country to be utilized for breeding.

In studying the charts of the lines as presented here, note that each indentation represents a successive new generation. Virtually all top producing males of the line (those that sired five or more champions) are traced. The color of each dog is identified, and the number in parenthesis at the end of each name indicates the number of champions the dog sired.

The charts serve as an outline to guide students of the breed in their search for bloodlines and pedigrees. Each chart is proceeded by a commentary that aims to point out the high spots of the line.

80

15

Mrs. Jack Taylor's Kennel

MRS. JACK TAYLOR'S name is a household word among Poodle fanciers in England. She showed her first Poodle in Cork in 1897 and won with it. She soon obtained Trillo, bred by Mrs. Jerome, as was Bizarre, the Poodle mentioned as winning at Cork, and both won at Edinburgh in 1900.

Mrs. Taylor and her husband soon thereafter were ordered to China and were not allowed to take their Poodles with them. Bizarre died of grief, but Trillo was bred to Ch. Orchard Minstrel, owned by Mrs. Crouch, and produced two puppies of which the famous Rio Grande was one. He won 98 prizes and the championship certificate at Belfast in 1905, and from him are descended all the Taylor Miniatures, although he was a Standard of Standard breeding.

The first champion was Ch. Mons, a grandson of Rio Grande's, who finished his championship in 1914. Wisteria was the dwarf of a litter by Rio Grande x Dolly Varden, the smallest in a Standard litter, and, bred to Miss Brunker's Whippendell Corbillat, produced Star Spangle, who, in turn, was bred to Moufflon Bleu (Whippendell) to produce Joan of Arc. Joan of Arc was bred to Mickey Free (by Puck of Pre-Fleuri ex Star Spangle) to produce Ch. Arc Angel, who accumulated six challenge certificates before she was run over and killed. However, before her death she became the dam of Ch. The Blue Boy and Ch. Angel of Mine (by Chic of Watercroft), and of Ch. Angelica.

Ch. The Blue Boy bred to Ch. Angelica produced Ch. Somebody. The Blue Boy bred to The Sprite (by Whippendell Azor ex Babette Grise, the dam of

Blue Jewel of Misty Isles (by Romance of Rio Grande ex Eng. Ch. Angel of Mine), bred by Mrs. Jack Taylor, owned by Mrs. Byron Rogers.

Mrs. Tyndall's Leila) gave the undefeated silver Ch. The Silver Gnome. The Gnome's daughter, Ch. Fee D'Argent of Piperscroft, came to this country and finished her title here. Ch. Angel of Mine was bred to Hunningham Silver (by Ch. The Silver Gnome) to produce Venda's Arrow of Silver and Romance of Rio Grande. Venda's Arrow of Silver was bred to Leila to produce the famous Venda's Blue Masterpiece. Romance of Rio Grande was bred back to his dam, Ch. Angel of Mine, to produce Mrs. Byron Rogers' two foundation bitches, Blue Jewel of Misty Isles and Venda's The Silver Sylph, bought directly from Mrs. Jack Taylor. Handled in accordance with Mrs. Taylor's advice, these two bitches established the Misty Isles Miniature line with great success.

Ch. Angel of Mine was bred to The Diplomat to produce the great Ch. The Monarch who heads one of the great Miniature sire lines. The Monarch, a blue, finished his championship in 1928. The Monarch sired four champion sons: Am. Ch. King Johnny of Marcourt and Eng. Ch. Blue Zenith (x Blue Love Bird, full sister of Ch. Angel of Mine and Ch. The Blue Boy), Am. Ch. Whippendell Picot (x Bougee Bleue, daughter of Ch. The Blue Boy and Leila), and Eng. Ch. Spriggan Bell (x Toy Bell).

The Monarch's sire, The Diplomat, was a black, as were his parents Mannifred and Campden Rena. The Monarch's dam, Ch. Angel of Mine, was registered as a silver. In these early days of color breeding the blacks, blues, and grays were of necessity bred together in order to use the best individuals produced up to that time. Many dogs registered as blacks turned gray in their later years. The graying genes which turned the blacks into blues and grays were also responsible for the production of the silvers when sufficiently concentrated. Although Mrs. Taylor and others combined these colors with success, she cautioned against the introduction of any white or brown into these lines. Breeders today are aware of the difficulty of breeding good jet non-fading blacks when gray genes are present in the pedigree.

The Monarch line is by all odds the most successful Miniature line of all, combining well with all others.

82

16

Characteristics of
the "Monarch" Line

THE outstanding virtue in this line is, in my opinion, the head. It has produced the most beautiful heads in Miniatures; in many cases quite up to the Standards in quality. The skulls are lean, the forefaces long and not deeply hollowed out under the eyes. The eyes themselves are oval and of a velvety darkness, and the expressions beautiful and typical. Ears are well placed, the leathers sometimes long, sometimes not. The bone is rather fine as a rule, and the backs sometimes short, but not always so. Coats are profuse, and, if there is not too much blue blood, they are soundly black.

The faults include the one greatest defect, a definite tendency toward flat and open feet, varying in degree. The legs are sometimes too short. Bodies, as a whole, are not as short backed or as round ribbed as the Chieveleys, and at times show a tendency towards roach. They are not always stylish movers. The hocks, while well bent and let down, now and then show a weakness which, at its worst, extends to the whole hindquarters. In my experience, they are not generally as sound as the Chieveleys and, at times, lack style. They sometimes show a snipiness of head and general build, a sort of "Whippety" quality.

It must be remembered that this is the largest line, and there are many branches of it which differ in type somewhat from each other; what might be true of one branch would not, perhaps, apply to another. These variations result, without doubt, from the breeders' manipulations of it and from the bitches used to correct the faults in it.

Unlike the Chieveleys, this is not a purely black line, and there are a number of blues and silvers in it.

Ch. Barty of Piperscroft with his daughter, Elise.

In disposition, I have found the Monarch dogs sweet, gay, obliging and much easier to train and handle than the Chieveleys. Though rather bold, they are also much more the friends of all the world, more everybody's dogs. They are affectionate, and much more adaptable than the Chieveley line, but not nearly as single hearted.

17

The "Monarch" Line
Eng. Ch. The Monarch

ENG. Ch. The Monarch was an extremely well-bred dog and he was in demand at stud. He sired six sons who were to head sub-divisions of this famous sire line: Success of Piperscroft, Marcourt Carnot, Dare Devil Dink, Popinjay, Am. Ch. King Johnny of Marcourt and Eng. Ch. Spriggan Bell.

SUCCESS OF PIPERSCROFT

The largest and most widespread influence from the line has come through Success of Piperscroft. Success sired Conceit of Piperscroft, and he in turn sired the famous litter brothers Monty of Piperscroft and Ch. Misty Isles Algie of Piperscroft. Monty exerted a great influence and sired many English winners and two American champions—Ch. Jingle of Piperscroft, who was a force in Massachusetts, and Ch. Leader of Piperscroft of Blakeen. Leader was brought to the West Coast by Gary Cooper of movie fame but later became the property of Miss Freddie Weis, under whose affectionate care he responded rapidly, and gained his championship and fame as a sire. His first litter was from a lovely brown bitch, Ch. Round Table Constance, but all died from distemper except one exquisite small brown dog, Ch. Leader's Brown Topper. Topper, bred to a daughter of his sire, gave Geneva Christine and she, bred back to Topper, gave that well-known brown, Ch. Tommy K, sire of 10 champions including Am. and Can. Ch. Norcrest Surrey Sahib, a Best in Show winner and sire of nine champions. Ch. Leader also sired Ch. Galcit's Priority of Ste. Elmo, who sired five champions.

Am. & Can. Ch. Poodhall Gus, owned by Poodhall Kennels.

Another important son of Monty was the handsome black Eng. Ch. Barty of Piperscroft. Barty was in the final five for Best in Show at the last Crufts Dog Show to be held before World War II. Barty was a tremendous success at stud. His daughter, Ch. Pitter Patter of Piperscroft, was brought to this country and became the first Miniature to go Best in Show at Westminster, this in 1943. Barty had four important sons: Robin, Ruffles, Russet and Am. Ch. Sabu—all of Piperscroft. Robin of Piperscroft sired, among other winners, Blakeen's import Firebrave Alphonse. Alphonse sired, in England, Am. Can. and Eng. Ch. Firebrave Pimpernel (six champion get). Pimpernel sired the great black Am. Can. and Eng. Ch. Pixholme Firebrave Gustav C.D. who had 23 champion get in all parts of the world. At Poodhall Kennels, in Texas, Gustav sired Am. and Can. Ch. Poodhall Gus. Gus was the top winning Poodle in Canada from 1957 through 1961, and was retired after winning his 100th Group first with a total of 26 Bests in Show. Gus sired 19 champions in Canada and the U.S.

Barty's son, Ruffles of Piperscroft (full brother of Pitter Patter), sired Eng. Ch. Top Hat of Piperscroft. Top Hat sired Highland Sand Kennels' Ch.

Ch. Pitter Patter of Piperscroft

Busby of Piperscroft, who sired 15 champions. Another son of Ruffles, Tiptop of Piperscroft, gave Cartlane Kennels the valuable stud Tais Toi of Piperscroft. Tiptop also sired Voila of Piperscroft whose son, Clipper of Piperscroft, sired the great Eng. Ch. Rudolph of Piperscroft.

On my last visit to England in 1956 I thought Rudolph possessed one of the most perfect and exquisite Poodle heads of my experience. So beautiful, in fact, that it was hard to look at the rest of him, which was unjust, as he was a good, sound, well-put-together dog with a nice way of going and a lovely inky black, well-textured coat. Rudi's character was delightful—friendly, gay and sweet. Despite several rather large offers, Rudi's devoted owner, Mrs. A. D. Jenkins, refused to part with her treasured pet. Rudi is now the top producing black Miniature sire of all time with 28 champions to his credit.

Rudolf has four top producing sons and three top producing daughters. These sons are Eng. Ch. Baroque of Montfleuri (sire of eight champions), Eng. Ch. Rippwood Milord of Eldonwood (sire of five champions), New Hat of Montfleuri (sire of nine champions) and Eng. Ch. Moensfarm Mascot of Montfleuri (sire of 18 champions). New Hat came to this country and, although he did not finish his title, he was good enough to go best of winners at the Poodle Club of America Specialty in 1957. New Hat was the sire of Surrey New Broom who sired five champions. Moensfarm Mascot sired Dunwalke Kennels' Ch. Dunwalke Lorenzo of Montfleuri. Rudolph's most famous offspring was Dunwalke Kennels' Ch. Fontclair Festoon, winner of numerous Bests in Show including Westminster 1959. Festoon was the dam of 10 champions. Festoon's full sister, Eng. Ch. Fontclair Fleur of Burdiesel, was the dam of three champions. Another Rudolph daughter, Emmrill

Russet of Piperscroft

Lindabelle, was the dam of three champions. The influence of Rudolph is widespread both in this country and England.

Now to return to Barty. His son Russet of Piperscroft appears in many pedigrees as he was the sire of the brown Sienna of Piperscroft who produced one of England's most famous sires and winners, Eng. Ch. Firebrave Gaulois. Gaulois sired Firebrave Patapan (6 champions), who in turn sired Eng. and Am. Ch. Firebrave Sanka of Montfleuri (sire of seven champions) and his full brother Firebrave Spiro of Braebeck. Sanka sired Am. and Eng. Ch. Merrymorn Antoine (sire of nine champions). Firebrave Spiro sired the great English winner of 17 challenge certificates Eng. and Am. Ch. Braebeck Toni of Montfleuri (sire of six champions).

Another important brown son of Barty was Am. Ch. Sabu of Piperscroft. Sabu sired the brown Ch. Smilestone's Sirprise (sire of five champions), who in turn sired Ch. Hollycourt Bronze Knight (sire of 10 champions). Bronze Knight sired Ch. Cappoquin Bon Fiston (sire of 17 champions) and Ch. Hollycourt Ensign (sire of five champions). Bon Fiston sired Ch. Cappoquin Carriage Trade, winner of eight Bests in Show and sire of a number of champions.

Monty's litter brother, Ch. Misty Isles Algie of Piperscroft, was the first Miniature to go Best in Show in America. Algie sired five champions, and his sons and daughters were noted producers. Bred to his granddaughter he produced Bibelot of Misty Isles, who sired eight champions. Bibelot's son, Bibelot Cadet of Misty Isles, sired six champions including Hollycourt's Ch. Petit Pierre. Another Bibelot son was Ch. Clairwell Ce Soir, whose son Hollycourt Chevalier D'Argent sired Ch. Hollycourt Grillon Argente (sire of five champions). Due to the fact that the Misty Isles kennels were founded on Mrs. Taylor's silver bitches, most of the Algie descendents from this line were grays or silvers.

Another distinguished line descended from Success of Piperscroft through his black son Harpendale Little Tich through six generations to the blue Spotlight of Summercourt. Spotlight sired Fircot Silvafuzz of Summercourt and he, bred to a granddaughter of Ch. Hollycourt Platinum and Ch. Petit Pierre, gave the handsome Ch. Freeland's Flashlight. Flashlight possessed an exceptionally long well-made head, especially for a silver, and he was a success both in the show ring (Best of Variety at the 1961 Poodle Club of America Specialty) and at stud with five champions to his credit.

Spotlight also sired the light cream, Am. and Can. Ch. Summercourt Square Dancer of Fircot, who is the leading sire in the breed with 61 champions to his credit. Square Dancer, a Best in Show winner himself, is the sire of the greatest winning white Miniature dog, Ch. Tedwin's Top Billing (56 all breed and 5 specialty Bests in Show), and the greatest winning white bitch, Ch. Estid Ballet Dancer. Top Billing is the sire of eight champions. Square

Mrs. Campbell Inglis' black Miniature, Dare Devil Dink (Eng. Ch. The Monarch ex Bonny Forget Me Not), and his son Am. Ch. Sparkling Jet of Misty Isles (ex Crystal Ball).

Dancer comes from a primarily colored family, and has not transmitted the faults often prevalent in the whites. Some breeders consider him to be a mutation as he is so dominant in passing on his own easily recognizable qualities to his offspring. He has produced only white, cream or apricot. Two other Square Dancer sons, Ch. Barbree Round Dancer and Ch. Midcrest The Cosmopolitan, are both Best in Show winners and top producers.

MARCOURT CARNOT

Marcourt Carnot, a son of Ch. The Monarch, sired Sherwood Hall's Ch. Marcourt Tricot, the sire of five champions.

DARE DEVIL DINK

Ch. The Monarch also sired the black Dare Devil Dink, who was the sire of the famous black Ch. Sparkling Jet of Misty Isles. Before Jet left England he was bred to his granddam Bonny Forget Me Not, and produced the famous brothers Eng. Ch. The Laird of Mannerhead and Eng. Ch. Limelight of Mannerhead. Jet sired 11 champions and with Ch. Misty Isles Algie of Piperscroft dominated the world of Miniature Poodles for many years. Jet's son, Ch. Demon of Misty Isles, sired three champions including Ch. Clairwell Him Especially. Him Especially sired six champions including Ch. Diablotin Onyx who in turn sired seven champions. Onyx sired Duncount's Dauphin who sired Am. and Can. Ch. Chriscrest Jamboree (sire of six champions). Jamboree, a Best in Show winner, sired the Best in Show winner Ch. Chriscrest The Fiddler, who is the sire of 16 champions. Ch. Clairwell Him Especially also sired Ch. Periwig Surrey Peter Pan who sired Ch. Touchstone Top Kick, who is the sire of five champions. Ch. Demon of Misty Isles also sired Ch. Barrack Hill Bomber. Bomber sired Ch. Hollycourt Philippe, the sire of 20 champions. Philippe is the sire of Ch. Hollycourt Phillipson, who has eight champions to his credit, including Ch. Hollycourt Blackamoor. Blackamoor's son, Ch. Hollycourt Black Bobbin, is the sire of the magnificent brown Ch. Cappoquin Bon Jongleur.

89

Eng. Ch. Eric Brighteyes (by Popinjay ex Bonny Forget Me Not), owned by Mrs. Campbell Inglis, Mannerhead Kennels, England.

POPINJAY

I will now connect Ch. The Monarch with another great English line. His son, Popinjay, sired Mannerhead Kennel's famous Ch. Eric Brighteyes, a big winner and sire of champions. Brighteyes' son, Harwee of Mannerhead (ex Eng. Ch. The Mistress of Mannerhead—Chieveley bred) sired Blakeen's famous Ch. Snow Boy of Fircot. Snow Boy's sire was a black and his dam was a gray. There was no white in his pedigree for many generations, consequently Snow Boy did not possess or produce the faults that were so common in the whites of his day. Snow Boy was a big winner at important shows and exerted a great deal of improvement in the whites, both in England and the States. Before leaving England, Snow Boy sired Fircot Garcon de Neige who sired five champions. At Blakeen, Snow Boy produced Blakeen Oscar of the Waldorf, who went to England where he completed his championship and became an important sire. Oscar sired 10 champions and several of his get came back to this country to win honors. One son, Eng. and Am. Ch. Adastra Magic Fame, became one of the greatest winners of the breed with 53 Bests in Show to his credit. Fame was the sire of 14 champions. Another Oscar son, Ch. Rothara The Ragamuffin, won five Bests in Show and sired 11 champions. Another imported Oscar son, Ch. Wychwood White Winter, produced the Best in Show winner Am. and Can. Ch. Plaza-Toro Snow Fantasy who sired eight champions. This is just a brief resume of the influence of Snow Boy and his sons and grandsons on the whites. There were a number of bitches from these males that also made important contributions. Snow Boy was the single greatest influence on white Miniatures until the advent of Square Dancer, and Square Dancer benefited from the Snow Boy legacy in compiling his amazing record at stud.

90

CH. KING JOHNNY OF MARCOURT

Among Ch. The Monarch's earliest American sons were two dogs that exerted a great influence upon the Miniatures of their day: the silver Ch. Whippendell Picot and the black Ch. King Johnny of Marcourt, considered by many the best Marcourt of his period. King Johnny was bred to Whippendell Garconette Bleu to produce Ch. Marcourt Armand, who was bred to the gray Marcourt Mimi of Meredick (by Ch. Whippendell Picot) to produce the silver Ch. Talon's D'Argent of Meredick. Talon's D'Argent in turn sired Ch. Aucassin, who was an important early day sire in silvers. His son, Ch. Smilestone's Silvern, sired six champions including Ch. Hollycourt Light of Star Tavern (sire of 12 champions), Ch. Hollycourt Platinum (sire of 13 champions) and Ch. Hollycourt Ozmium of Paragon (sire of four champions). Light sired the beautiful Best in Show winner on the West Coast, Ch. Barclay Summer Smoke. Smoke was noted for his lovely head and excellent balance, and he sired 10 champions. Ozmium sired Ch. Paragon Dorien of Hollycourt and he in turn sired the Best in Show winner, Ch. Round Table's Avocat (sire of five champions).

ENG. CH. SPRIGGAN BELL

Ch. The Monarch also sired the black Eng. Ch. Spriggan Bell. A son of Spriggan Bell went to France, where his name was changed from Kinsoe Dapper to Footit de Madjige. Footit finished his championship and became an important Miniature sire on the continent. Footit sired French Ch. Illico de Madjige and Am. Ch. Moutit de Madjige, who came to the Blakeen Kennels where she produced Ch. Blakeen Tito and Ch. Blakeen Paper Doll. Spriggan Bell bred to the silver Hunningham Virginia produced Smoke Ring of Eathorpe. Smoke Ring sired Am. Ch. Grayling of Eathorpe-Carillon and Gunmetal of Eathorpe. Gunmetal was the sire of Silda of Eathorpe, who in turn sired the silvers Eng. Ch. Frenches Comet, Frenches Silverstar and Eng. Ch. Vendas Silver Pickles. Silverstar sired Poodhall Kennels Am. Ch. Frenches Mercury, who was a Group winner and sire of Ch. Bayou Breeze L'Argent Puppet (dam of four champions). Ch. Vendas Silver Pickles sired Swandora Gypsyheath Silver Sequins, who in turn sired Eng. Ch. Gypsyheath Silver Wings (sire of four champions). Another Silda of Eathorpe son, Berinshill Patta Pouf of Ronada, sired the Best in Show winner Am. Ch. Wychwood Peroquet of Blakeen (sire of three champions).

The Monarch line is the largest and most successful in the Miniature variety. A study of the foregoing will show that it has exerted tremendous influence in blacks, and even in the whites and silvers, although The Monarch himself was a blue. And, of course, in the intervening years not only color, but type as well, has been affected by the bitches that breeders have brought to the line.

Ruffles of Piperscroft

Ch. Tommy K

Clipper of Piperscroft

Conceit of Piperscroft

Ch. Cappoquin Carriage Trade

Eng. Ch. Baroque of Montfleuri

ENG. CH. THE MONARCH
    Success of Piperscroft (blk)
        Conceit of Piperscroft (blk)
            Monty of Piperscroft (blk)
                Ch. Jingle of Piperscroft (blk)
                    Ch. Leader of Piperscroft of Blakeen (blk) 5
                        Ch. Galcit's Priority of Ste. Elmo (blk) 5
                        Ch. Leader's Brown Topper (brn)
                            Ch. Tommy K (brn) 10
                                Am. & Can. Ch. Norcrest Surrey Sahib (brn) 9
                    Eng. Ch. Barty of Piperscroft (blk) 2
                        Robin of Piperscroft (blk)
                            Firebrave Alphonse (blk) 4
                                Int. Ch. Firebrave Pimpernel (blk) 6
                                    Int. Ch. Pixholme Firebrave Gustav (blk) 23
                                        Ch. Poodhall Gus (blk) 19
                        Ruffles of Piperscroft (blk)
                            Eng. Ch. Top Hat of Piperscroft (blk)
                                Ch. Busby of Piperscroft (blk) 15
                            Tiptop of Piperscroft (blk)
                                Tais-Toi of Piperscroft (blk) 6
                                Voila of Piperscroft (blk)
                                    Clipper of Piperscroft (blk)
                                        Eng. Ch. Rudolph of Piperscroft (blk) 26
                                            Eng. Ch. Baroque of Montfleuri (blk) 8
                                            Eng. Ch. Moensfarm Mascot of Montfleuri (blk) 18
                                                Ch. Dunwalke Lorenzo of Montfleuri (blk) 5
                                            Eng. Ch. Rippwood Milord of Eldonwood (blk) 5
                                            New Hat of Montfleuri (blk) 9
                                                Surrey New Broom (blk) 5
                    Russet of Piperscroft (brn)
                        Sienna of Piperscroft (brn)
                            Eng. Ch. Firebrave Gaulois (blk) 6
                                Firebrave Patapan (blk) 6
                                    Int. Ch. Firebrave Sanka of Montfleuri (blk) 7
                                        Int. Ch. Merrymorn Antoine (blk) 9
                                    Firebrave Spiro of Braebeck (blk) 7
                                        Int. Ch. Braebeck Toni of Montfleuri (blk) 6
                    Ch. Sabu of Piperscroft (brn)
                        Ch. Smilestone's Sirprise (brn) 5
                            Ch. Hollycourt Bronze Knight (brn) 10
                            Ch. Hollycourt Ensign (blk) 5
                            Ch. Cappoquin Bon Fiston (blk) 17
                                Ch. Cappoquin Carriage Trade (blk) 6
            Ch. Misty Isles Algie of Piperscroft (gr) 5
                Bibelot of Misty Isles (gr) 8
                Bibelot Cadet of Misty Isles (gr) 6
                    Ch. Petit Pierre (gr) 9
                        Ch. Hollycourt Manicamp (si)
                    Ch. Clairwell Ce Soir (gr)
                        Hollycourt Chevalier d'Argent (si)
                            Ch. Hollycourt Grillon Argente (si) 5

Spotlight of Summercourt

Ch. Sparkling Jet of Misty Isles

Ch. Freeland's Flashlight

Ch. Barrack Hill Bomber

Ch. Summercourt Square Dancer
of Fircot (as a puppy).

Ch. Hollycourt Phillipson

```
    Success of Piperscroft (continued)
      Harpendale Little Tich (blk)
        Harpendale John Brown (brn)
          Harpendale Admiration (brn)
            Chocolat of Swanhill (brn)
              Eng. Ch. Cremola of Swanhill (crm)
                Victor of Fircot (apr)
                  Spotlight of Summercourt (blu)
                    Fircot Silvafuzz of Summercourt (si)
                      Ch. Freeland's Flashlight (si) 5
                    Ch. Summercourt Square Dancer of Fircot (crm) 61
                      Ch. Tedwin's Top Billing (wh) 8
                      Ch. Barbree Round Dancer (wh) 5
                      Ch. Midcrest The Cosmopolitan (wh) 6
    Marcourt Carnot (blk)
      Ch. Marcourt Tricot (blk) 5
    Dare Devil Dink (blk)
      Ch. Sparkling Jet of Misty Isles (blk) 11
        Ch. Demon of Misty Isles (blk) 3
          Ch. Barrack Hill Bomber (blk) 2
            Ch. Hollycourt Philippe (blk) 20
              Ch. Hollycourt Blackamoor (blk) 5
                Ch. Hollycourt Black Bobbin (blk)
                  Ch. Cappoquin Bon Jongleur (brn) 20
              Ch. Hollycourt Phillipson (blk) 8
          Ch. Clairwell Him Especially (blk) 6
            Ch. Diablotin Onyx (blk) 7
              Duncount's Dauphin (blk) 3
                Ch. Chriscrest Jamboree (blk) 6
                  Ch. Chriscrest The Fiddler (blk) 16
            Ch. Perriwig Surrey Peter Pan (blk)
              Ch. Touchstone Top Kick (blk) 5
```

Ch. Touchstone Top Kick

Harwee of Mannerhead

Eng. Ch. Toomai of Montfleuri

Eng. Ch. Blakeen Oscar
of the Waldorf

Ch. Smilestone's Silvern

Ch. Rothara The Ragmuffin

Eng. Ch. Gypsyheath Silver Wings

Popinjay (blk)
   Eng. Ch. Eric Brighteyes (blk)
      Harwee of Mannerhead (blk) 3
         Eng. Ch. Toomai of Montfleuri (blk) 2
         Ch. Snow Boy of Fircot (wh) 10
            Fircot Garcon de Neige (wh) 5
            Eng. Ch. Blakeen Oscar of the Waldorf (wh) 10
               Int. Ch. Adastra Magic Fame (wh) 14
               Ch. Rothara The Ragamuffin (wh) 11
               Ch. Wychwood White Winter (wh)
                  Ch. Plaza-Toro Snow Fantasy (wh) 8
Ch. King Johnny of Marcourt (blk)
   Ch. Marcourt Armand (blk)
      Ch. Talon's D'Argent of Meredick (si) 4
         Ch. Aucassin (gr)
            Ch. Smilestone's Silvern (si) 6
               Ch. Hollycourt Light of Star Tavern (si) 12
                 Ch. Barclay Summer Smoke (si) 10
               Ch. Hollycourt Platinum (si) 13
               Ch. Hollycourt Ozmium of Paragon (si) 4
                 Ch. Paragon Dorien of Hollycourt (si)
                  Ch. Round Table's Avocat (gr) 5

  Eng. Ch. Spriggan Bell (blk)
    Int. Ch. Footit de Madjige (France) 2
      Ch. Illico de Madjige (France)
    Smoke Ring of Eathorpe (gr)
      Ch. Grayling of Eathorpe-Carillon (si)
      Gunmetal of Eathorpe (si)
        Silda of Eathorpe (si) 2
          Eng. Ch. Frenches Comet (si)
          Frenches Silverstar (si)
            Ch. Frenches Mercury (si)
          Eng. Ch. Venda's Silver Pickles (si)
            Swandora Gypsyheath Silver Sequins (si)
               Eng. Ch. Gypsyheath Silver Wings (si) 4
          Berinshill Patta Pouf of Ronada (si)
            Ch. Wychwood Peroquet of Blakeen (si) 3

Four generations from the Chieveley Kennels: Eng. Ch. Harcourt Jack, Eng. Ch. Chieveley Choufleur, Chieveley Clarence and Chieveley Chub (as a puppy).

Eng. Ch. Chieveley Chintz

18

Chieveley Kennels

AT the time of the death of Miss Morehouse and the dispersal of the inmates of her Chieveley Kennels in 1924, the institution housed some sixty Poodles, and had won more prizes up until that time than any other kennel with any breed of dogs. The Chieveley Line is the only one of the old black lines to come directly down to the dogs of this time. It is, of course, because of the merits of the Chieveley dogs more than because of their numbers that their blood has survived.

A bitch named Jill, of whose pedigree there is no record, a gift to Miss Morehouse, was the foundation of the kennel that was soon to become famous as Chieveley. Jill was the dam of Ch. Harcourt Jack, the first of Miss Morehouse's many distinguished champions. Harcourt Jack, mated to Harcourt Bijou, produced Chieveley Bunty, who, as a result of her union with Whippendell Petit Chou, was to produce the sensational Ch. Chieveley Chouflour.

However, of the earlier Chieveleys, old breeders are almost unanimous in considering Chouflour's son, Ch. Cheeky Boy, to be the best. From pictures of Cheeky Boy, we may judge his length of foreface, body type and wealth of coat to be quite up to our modern concepts. He was by the small Chouflour out of Desdemona of Monte Christo, a small Standard Poodle of a well-known line. Desdemona was also the dam of Chieveley Gypsy, by Harcourt Jack. Gypsy was another with an excellent head, cobby body, and magnificent coat.

Ch. Chieveley Cheeky Boy died of distemper while he was yet a young dog and left few progeny. However, included was a bitch called Chieveley Char-

Eng. & Am. Ch. Chieveley Chopstick

meuse (who became the dam of the great Eng. and Am. Ch. Chieveley Chopstick) and Eng. Ch. Naughty Boy. It was her admiration of Cheeky Boy that prompted Mrs. Audrey Tyndall, owner of the famous Venda's Kennels, to mate Belinda Bleue to Aide do Camp—both were by Ch. Naughty Boy. The resultant litter justified its breeder's judgment, for it included two of the most famous brood bitches of their time, La Pompadour of Piperscroft and Bonny Forget-Me-Not.

La Pompadour was the dam of Eng. Ch. Louis of Piperscroft (by Ch. Pronto of Gotton), and of Manon of Piperscroft (by Petit Ami of Piperscroft, who was by Chieveley Chanter ex Ch. Chieveley Chess). Manon was Mrs. Alida Monro's first Poodle. She was the dam of the great foundation sire, Eng. Ch. Barty of Piperscroft, and of Am. Ch. Leader of Piperscroft and Blakeen.

Bonny Forget-Me-Not went to Mrs. Campbell Inglis' Mannerhead Kennels, where she produced four champions. Bonny bred to Venda's Blue Masterpiece produced Eng. Ch. Flashlight of Mannerhead. Bred to Popinjay (by Ch. The Monarch), Bonny produced Eng. Ch. Eric Brighteyes. Bonny bred to Ch. The Monarch produced Dare Devil Dink. Dink bred to Crystal Bell gave Eng. Ch. The Ghost and Am. Ch. Sparkling Jet of Misty Isles. Sparkling Jet, bred to his grand-dam Bonny Forget-Me-Not, produced Eng. Ch. The Laird of Mannerhead (sire of three champions) and Eng. Ch. Limelight of Mannerhead.

Shortly after the end of World War I, Miss Morehouse died and her brother, Sir Henry Morehouse, saw fit to disperse the many dogs in her kennel, retaining Chieveley Cheepress (by Ch. Chieveley Chopstick) as a pet.

100

Cheepress, when mated to Eng. Ch. Spriggan Bell, produced the famous winner and International Ch. Footit de Madjige. Sir Henry presented two of the Chieveleys to Mrs. Grace Boyd: Chieveley Chatty and Petit Ami of Piperscroft, both out of the tiny Eng. Ch. Chieveley Chess (by Chieveley Chaps ex Eng. Ch. Anita).

The cream of the Chieveley Kennels at its dispersement went to Mr. Price's Marcourt Kennels in Boston, Massachusetts, the most notable being the three champions Chopstick, Chess and her son Chump. Chopstick and Chump soon added American championships to their English titles, and were the first two Miniature Poodles to attain this double distinction. Chess was bred again to Chopstick to produce Ch. Marcourt Andre. This was a repeat of the breeding that had produced Chieveley Chatty, who remained in England. Chump was bred to Marcourt Justine (a Chopstick daughter) to produce Ch. Marcourt Petit Pierre. Chump's English son, Jambo, was the sire of Ch. Venda's The Black Imp of Catawba.

Perhaps the most famous of all the Chieveleys was the black Eng. and Am. Ch. Chieveley Chopstick. Chopstick was by Chieveley Chaps (by Eng. Ch. Chieveley Choufleur ex Sue) out of Chieveley Charmeuse (by Eng. Ch. Chieveley Cheeky Boy ex Chieveley Charlotte). Chopstick was the sire of four champions: Eng. Ch. Caddy of Wymerling, Ch. Marcourt Andre, Ch. Marcourt Sabot (dam of four champions at Sherwood Hall) and Ch. Marcourt Julia (dam of Sherwood Hall's Ch. Marcourt Tricot, sire of five champions). Chopstick's son, Tinker of Marcourt, sired Cartlane Augustin, a great stud force in his day. In the Venda's Kennel, in the Wymering Kennels, in the Harpendale Kennels, in the Piperscroft Kennels, and elsewhere in England, bitches by Chopstick were treasured and bred from to produce notable Poodles.

Although most of the Chieveleys were black, there were occasional browns due to the influence of the brown Sue, who was from small brown French stock. Bred to Ch. Chieveley Choufleur, Sue produced Chieveley Peggy (dam of Eng. Ch. Naughty Boy) and Chieveley Chaps. Chaps was the sire of Am. and Eng. Ch. Chieveley Chopstick and Eng. Ch. Chieveley Chess. Chess was the dam of Am. and Eng. Ch. Chieveley Chump and Petit Ami of Piperscroft (by Chieveley Chanter, a double grandson of Choufleur). Petit Ami proved of tremendous worth to the Piperscroft Kennel, and through his son, Petit Morceau of Piperscroft, of equal value to the Venda's line. Chess bred to Ch. Chieveley Chopstick produced Am. Ch. Marcourt Andre and the 12-inch Chieveley Chatty, whose daughter was to found the world-famous Firebraves of Mrs. Alida Monro.

Mrs. Monro was a great admirer of the Chieveleys and her kennel contains the strongest concentration of these bloodlines to be found anywhere. Chieveley Chatty bred to Francois of Piperscroft produced Firebrave Mam'-

Eng. Ch. Chieveley Cheeky Boy

selle. Mam'selle was bred to Firebrave Copperfield to produce the Eng. Ch. Firebrave Nicolette, dam of four champions. Nicolette bred to Firebrave Alphonse produced Eng. Am. and Can. Ch. Firebrave Pimpernel (sire of six champions. Nicolette bred to Firebrave Patapan (by Eng. Ch. Firebrave Gaulois ex Firebrave Mam'selle) produced Eng. Ch. Firebrave Olympia, Eng. Ch. Firebrave Marie, Eng. and Am. Ch. Firebrave Sanka of Montfleuri (sire of seven champions) and Firebrave Spiro of Braebeck (sire of seven champions). Mam'selle bred to her grandson Eng. Ch. Firebrave Gaulois produced Firebrave Patapan (sire of six champions). Mam'selle bred to another grandson, Ch. Firebrave Pimpernel, produced Eng. Am. and Can. Ch. Pixholme Firebrave Gustav C.D. (sire of 23 champions). As can be seen by the foregoing Mrs. Monro carefully interwove and concentrated her precious Chieveley blood through Mam'selle and Nicolette.

This brief study will help to point up the tremendous effect that the Chieveleys exerted in a number of important kennels in England and America.

102

19

Characteristics of
the "Chieveley" Line

THE faults and virtues that characterized the Chieveley dogs, the oldest distinct line of Miniature Poodles of which any record exists, are persistent, even though the Chieveley Kennels were disbanded and the inmates scattered in the 1920's. The Chieveley blood has been diluted and attenuated by the admixture of other strains, but its influence upon the Miniature Poodle family remains evident. The best of it is very good indeed, producing a daintiness and a Miniature quality that is difficult to find in other strains. In a letter written on September 5, 1935, Miss Brunker, the dean of the English Poodle fancy, says, "I consider the Chieveleys excelled all over, some, of course, better than others. They excelled in coat, were beautifully put down, and showed well. Ch. Chieveley Cheeky Boy was the best, and I always look for his descendants."

The Chieveley is the one strain that can be depended upon to keep size down. It has been used for this purpose for many years in England, where large bitches or those with Standard blood close behind them have been mated to small Chieveley-bred dogs with excellent results. Used wisely, it will produce tiny dogs, such as those in my own kennels, of actual Toy measurement and the equals in type of Miniatures four times their size.

In my many years' experience with the Chieveley strain, I learned to expect from it beautiful, short bodies, straight backed and round ribbed, with tails set high. Chieveley feet are excellent, high-arched and tight-toed. At their best, dogs with this blood exhibit great refinement of head, although skulls and muzzles are seldom as long as those from the Monarch line.

Eng. Ch. Chieveley Choufleur

The Chieveleys have typical expressions together with an elfin charm difficult to define.

The reverse of the Chieveley medal—and, alas, a medal always has a reverse —is a tendency toward eyes too round and too light; sometimes skulls that are too thick, short forefaces, and, worst of all, undershot jaws. The hocks of many Chieveley-bred Poodles are too straight, and their shoulders are straight instead of sloping, which causes fronts to appear too wide. In some branches of the strain there exists a tendency toward thickness of bone and general coarseness of heads; but, in well nigh every Chieveley, the body can be depended upon to be superb.

The strain is basically black, with a dash of brown blood, which is treated at greater length in the chapter about browns.

Your Chieveley is a distinct individualist, no two of them being alike in their characters. They have a quaint charm and a distinction, different from that of other strains, along with odd crotchets that are all the individual's own and most amusing. They are not friends to all the world, but quite the contrary. Their devotion to those persons they love, however, is deep and unswerving. Their intelligence is uncanny. Sometimes their traits are difficult and they are quarrelsome, but I have never had a dog of Chieveley blood that failed to respond to loving human companionship and understanding. Given the affection they crave, the Chieveleys make ideal companions.

20

The "Chieveley" Line
Eng. Ch. Chieveley Choufleur

THE key dog in the Chieveley tail male line was Eng. Ch. Chieveley Choufleur. Choufleur's most important sons were Eng. Ch. Chieveley Cheeky Boy who died early, Chieveley Chaps and Chieveley Challenger. Chaps was the sire of the famous Eng. and Am. Ch. Chieveley Chopstick who was the sire of four champions. Chopstick's son, Tinker of Marcourt, produced Cartlane Augustin who was a vital stud force in the early days. Chieveley Challenger bred to Chieveley Chatterer (also by Choufleur) produced Chieveley Chanter. Chanter produced two sons, full brothers, which were to be of great importance to the breed—Am. and Eng. Ch. Chieveley Chump and Petit Ami of Piperscroft. These were out of Eng. Ch. Chieveley Chess who was a granddaughter of Choufleur.

Before going to America, Chump sired a black dog called Jambo, who was bred to Venda's Maid of Honor to produce Ch. Venda's the Black Imp of Catawba. The Black Imp was a truly great sire. His main contributions were an excellent body type, the good feet of the Chieveley line, and a profuse stiff-textured coat. There were some that were too light in the eye, some that were too heavy-boned, and some could have been finer in the skull but the appearance of these faults and virtues depended to a degree on the bitches to which he was bred. There is no doubt that he was a great sire, and his appearance on the American scene was well-timed.

The Black Imp sired eight champions including Ch. Blakeen Eldorado. Eldorado was probably the greatest brown Miniature in America up to his time, and he had a sensational career with seven Bests in Show to his credit. Eldorado in turn sired Ch. Diablotin Demi-Setier who sired five champions.

The Black Imp also sired Ch. Blakeen Bitzie Boy (sire of five champions) and Sherwood Hall's Blakeen Chieveley (sire of five champions). Another Black Imp son, Ch. Black Magic, was bred to Bric A Brac Ballerina, to produce the great winner, Am. and Can. Ch. Magic Fate of Blakeen, who won 25 Bests in Show. Magic Fate went to California where he was very popular at stud and produced 13 champions. Magic Fate was the sire of another top winner (11 Bests in Show) and producer, Am. and Can. Ch. Highland Sand Magic Star. Magic Star was the sire of Ch. Highland Sand George who was a notable winner in the Mid-West with five Bests in Show to his credit. George sired 16 champions. Another Magic Star son, Beaujeu Kennels' Ch. Highland Sand Star Baby, is the sire of six champions. Ch. Black Magic's son, the non-titled Bric A Brac Barker, was the sire of five champions, including Ch. Bric A Brac Best Man (sire of five champions). Best Man's son, Hollycourt Excalibur II, also sired five champions.

A full brother of Ch. Chieveley Chump, Petit Ami of Piperscroft, remained in England to perform great service to the breed. He sired Vulcan Muscat who in turn sired The Elfin Boy of Toytown. The Elfin Boy sired the famous Eng. Ch. Toy Boy of Toytown. Toy Boy, a Best in Show winner, was described as "full of quality from his nicely-proportioned and quality head, dark eyes and thick ears to his well-muscled hindquarters, and thick harsh coat." His owner reportedly refused an offer of 2,000 pounds for him, and this was in the days when the pound was worth more than twice what it is today. Howard Price, of the famous Montfleuri Kennels, described Toyboy as "a small, very smart and ultra-compact little dog with a huge, dense black coat." Toy Boy sired Eng. Ch. Jacqueline Jegu, Eng. Ch. Braeval Bobo and Eng. Ch. Glendoune Dapper. In addition to these, three of Toy Boy's sons and six of his daughters were producers of champions.

Bobo and Dapper head important families that are currently winning and producing. Bobo bred to his double granddaughter, Braeval Burnt Grass, produced Eng. Am. and Can. Ch. Braeval Boomerang. Boomerang, a Group winner, went to the Beaujeu Kennels in Texas where he sired 15 champions. Boomerang sired the Best in Show winning brothers, Ch. Beaujeu Royal and Ch. Beaujeu Regal. Regal in turn sired the Best in Show winner Ch. Crikora Commotion (sire of five champions). Bobo bred to Braeval Brighteyes (by Harwee of Mannerhead) produced three important individuals: Eng. Ch. Braeval Bolero, Eng. Ch. Braeval Brioche (dam of five champions) and Braeval Brown Bella (dam of four champions). Bolero was a big winner with many Bests in Show and 10 challenge certificates to his credit. Bolero was also one of England's greatest stud dogs with 21 champions to his credit. Bolero bred to his daughter, Braeval Best Bet, gave Eng. Ch. Braeval Barty who has five champion daughters in America (all out of Aspen Arraminta— a double granddaughter to Montmartre What-A-Boy). Bolero also sired Eng. Ch. Braeval Brave. Brave's son, Braeval Bingo, was the sire of four champions including Am. Ch. Braeval Busker. Busker, a group winner, was the sire of five champions including the outstanding Best in Show winner Eng. Ch. Braeval Bentley. Bentley sired the outstanding winner in England (14 challenge certificates) and American (several Bests in Show) Eng. Am. Can. and Mex. Ch. Montmartre Bartat By Jingo, who is a current popular sire at Beaujeu and has nine champions to his credit. In England, By Jingo's son, Eng. Ch. Beritas Bonaparte has won 12 c.c.'s. Bonaparte is the sire of 12 champions to date.

Ch. Toyboy of Toytown bred to his granddaughter, Braeval Brown Bella, produced Eng. Ch. Glendoune Dapper. Dapper bred to his dam, Brown Bella, produced Eng. Ch. Glendoune Dazzle, Eng. Ch. Glendoune Dinah and Am. Ch. Glendoune Brunetta. Dapper produced a total of six champions. Dapper's son, Faskine Velutina, sired Faskine Talpatina. Talpatina was a Best in Show winner with two challenge certificates and three reserve c.c.'s. Talpatina bred to Eng. Ch. Braeval Betta (a granddaughter of Ch. Braeval Bobo and Ch. Toy Boy of Toytown) gave the Best in Show winner in England, Montmartre What-A-Boy. What-A-Boy was used extensively at Montmartre before coming to the Dunwalke Kennels in America. He sired 15 champions—seven of them out of Dunwalke's Ch. Fontclair Festoon. This was a prime example of the wisdom of combining the Chieveley—Monarch lines. What-A-Boy possessed a small gene and his Toy-sized daughter Eng. Ch. Montmartre Miss Muffet was the dam of three champions. What-A-Boy bred to his daughter, Ch. Montmartre Marcella, produced Ch. Dunwalke Marcellus who went to the Challendon Kennels on the West Coast where he sired 13 champions. Marcellus has returned to the East Coast to the Highlane Kennels, where he should continue to add to his outstanding record as a sire.

What-A-Boy left in England a Best in Show son, Eng. Ch. Montmartre Marksman. Marksman, bred to a litter sister of his sire What-A-Boy, Eng. Ch. Montmartre Little Mo, produced Eng. Ch. Montmartre Marco Polo who is the sire of 14 champions.

This is perhaps the strongest black-bred line in existence in the world. There have been crosses to the Monarch line but always the return to the Chieveley heritage. The present day specimens whose success has been outlined attest to quality inherent in this line and represent many, many crosses to the Chieveley line. Mrs. Monro's Firebraves, Mrs. Conn's Montmartres and Mrs. Austin-Smith's Braevals are rich in Chieveley breeding and have rewarded their breeders for their faith in this great family line.

Petit Ami of Piperscroft

Ch. Crikora Commotion

Eng. Ch. Toyboy of Toytown

Eng. Ch. Beritas Bonaparte

Ch. Highland Sand George

Montmartre What-A-Boy

ENG. CH. CHIEVELEY CHOUFLEUR
    Chieveley Chaps (blk) 2
        Eng. & Am. Ch. Chieveley Chopstick (blk) 4
            Tinker of Marcourt (blk)
                Cartlane Augustin (blk) 5
    Chieveley Challenger (blk)
        Chieveley Chanter (blk)
            Eng. & Am. Ch. Chieveley Chump (blk)
                Jambo (blk) 1
                    Ch. Venda's The Black Imp of Catawba (blk) 8
                        Ch. Blakeen Eldorado (brn) 7
                            Ch. Diablotin Demi-Setier (blk) 5
                        Ch. Blakeen Bitzie Boy (blk) 5
                        Blakeen Chieveley (blk) 5
                        Ch. Black Magic (blk) 2
                            Am. & Can. Ch. Magic Fate of Blakeen (blk) 13
                                Am. & Can. Ch. Highland Sand Magic Star (blk) 23
                                    Ch. Highland Sand George (blk) 16
                                    Ch. Highland Sand Star Baby (blk) 6
                            Bric A Brac Barker (blk) 5
                                Ch. Bric A Brac Best Man (blk) 5
                                    Hollycourt Excalibur II (blk) 5
        Petit Ami of Piperscroft (blk)
            Petit Morceau of Piperscroft (blk) 2
                Vulcan Champagne Muscat (blk)
                    The Chocolate Tin Soldier of Toytown (blk) 3
                        The Elfin Boy of Toytown (blk) 1
                            Eng. Ch. Toy Boy of Toytown (blk) 3
                                Eng. Ch. Braeval Bobo (blk) 6
                                    Int. Ch. Braeval Boomerang (blk) 15
                                        Ch. Beaujeu Regal (blk) 6
                                            Ch. Crikora Commotion (blk) 5
                                    Eng. Ch. Braeval Bolero (blk) 21
                                        Eng. Ch. Braeval Barty (blk) 5
                                        Eng. Ch. Braeval Brave (blk)
                                        Braeval Bingo (blk) 4
                                            Ch. Braeval Busker (blk) 5
                                                Eng. Ch. Braeval Bentley (blk)
                                                    Ch. Montmartre Bartat By Jingo (blk) 9
                                                        Eng. Ch. Beritas Bonaparte (blk) 13
                            Eng. Ch. Glendoune Dapper (blk) 6
                                Faskine Velutina (blk)
                                    Faskine Talpatina (blk) 1
                                        Montmartre What-A-Boy (blk) 15
                                            Ch. Dunwalke Marcellus (blk) 13
                                            Eng. Ch. Montmartre Marksman (blk) 7
                                                Eng. Ch. Montmartre Marco Polo (blk) 14
                                                Aus. Ch. Montmartre Mighty Tiny (blk) Eng. Toy 1
                                                    Montmartre Louis Miguel (brn) Eng. Toy 2
                                                        Eng. Ch. Montmartre Mastersinger (blk) Eng. Toy 3
                                                            Montmartre Ring-Master (blk) Eng. Toy 5
                                                                Montmartre Minute Man (blk) Eng. Toy 2

Berinshill Dancing Boy (white Miniature) by Berinshill Polar ex Berinshill Dancing Shoes, bred by Berinshill Kennels.

Ch. Rothara The Cavalier

21

The "Dancing Boy" Line
Berinshill Dancing Boy

T̲HE importance of this line is far greater than its size indicates. It has its origins in the white German dog, Bodo V. Kurpark. The foundation dogs were unrelated to either the Monarch or Chieveley lines, although in later generations other lines were added through the bitches brought to it. The line is primarily white and cream in descent in the tail male line. Bodo V. Kurpark sired Whippendell Perce Neige Deux who in turn sired Whippendell Duvet. Duvet sired Whippendell Petit Eclair who was the sire of Petit Jean of Toytown, and of Aureolin of Toytown who is discussed in the section on the breeding of apricots. Petit Jean bred to the silver Storyval Maree of Fircot (sister of the great white Ch. Snow Boy of Fircot) produced the white Berinshill Polar. Polar bred to a granddaughter of Whippendell Petit Eclair produced the silver Am. Ch. Berinshill Tarrywood Silver Glow (Best in Show winner) and Berinshill Dancing Boy.

In England, Dancing Boy was a Best in Show winner and won two challenge certificates. He was a popular stud, and a number of his sons came to this country and were outstanding winners. These include Ch. Fircot L'Ballerine of Maryland, Ch. Icarus Duke Otto (Best in Show winner and sire of nine champions), Ch. Nikora of Manapouri (Best in Show winner), Ch. Pita of Manapouri and Ch. Berinshill Silver Nickle. Another son, Eng. Ch. Kannishon Venda's White Lancer, remained in England. When Diana Waugh moved to Canada she brought Dancing Boy with her. Upon her return to England she felt Dancing Boy was too old to be put through the six-month quarantine period, so she left him in the care of the Harbridge Kennels in Michigan, where he lived to an advanced age, siring right up to

Ch. Icarus Duke Otto (by Berinshill Dancing Boy ex Wychwood Georgia). Bred by G. Till, England. Owned by Beaujeu Kennels.

the end of his long life. On this side of the Atlantic, he sired Ch. Silhou-Jette's Dancing Shoes and Can. Ch. Tarna's Vanessa.

Dancing Boy's most famous son was Ch. Fircot L'Ballerine of Maryland who went Best in Show at the famous Morris and Essex Kennel Club Show and at the Poodle Club of America Specialty. L'Ballerine sired Ch. Bric A Brac Ballet Star and Am. and Mex. Ch. Hawesdown Blanche Neige, and a number of champions in later generations. An untitled English son of Dancing Boy, Rothara The Rake, sired Am. and Can. Ch. Rothara The Cavalier who was a Best in Show winner in England and the States. The Cavalier was the sire of five champions. This line has combined well with the descendants of Ch. Snow Boy of Fircot and Ch. Summercourt Square Dancer of Fircot.

```
BODO V. KURPARK (German)
    Whippendell Perce Neige Deux
        Whippendell Duvet (apr)
            Whippendell Petit Eclair (apr)
                Petit Jean of Toytown (apr)
                    Berinshill Polar (wh)
                        Berinshill Dancing Boy (wh) 7
                            Ch. Fircot L'Ballerine of Maryland (crm) 2
                            Ch. Icarus Duke Otto (wh) 9
                            Rothara The Rake (wh)
                                Ch. Rothara The Cavalier (wh) 5
                    Aureolin of Toytown (apr)
                        Frenches Lil' Goldsmith (apr)
                            Fircot Sunshine of Zizi Pompom (apr)
                                Tio Pepe of Greatcoats (apr)
                                    Puckshill Amberglaze (apr)
                                        Puckshill Ambersuncrush (apr)
                                            Eng. Ch. Oakington Puckshill Ambersunblush
                                            (Eng. T apr. bitch, BIS Crufts)
                                        Puckshill Marmalade of Greatcoats (apr)
                                            Eng. Ch. Rhosbridge Golden Shred (apr) Eng.T
```

Eng. Ch. The Silver Gnome

Ch. Blakeen Quicksilver (silver Miniature) by Ch. Platinum of Eathorpe ex Ma Foi of Misty Isles, bred and owned by Mrs. Sherman Hoyt.

22

The "Blue Boy" Line
Eng. Ch. The Blue Boy

THE "Blue Boy" sire line, although not directly descended from Eng. Ch. The Monarch, is very closely related. Chic of Watercroft sired Eng. Ch. Angel of Mine (dam of Ch. The Monarch) and her full brother Ch. The Blue Boy. Blue Boy sired Eng. Ch. The Silver Gnome, who in turn sired Am. Ch. Fee D'Argent of Piperscroft and the silver full brothers Hunningham D'Argent and Hunningham Silver (ex Hunningham Rikki-Tikki, a silver). Hunningham D'Argent was bred to Griz Nez of Eathorpe (by Eng. Ch. Spriggan Bell ex Hunningham Virginia—a full sister to Hunningham D'Argent) to produce Am. Ch. Blue Streak of Eathorpe-Mansard and Am. Ch. Platinum of Eathorpe of Blakeen. Platinum sired Ch. Blakeen Hi Ho Silver, Ch. Blakeen Quicksilver, Ch. Snappy Morn and Hollycourt's great foundation bitch Ch. Platina. Hunningham Silver was bred to Ch. Angel of Mine to produce Venda's Arrow of Silver (who later went to Misty Isles). Arrow of Silver was bred to Leila to produce England's great silver foundation sire, Venda's Blue Masterpiece (2 Challenge Certificates, 6 reserve c.c.'s).

Blue Masterpiece bred to the blue Bonny Forget-Me-Not (dam of four champions) produced Eng. Ch. Flashlight of Mannerhead. Flashlight won 9 c.c.'s. His color was described as being a rich, even, almost persian-cat blue. Flashlight was bred to Eng. Ch. The Mistress of Mannerhead to produce the gray Francois of Mannerhead, who came to the States. Francois sired Roadcoach Qui Vive (sire of three champions), Ch. Dunwandrin Pepe Le Moko, and Ch. Hollycourt Venture (sire of five champions). Venture in turn was bred to Ch. Hollycourt Aure de Montalais to give Ch. Hollycourt Mercure.

```
ENG. CH. THE BLUE BOY*
    Eng. Ch. The Silver Gnome (si)
        Hunningham D'Argent (si) 2
            Ch. Platinum of Eathorpe of Blakeen (si) 4
        Hunningham Silver (si)
            Venda's Arrow of Silver (si)
                Venda's Blue Masterpiece (gr)
                    Eng. Ch. Flashlight of Mannerhead (gr)
                        Francois of Mannerhead (gr) 2
                            Roadcoach Qui Vive (si) 3
                        Ch. Hollycourt Venture (si) 5
                            Ch. Hollycourt Mercure (si)
                                Ch. Hollycourt Vaillant (si) 8
                                    Ch. Hollycourt Talent of Silver (si) 10
                                    Ch. Touchstone Silversmith (si) 5


* Brother of Eng. Ch. Angel of Mine (dam of Eng. Ch. The Monarch)
```

Ch. Hollycourt Talent of Silver

Am. & Can. Ch. Touchstone Silversmith

Mercure was bred to Hollycourt Iridium (ex Ch. Platina) to give Ch. Holly-Court Vaillant who was the sire of eight champions including Ch. Hollycourt Talent of Silver (sire of 10 champions) and Am. and Can. Ch. Touchstone Silversmith (sire of five champions).

Ch. Platinum of Eathorpe
of Blakeen

Venda's
Blue Masterpiece

Nanette Grise. One of the first silver Miniatures in England. Bred and owned by Millie Brunker.

Moufflon Bleu

23

The Silver Miniature

WHIPPENDELL BLUES AND SILVERS

THE silver Miniature started in England with the birth of the silver-gray bitch Pierrette Jackson, who was whelped in 1895. Her breeder Millie Brunker stated that she was the first silver-gray bred in England. Pierrette's sire Moustache and her dam Toupet were both coal-black. The entire litter was born black, but three of them started changing to gray at three months of age. Moustache and Toupet were both sired by Peter Jackson, but their dams were listed as unknown so we can only speculate as to where the gray gene came from. Pierrette Jackson made her debut at the L.K.A. Show at Holland House in 1896 where she created a sensation when she won the premiership over all the established black and white prize winners. Bred to London Pride, a gray imported from the Continent, Pierrette Jackson produced La Poupee and Nanette Grise.

It is important to remember that breeders used the terms blue to cover a range of colors. Miss Brunker herself stated, "These blues range from a deep smoke gray to the palest silver and are very attractive." Miss Brunker further stated that the silver Moufflon Bleu (whelped 1902) was the sire of more champions and winners than any other Toy Poodle (actually Miniature at this stage of the development of the breed), including the beautiful champions Fanchette, Wendette and Mariette of Hook. Moufflon Bleu's son, Whippendell Grison, sired Eng. Ch. Whippendell Azor. Azor sired Hunningham Rikki Tikki and Jacques of Hook. Jacques in turn sired Chic of Watercroft who was the sire of Eng. Ch. Angel of Mine and Ch. The Blue Boy. Eng. Ch. Whippendell Crepon was from a grandson of Moufflon Bleu bred to a Moufflon Bleu daughter. Crepon bred to a double granddaughter of

Moufflon Bleu produced Mrs. Tyndall's Leila (founder of the Venda's line). Practically all the famous blue strains contain Whippendell breeding: Mrs. Jack Taylor's, Mrs. Tyndall's Venda's, and Mrs. Twist's Eathorpe and Hunningham. These are the three most important blue and silver lines, and served as the foundation blood upon which other important kennels were founded.

In England it has been well known among the older breeders of blue and silver Miniatures that certain dishonest and irresponsible breeders introduced Bedlington Terrier blood into their lines of silver Miniatures. Silver has been used in the creation of apricots and creams, so introduction of Bedlington blood has affected them also. Like all *sub rosa* and hidden things, this has revealed itself in various ways. The most startling one is the sudden appearance of puppies with typical Terrier coats, flat and stiff, that can be stripped or plucked. Another distinct Terrier characteristic is the Terrier-shaped ear. And the gait has also been affected and is distinctly that of a Terrier rather than the Poodle way of going. To an apparently lesser degree, really serious faults appear in otherwise normal Poodles. One of these faults is in the formation of the muzzle, which starts at the eyes and goes straight forward with no modeling whatever. Such a formation is, again, correct in a Bedlington but not in a Poodle and gives an untypical and unattractive expression to the whole face. This is seen in a great many silver and blue Miniatures. Other signs are the rounded spine instead of the straight back required by our Poodle Standard. This fault of "roaching" is particularly discouraging as it often does not appear until the dog is well out of puppyhood. In Bedlingtons, I understand, this is called "the wheel" and does not develop until the dogs are a year old or more, and is correct for this breed. The curve draws the hindquarters forward and under the dog's body, which is, again, a common fault in silver Miniature Poodles with notoriously faulty hindquarters. A really correct, sound, well-let-down hindquarter is rare in silver Miniatures.

My reason for including this information in the book is that I hope once the source of the common defects in this color is known, some solution may be reached.

VENDA'S SILVERS

The Venda's silvers of Mrs. Audrey Tyndall are famous all over the world. The foundation of Mrs. Tyndall's silvers was Leila. Mrs. Tyndall applied for the name of Lavender Blue which was turned down by the English Kennel Club, so she registered her as Leila. However, she continued to call her by her pet name "Venda" at home, and this later became the kennel name. Through Leila, Venda's has exerted an enormous influence on silver Miniatures and Toys throughout the world.

Mrs. Tyndall's special interest throughout the years have been the Venda's silvers, and she has been especially insistent on keeping the silver line pure without mixing with white or other colors, mixtures she considers most detrimental. In her own breeding program she has bred to keep the silver silver —not a dirty gray. She has also bred for good points—small dark eyes, good feet and stance, and soundness. She considers the shortness of ear leathers one of the main problems in Miniatures. Most, if not all, silver Miniatures today trace directly back to the Venda's line.

On the subject of breeding silver, Mrs. Tyndall has this advice to offer, "As I have been breeding silver Poodles since 1926 I have surely fixed the colour of my own strain. I started with one of a lovely colour, Leila, which was by Eng. Ch. Whippendell Crepon out of Babette Gris, and I also got Venda's Arrow of Silver, from Mrs. Jack Taylor, whose silvers were really out of this world. One of the sires I used was Eng. Ch. Spriggan Bell, son of Ch. The Monarch. Several people have written to me about breeding silvers, but I fear that some of them may not have relished my replies when I told them that, judging from the pedigrees they sent me, they will never succeed. If people really want to go in for this lovely colour, and it is not an easy colour to breed, then my advice is to scrap the unattractive grays they have now, and start again with true silver. Never mate to any other colour, and when mating to a silver, make sure that it is silver-bred. In the pioneering days of long ago, breeders were faced with the problem of evolving the new colour by judicious practical experimentation. People such as Miss Brunker and Mrs. Taylor had a clear mental picture of what they wanted to achieve, but at that time it was a matter of sheer necessity to use one's intelligent imagination to discover the best methods of bringing the ideal to life. Sometimes we succeeded and sometimes we failed, but whenever we succeeded we had the sense to consolidate our successes by refraining as much as possible from introducing (or rather, re-introducing) other colours, particularly white or brown. The silver colour is delicate, and the factors which produce it must be inherited in the right proportions. This was achieved, and the next stage was to consolidate what had been achieved by evolving true-breeding strains which still survive. It is folly to reintroduce any of the factors which were the original 'raw materials,' because by doing so one risks upsetting the delicate balance. The best recipe for improving silvers today is to mate to a good representative of one of the long established silver strains, choosing one which has the least contamination with other colours."

The first champion that Mrs. Tyndall bred was Ch. Whippendell Picot who was whelped in 1926. She considers Venda's Blue Masterpiece and his son Venda's Somebody In Silver as coming closest to her ideal of what a Poodle should be.

It is all but impossible in America to find a purebred blue and silver pedigree free from a contaminating mixture with blacks. For the production of clear, light silvers without any shadings, generation after generation, it is important to have foundation breeding stock free from black blood. The employment of black blood is likely to result in uncertain and unpleasant shades of sad, dark steel and brownish taupe. It is impossible to tell how the color of a blue puppy with an infusion of black in his pedigree is going to turn out; sometimes such a dog is still changing colors at five years of age. It is disheartening. It keeps otherwise excellent dogs out of the show ring until they have decided what color they are going to be.

However, many fanciers have made no effort to keep the colors of their dogs clear and sound—so many, in fact, that it is almost impossible to obtain blue foundation stock free from mixtures with blacks. The time will come, at least one hopes so, when the colors will be maintained absolutely pure. It will be good not only for the blues, but for the blacks and other colors as well. The time to begin that purification is now. The best advice I can offer to breeders of blues and silvers is not to permit any admixture of black to your strains. Silver and blue are dilute and recessive colors. Silver bred to silver will produce silver with two exceptions. If both parents carry a white gene there may be whites, or if both parents carry beige genes there may be silver-beiges as part of the litter. Silver is a recessive color and two recessives cannot produce a dominant (such as black). One of the most common mistakes made by the novice is to breed a silver to a white hoping the white will dilute the silver to platinum. Nothing could be further from the truth. The most probable results would be bad blacks or dark grays with the possibility of white toes, white chest marks or particolors, not only in the first but also in later generations. A brown gene on both sides as far removed as five generations can result in two silvers producing brown puppies which will in time turn into silver-beiges. All of this points up the importance of breeding silver to silver and keeping the pedigrees free of contaminating mixtures with any and all other colors.

AMERICAN SILVERS

In America, the sources of blue and silver were Ch. Whippendell Picot (Ch. The Monarch line) and the much more influential brood bitch, Whippendell Garconette Bleue, who were responsible for several blue and silver champions, and to whose blood the small Meredick Kennels rigidly adhered with excellent results. Mrs. Byron Rogers' two bitches, Blue Jewel of Misty Isles and Venda's The Silver Sylph, have contributed their share of good silvers to the Misty Isles Kennels, to Cartlane Kennels, and elsewhere. Mrs. Hoyt's imports, Ch. Platinum of Eathorpe of Blakeen and Flora of Pipers-

Ch. Petit Pierre (by Bibelot Cadet of Misty Isles ex Ch. Platina), bred and owned by Hollycourt Kennels.

croft of Blakeen, have also proved valuable in the production of sound colored silvers and blues. Platinum and Flora's daughter, Ch. Platina, heads the greatest family of winning and producing silvers in this country. Hollycourt has carefully preserved its silver-to-silver breeding to the benefit of all those interested in breeding silvers.

123

Ch. Highland Sand Buzzette (by Ch. Busby of Piperscroft ex Ch. Phillippa of Piperscroft), dam of 10 champions at Highland Sand Kennels.

Ch. Silverette of Ledahof (by Smilestone's Spinner ex Starlet of Ledahof), pictured going Best of Opposite Sex to the Best of Variety at Westminster 1955, under judge Miss M. Ruelle Kelchner, handled by owner Betty VanSciver Atkinson. Dam of seven Perrevan champions.

24

Leading Miniature Dams

THE great producing bitches are relatively unknown, and never receive the recognition given the more popular stud dogs. A noted stud may sire hundreds of offspring during his lifetime, but a bitch—even the most prolific, properly rested between matings—can produce but a limited number of puppies. In the case of Miniatures, it is generally not more than 20 or 25. Because of this limitation, it is unlikely that a bitch will ever approach the production records of the leading sires, although some bitches actually have a much higher *percentage* of champion offspring.

Whereas the genetic influence of the sire and dam are of approximate equal importance at the time of mating, the dam's role becomes the greater in the development of the puppies. For here her health and maternal instinct become significant. A litter of puppies from a poor "doer" with a nervous temperament will rarely live up to its full potential. Breeders of livestock are well aware of the virtues of vigor and maternal instinct, and females lacking in these qualities are promptly weeded out of a breeding program.

There are few breeds, if any, in which the bitches have to overcome so many handicaps to a show career as in Poodles. The growing of a full show coat on a Poodle takes considerable time and effort, and it is almost impossible to maintain a show coat on a bitch while raising a litter from her. For this reason, maternal duties are usually deferred until after the chance in the show ring. By the time the bitch wins the coveted title she may be well past her peak years as a producer. Studies have shown that the younger bitches have less trouble during gestation, whelp easier, and produce larger litters.

Despite all this, it is amazing to learn that the champion Poodle bitch more than holds her own in competition with the vastly greater number of non-champion producers in the breed. In a study of the Miniature bitches that have been Top Producers (that is producers of three or more champions) it was discovered that of the 85 total, 39—or almost half—were champions.

Many breeders, myself among them, believe that once a fine bitch line is firmly established in a kennel, the battle for successful production of show dogs is more than half won.

The leading producing Miniature bitch has been the black Ch. Diablotin Star of Elblac, with 11 champions. Star, and her kennelmate Ch. Highland Sand Buzzette with 10 champions, helped put Highland Sand Kennels in the top ranks.

Although starting late because of a great show career that was climaxed with Best in Show at Westminster, Ch. Fontclair Festoon, also a black, proved to be an equally great producer with 10 champion get, and was the important influence in the success of Dunwalke Kennels.

The leading producing brown Miniature bitch has been Ch. Diablotin Autumn Leaf, who produced five champions at Beaujeu Kennels.

The leading producing white Miniature bitches have been Blakeen Solitaire, who produced nine champions at Blakeen and later at Loabelo Kennels, and Am. & Can. Ch. Simloch Ice de la Fontaine, dam of eight champions at Poodanne Kennels.

The leading silver Miniature dams have been Ch. Hollycourt Aure de Montalais, dam of eight Hollycourt champions, and Ch. Silverette of Ledahof, dam of seven champions at Perrevan Kennels.

Ch. Charda's Perdita of Sassafras, CDX, platinum Miniature bitch, Best in Show winner and many times Group winner, owned by Hilda S. Charbonneau, bred by Sassafras Kennels, handled by Frank T. Sabella.

Ch. Whippendell Picot (by Ch. The Monarch ex
Bougee Bleue, daughter of Leila).

Whippendell Garconette Bleue, by
Ch. The Monarch ex Leila. Most
American champions come through
Garconette, bred by Mrs. Tyndall.

Ch. King Johnny of Marcourt, and Eng. and Am. Ch.
Chieveley Chump. This is a rare old snapshot from
the Marcourt Kennels.

25

The Marcourt Kennels

M R. PRICE of the Marcourt Kennels, in Boston, was among the first, if not the very first, to own a kennel of English-bred Miniatures in America. With the purchase of what remained of Miss Morehouse's Chieveley Kennels after her death, came three English champions, Ch. Chieveley Chopstick, Ch. Chieveley Chump, both of which became our first dual champions in America, and the tiny bitch, Ch. Chieveley Chess, together, I believe, with several brood bitches. Ch. Chieveley Chopstick was whelped August 12, 1925. He finished his title here in March 1933.

So far as I have been able to find out, there have been only two sons of Ch. Chieveley Chump that have carried on in America: Mrs. Winthrop's Ch. Marcourt Petit Pierre and Mrs. Hoyt's dark brown dog, Marcourt Nardini. Many more descendants of Chump appear in English pedigrees, and the famous winner and notable sire, Ch. Venda's The Black Imp of Catawba, is a grandson of Chump.

Ch. Chieveley Chopstick's American descendants are the well known Tinker of Marcourt (Cartlane), Ch. Marcourt Andre and Ch. Marcourt Josephine, of whom I have no extensive record, the lovely chocolate brown Ch. Marcourt Julia, the dam of my own first Miniature Poodle, Ch. Marcourt Tricot, of Marcourt Joan, also in my kennels with a number of her winning descendants, and of my lovely little Ch. Marcourt Sabot, dam of four champions.

Another imported black dog in the Marcourt Kennel was Ch. King Johnny of Marcourt, from a blue line, by Ch. The Monarch. He was advertised as always throwing black puppies, even when bred to blue bitches,

Ch. Misty Isles Algie of Piperscroft, the first Miniature Poodle to win Best in Show in America.

and was considered by some of our older breeders as the best among the Marcourts. He was from Mrs. Jack Taylor's blue strain and was a litter brother of her Ch. Blue Zenith.

American Ch. Whippendell Picot was the foundation of the blue and silver line at Marcourt. He was another son of Ch. The Monarch, and his mother was Bougee Bleue, a daughter of Mrs. Tyndall's famous Leila. The brood bitch, Whippendell Garconette Bleue, was another daughter of Leila's, by Ch. The Blue Boy.

The combination of Ch. Picot and Garconette doubled the blood of Leila. And from this combination came Ch. Marcourt Armand, the best producer among the later Marcourts, and his litter sister, Ch. Marcourt Amana.

Mr. Price disbanded the kennels some years ago, after a disastrous fire in the kennel property, and made over the rights to ownership of this well-known old prefix to Mrs. Helen Crowell Bacon, to whom I am indebted for the photographs of the famous old Marcourt and Chieveley dogs that are in this book.

This kennel had eleven champions in all—seven of them homebred. Although it is no longer in operation, it has played such an important part in the foundation and growth of our American Miniatures that its influence is still felt and will continue to be felt for generations to come.

130

26

Misty Isles Kennels

MRS. BYRON ROGERS, whose delightful affix, of Misty Isles, had its origin in her earlier fancy for Cairn Terriers, began her Poodle career with Standards, which were among the earliest in the revival of the breed and most famous, and later added Miniatures. The two first Poodles, both Standard and Miniature, at Blakeen were obtained by Mrs. Hoyt from Misty Isles.

Mrs. Rogers' first important Miniatures were, I believe, the two dogs purchased in England for her by Mrs. Hoyt, who, commissioned to buy one dog, was unable to make a choice between two equally good ones, and so brought them both to America with the mental reservation that she would keep for herself, the one Mrs. Rogers did not want. Upon their arrival, Mrs. Rogers found herself in the same predicament of being unable to choose and decided to have them both. They were none other than the two famous stars of the Miniature Poodle world, Sparkling Jet and Algie of Piperscroft, who, with the Misty Isles affix added to their names, speedily became American champions and the foundation of all the best American-bred show dogs of their day. This little story is a commentary upon the knowledge and foresight of these two clever fanciers, to whom the Poodles in America, both Standard and Miniature, owe so much.

Ch. Sparkling Jet was by Dare Devil Dink, one of Ch. Monarch's sons, from the famous producer, Bonny Forget Me Not. Jet's dam, Crystal Bell, was a litter sister of Ch. Spriggan Bell, winner of two championship certificates, and of Joy Bell and Ch. The Ghost. As a sire, Ch. Sparkling Jet had already proven his worth, since bred back to his grandmother, Bonny

Forget Me Not, he produced in one litter two of the most famous champions of their day, Ch. The Laird of Mannerhead (eleven certificates), and his litter brother, Ch. Limelight of Mannerhead. Ch. Jet was one of the greatest sires in Miniature Poodle history, and, not only did he sire seven American champions, but his sons and daughters also carried on.

Ch. Jet was a handsome little dog with a lovely type of head, with dark oval eyes, well set ears, short body, and a heavy, jet-black coat. His bone was fine and he gave the impression of extreme refinement all over. He had a sweet and winning disposition. All of these qualities he handed on to his descendants.

If Jet at the time was perhaps the best sire, Ch. Algie was the best show dog. Even after the many years and the many beautiful Miniatures I have seen since, he still remains in my mind as a perfect model of what a Miniature should be, although he was past his prime when I saw him. It was as if I were looking at a beautiful Standard when some Alice in Wonderland creature came along and gave it a bite of something that caused it to shrink and, presto, there stood Algie. He was perfectly proportioned and I have never seen another small dog that gave me the same feeling of a Standard in miniature. His balance was perfection, he had superb legs and feet, well let down hocks, and magnificent hindquarters; because of these, Algie was an absolutely sound mover with great style and a proud carriage. His head was excellent, and he had dark oval eyes and good ears.

Ch. Algie of Piperscroft was bred by Mrs. Boyd, by her Conceit of Piperscroft x her noted Ch. Vanity of Piperscroft. Vanity's dam, Twinkle, was a small Standard, and her sire was Presto of Gotton, a small dog from a very old, very small English line. In England, Algie's litter brother, Monty of Piperscroft, sired many champions and winners. For awhile it looked as though Algie would carry on through his daughters; but his son, Bibelot of Misty Isles, has outdone him as the sire of seven champions; and his grandson, Bibelot Cadet, also carried on this famous line.

Jet and Algie dominated the show world in Miniatures for many years (Algie was the first of the variety to win Best in Show in America), and the daughter of one bred to the other was the recipe for good results. Both played a great part in founding winning strains in all the other earlier kennels, as well as Misty Isles. Jet ended his days at Blakeen, but Algie stayed with Mrs. Rogers, the apple of her eye until the end of his valuable little life.

Early in the foundation of her strain, Mrs. Rogers purchased from Mrs. Jack Taylor in England two daughters of Mrs. Taylor's famous Ch. Angel of Mine, litter sisters, by Romance of Rio Grande, one blue and one silver. These were Venda's The Silver Sylph and Blue Jewel of Misty Isles. In the same consignment came the gray dog, Venda's Arrow of Silver, who unfortunately died from distemper shortly afterward. Prior to his importation

Mrs. Byron Rogers with two of her Misty Isles Miniatures.

Arrow was bred to Mrs. Tyndall's great foundation bitch Leila to produce Venda's Blue Masterpiece (two c.c.'s), one of the most important foundation sires in silver Miniatures. Blue Jewel and The Silver Sylph both produced champions, and have many champion descendants. Another of Mrs. Rogers' bitches, Phayre's Mitzie, a black from an old American strain of undoubtedly French origin, has a large number of champion descendants. Ch. Lady in Waiting of Misty Isles (dam of three champions), was imported from England by Mrs. Rogers, and sold to Blakeen Kennels. A total of 18 Miniature champions were either bred or owned by Mrs. Rogers, but this total is only a slight indication of their tremendous influence on the American Miniature.

133

Ch. Sherwood Mademoiselle Bibi, first colored Toy to win a specialty (1948), and litter sister, Ch. Sherwood Vest Pocket Edition, shown here winning Best Brace (first Toy brace to be Best in Show).

27

Sherwood Hall Kennels

ALTHOUGH my own Sherwood Hall Kennel was founded in 1909 with Toys, especially Pekingese, Pomeranians, Brussels Griffons and other breeds, it ranks as third in point of time as far as the Miniature Poodles are concerned, since Blakeen at the time I undertook the breeding of Miniatures was still exclusively in Standards.

My kennel of Poodles was founded with two small Miniatures, both under 12 inches, purchased from Mrs. Leo Brady in 1934 and bred by Mr. Price at Marcourt. The little black dog Ch. Marcourt Tricot, was, however, a double grandson of English and American Ch. Chieveley Chopstick, being by Marcourt Carnot out of that lovely brown Ch. Marcourt Julia. Tricot, after some Eastern puppy wins, finished his championship speedily in the West. He was a particularly well built little fellow with the shortest of backs, beautiful feet and legs, and a good head. He became the sire of five champions, three daughters and two sons. Of these, his noted daughter, Ch. Sherwood Silhouette, was one of the first Group winners among the early Miniatures and became the dam of Ch. Sherwood Claude Antoine, and through Claude Antoine's daughters had a marked influence in the kennels. Silhouette's dam, Mignonne of Misty Isles, was by Ch. Sparkling Jet of Misty Isles out of Venda's The Silver Sylph.

Perhaps the most important son of Ch. Tricot was the very outstanding winner, the tiny 10½ inch, black Ch. Sherwood Pocket Edition, sired when his father was eleven years old. Ch. Pocket Edition was perhaps the smallest Miniature champion in America, and in his turn was the sire of many beautiful small dogs. Among these are the now noted Miniature-bred Toys,

135

Ch. Sherwood Mademoiselle Bibi and her litter sister, Sherwood Vest Pocket Edition, their older full brother, Sherwood Sporting Edition, Sherwood Petite Paillette, and her larger sister, Ch. Sherwood Petite Poupee. Little Pocket Edition was like his sire in build. He inherited Tricot's lovely feet, had a superlative head, and excelled in action, proudness of carriage and style. He retired undefeated by any Poodle, Standard or Miniature, the winner of Groups, to become the grand little old man of the kennels.

My first bitch was little Ch. Marcourt Sabot, by English and American Ch. Chieveley Chopstick. After winning at Westminster, she finished her championship in the West and was the first American-bred Miniature to win the Group. She was an extremely dainty little Poodle, full of true Poodle character and type, with an exquisite little head and body and beautiful feet. For me she never had a puppy that could not have won, although many of them were never shown. Through her daughters and her champion son, Ch. Sherwood Louis Philippe, she had a marked influence on the Sherwood strain and was the dam of four champions.

My second bitch of importance, Mignonne of Misty Isles, who through her daughter, Ch. Sherwood Silhouette, founded the second bitch line, was taken on breeder's terms for one litter only, after the death of her sister, Mimi, from distemper.

The third bitch line descends from an imported French bitch, Lindi de Madjige, a double granddaughter of Int. Ch. Footit de Madjige. Lindi was also taken on breeder's terms and bred to Ch. Marcourt Tricot.

From these three bitch lines came all the Sherwood Hall Miniatures, as practically no outcrosses were made from the purchase of outside bitches, and all the new blood was introduced by the stud dogs.

The second dog introduced into the Sherwood Hall line was Ch. Blakeen Dipsy Doodle (Ch. Sparkling Jet of Misty Isles x Ch. Mechancete of Misty Isles), whose dam was by Ch. Misty Isles Algie of Piperscroft x Phayre's Mitzie. She was also the dam of two other champions, Ch. Blakeen Bitzie Boy and his litter sister, Ch. Blakeen Hoity Toity, by Ch. Venda's The Black Imp of Catawba. Dipsy finished his title on the West Coast without defeat. He was a cobby little dog with (like most of Jet's descendants) a truly beautiful head and very dark eyes, carried a heavy black coat and had great style and carriage. Unfortunately, he was not used in the stud at first, because little Ch. Tricot was aging and giving us his last litters and we thought that as Dipsy was young there was plenty of time. However, this did not prove to be the case for Dipsy died in his sleep very suddenly, leaving behind him only two litters. Fortunately, they were from my two best bitches, Ch. Marcourt Sabot and Ch. Sherwood Silhouette; from Sabot's litter came Ch. Sherwood Louis Philippe, sire of Ch. Sherwood Louis Andre and Ch. Sherwood Soubrette; and from Silhouette I got Ch. Sherwood Claude

Antoine. These two litters also included three bitches, from whom are descended many of our winners.

The third stud purchased was Blakeen Chieveley, by Ch. Venda's The Black Imp of Catawba out of Crowell's Mightie Miss, and a full brother of Ch. Blakeen Ace High. Chieveley, the one son of Imp's in the West, had a notable career as a puppy in the East, but unfortunately our warmer western climate did not agree with his coat, and so he was not shown on the West Coast. However, he was worthily represented by his children, Ch. Sherwood Franchot, Ch. Sherwood The Chocolate Dandy, Ch. Sherwood His Highness, Ch. Meisen Chocolate Chip, and the black Toy, Ch. Sherwood Petite Mademoiselle.

The fourth stud purchased was Ch. Blakeen Tito, who finished his title in the East, and who produced Ch. Bric A Brac Blackbird. Tito sired a number of outstanding Sherwoods. He was by Ch. Blakeen Bitzie Boy out of Ch. Moutit de Madjige of Blakeen, and proved to be a fine mate for Sherwood bitches with the Madjige bloodlines, as well as others.

In the beginning, the kennel specialized in blacks alone, and black was bred to black for many generations. However, other colors were added later. These include the silver Ch. Blakeen Invincible and several silver-bred bitches, the small white Cottontail of Toytown, who sired some excellent whites, and several good browns.

Early in 1950 we started laying the foundation of a lighter colored strain with the purchase of the noted twelve-inch, black-eyed apricot sire, Victor of Fircot (Ch. Cremola of Swanhill x Cream Puff of Fircot). Victor left behind him some big English winners as well as American youngsters. We also imported the line-bred apricot puppy, Fircot Ray of Sunshine, a deep true apricot with black eyes, and a small silver bitch, Angela of Fircot.

But by far the most important purchase was that of the two sensational youngsters, Fircot Garcon Fils, admittedly the best bred at Fircot up until that time, and his lovely white sister, Sonia of Fircot, by Fircot Garcon de Neige x Vulcan Champagne Jouet.

The last several years at Sherwood Hall were devoted to the building up and concentrating of bloodlines in several color-bred strains. While the Sherwood Poodles have won whenever shown, it has never been the policy of the kennel to show more than just enough to prove the dogs' worth. And in the last years, because of my ill health, rather less.

The old small line of blacks was strengthened. And I believe that the creative work we have done in founding a small line of Miniatures that breeds true has not only been a foundation for Toys of the proper type but also has been of value in bringing down size in over-large Miniatures. No small dog or bitch was retained unless it was of champion quality, representing the cream of the crop of many years' breeding. Purely black-bred, they were of exquisite type, and though too small for the taste of many of our judges of Miniatures, they were fine little Poodles and dead sound in construction, but unshown. The three principal small stud dogs, all eleven inches or under and the proven sires of outstanding stock, were: Sherwood Busby Brown (Sherwood The Ace x Sherwood Miss Chiffon); Sherwood Antoine (Sherwood The Ace x Puttencove Dot, dam of two Blakeen Toy champions); and Sherwood The King Pin [Int. Ch. Pixholme Firebrave Gustav x Sherwood Topscore (Topscore, an eleven-inch litter sister of Sherwood The Ace, was by Ch. Busby of Piperscroft x Sherwood Ace High, by Blakeen Chieveley)]. All three of the aforementioned studs sired Toys as well as very small Miniatures, and our many very small Miniature bitches showed equal quality.

Among our normal sized black and brown Miniatures, our sensational young son of Ch. Rudolph of Piperscroft x a best-in-show bitch was the imported Willowbrae Foxtrot, who sired very outstanding stock. Ch. Yasmin de Peche (Int. Ch. Pixholme Firebrave Gustav, CD, x Poodhall Amala) and several imported English bitches, such as Olivia and Marcella of Priorsgate, were in the kennel, as well as bitches of our own old black strain.

The principal lighter colored dogs and bitches in the kennel came from Mrs. Thomas at Fircot and included Victor of Fircot (apricot), Fircot Ray of Sunshine (unfading apricot), and our beautiful deep cream Ch. Fircot Garcon Fils, sire of champions. Our creams have been deep in color and our apricots the most beautiful color of deep true apricot and have achieved a great reputation. We are very proud of the beautiful heads, so difficult to get in these colors, and their splendid, sound bodies and profuse coats.

The third and newest creation in the Miniatures was our ice white strain, headed by our sensational grandson of Ch. Fircot L'Ballerine of Maryland, Persil of Fircot, a prepotent sire. His son Sherwood Jack Frost also made a name for himself as a sire. The bitches of the ice white strain came from our own old white stock and from a fine German line of worth.

And now we come to the Sherwood Toys, both black and light colored. In the light colored Toys, pride of place must go to our imported white English Toy, Peaslake Peter Paul (Peaslake Little Tremendous x Peaslake Mistletoe, both big English winners). Peter Paul, of Miniature type, was very sound moving and carried an immense coat of harsh texture. Our little Barnes Alphonse, full brother of all the great Barnes winners, sired a number of winners and champions. Sherwood The Little Nob, our Toy son of Victor of Fircot and Barnes Nada (Alphonse's sister), gave us some excellent apricot and cream youngsters.

In the black Toys, pride of place goes to Sherwood the Black Bandit (Palmares Monsieur x a small Miniature bitch from the Diablotin strain). Bandit sired the sensational black Toy puppies, Sherwood Lil' Black Madcap

138

Ch. Sherwood Lil' Prize Package (by Palmares Monsieur Fabuleux ex Redland's Bonne Amie) bred by J. Berman, owned by Broughton Kennels.

and her litter sister Sherwood Mischievous Miss. Sherwood Thumbelina, Bandit's litter sister, was an outstanding little Toy bitch. Ch. Sherwood Lil' Prize Package, the property of the Broughton Kennels in the East, went best of all breeds in her second show. The daughters and granddaughters of our noted winner Ch. Sherwood Petite Mademoiselle headed the Toy division of black bitches. And we also had several Toy daughters of Puttencove Dot.

The year 1958 represented a change in the ownership of the kennels, but not in its policy, as Mrs. Helen Kincaid and Miss Virginia Hull, who had been my valuable assistants for twelve years, became my full partners. Their well-known winning Kinswood Shelties and our small sideline of Miniature Longhaired Dachshunds came under joint ownership, so that in the future, these valuable bloodlines will go forward, under the old prefix.

Ch. Venda's The Black Imp of Catawba

Ch. Blakeen Eldorado

Ch. Snow Boy of Fircot

28

Blakeen Kennels

ALTHOUGH the Blakeen Kennel was in point of time the fourth to acquire Miniatures, it is by achievement the greatest in America. Mrs. Hoyt, who was already the owner of a number of Standard champions and was instrumental in importing the foundation stud dogs for Misty Isles, in 1936 purchased her first Miniature, Mrs. Rogers' Ch. Mechancete of Misty Isles (Ch. Misty Isles Algie of Piperscroft x Phayre's Mitzie.) Ch. Mechancete was not only a big winner but was also the dam of three champions, my own Ch. Blakeen Dipsy Doodle, by Ch. Sparkling Jet, and Ch. Blakeen Bitzie Boy and his litter sister, Ch. Blakeen Hoity Toity, by Ch. Venda's The Black Imp of Catawba. Ch. Blakeen Bitzie Boy was a great winner and sire of my Ch. Blakeen Tito, himself the sire and grandsire of a number of champions, among them Ch. Bric A Brac Blackbird. Ch. Blakeen Hoity Toity produced Ch. Blakeen Seabee.

One of the most important among the black bitches at Blakeen was that beautiful winner and English and American Ch. Bonny Bright Eyes of Mannerhead, by Eng. Ch. Eric Brighteyes out of Ch. Vanity of Piperscroft. Bonny Bright Eyes is the only Miniature bitch to hold the title in both countries. Her head was a study of perfection. Her daughter by Ch. Venda's The Black Imp, Ch. Blakeen Bon Bon, was also a big winner.

The small French-bred bitch, Ch. Moutit de Madjige of Blakeen, by that famous Continental winner, International Ch. Footit de Madjige (Ch. Spriggan Bell ex Chieveley Cheepress) from a French-bred mother, was of great importance. Bred to Ch. Venda's The Black Imp of Catawba, she produced in one litter Ch. Blakeen Tito and Ch. Blakeen Paper Doll. (Tito is mentioned above.) Ch. Paper Doll became the dam of Ch. Blakeen Magic Dancer and Ch. Blakeen Paper Weight.

There were many other good black bitches at Blakeen, so many, in fact, that it is difficult to choose which to record.

The two most famous black sires at Blakeen were, of course, Ch. Sparkling Jet of Misty Isles in his later years and Ch. Venda's The Black Imp of Catawba, together, without question, the greatest Miniature sires in American history. Ch. Jet's international record lies in his earlier years, but Ch. Imp produced his greatest progeny at Blakeen. These include Ch. Blakeen Bitzie Boy, Ch. Blakeen Hoity Toity, Ch. Blakeen Bon Bon, that noted brown Ch. Blakeen Eldorado, Ch. Blakeen Ace High, all for Mrs. Hoyt, and in other kennels Ch. Black Magic, Ch. Seafren High Falutin, Ch. Seafren Harum Scarum and others. Many of Imp's non-champion progeny have been famous producers as well, such as Crowell's Dawn of a New Day, my own Blakeen Chieveley, and Mrs. Sayre's Bric A Brac Cinderella and Ballerina and many more. His grandchildren include such famous winners as Ch. Blakeen Magic Fate, Ch. Smilestone's Magic, Ch. Ensarr Salute, Ch. Blakeen Souvreign Gold, Ch. Blakeen Seabee, Ch. Blakeen Tito, Ch. Blakeen Paper Doll, Ch. Blakeen Bubbling Over, Ch. Diablotin Danseuse, Ch. Diablotin Dit On, Ch. Diablotin Dentelle, Ch. Sherwood Franchot, Ch. Sherwood The Chocolate Dandy and many, many others. His influence extends to great-grandchildren and further. No dog ever put his stamp of excellence any more definitely upon winning strains.

Mrs. Hoyt's importation of the black Firebrave Alphonse, sire of the well-known English winner, Ch. Firebrave Pimpernel, also proved of importance.

The famous white Blakeen Miniatures were founded with Ch. Arnim of Piperscroft, an English dog of German bloodlines, and the bitch Adastra Avalanche, which two mated together produced Ch. Blakeen Minnikin. Ch. Minnikin, mated to the cream bitch Fifi of Swanhill (from brown and gold breeding with a white grandmother), produced Ch. Blakeen Fleur de Lys, Ch. Blakeen Flurry (the dam by Ch. Snow Boy of Fircot of Ch. Blakeen Snow Flurry), Blakeen Baguette, and Blakeen Alba, who, bred back to her sire, Ch. Minnikin, produced that record breaker, Ch. Blakeen Christable.

The purchase of Ch. Snow Boy of Fircot, who was already responsible for some of the best whites in England, was to revolutionize the white Miniatures. Although himself a beautiful white, Ch. Snow Boy was by Harwee of Mannerhead (a noted black sire from a line known for perfection of heads) and his dam, Solitaire of Piperscroft, was a gray carrying a white factor, with a gray father and with silver and brown on her dam's side. A white bitch, Venda's Ice Fairy, maternal great-granddam, was the same bitch that was behind Fifi of Swanhill. Both descended from that prolific bitch, Venda's Gold Dollar, a daughter of Venda's Ice Fairy, who probably ac-

142

Divinity of Piperscroft, bitch (left), and Michel of Piperscroft, dog (right)—dam and sire of Am. Ch. Bubbles of Piperscroft of Blakeen.

counted for the white genes in both these colored strains. Ch. Snow Boy had so much colored blood and such excellent head properties behind him that when he was mated to white bitches, he produced beautiful headed whites. And as recessives breed true, he rapidly founded a strain with heads of a merit formerly unknown in whites. Ch. Snow Boy's brilliant show record is well known to all those interested in Poodles. Later importations of white Miniatures greatly strengthened this Blakeen white strain, already so strong.

The first brown at Blakeen was that well-known winner and sire, Harpendale John Brown, who unfortunately died shortly after his arrival in America. Another early brown dog was a very dark (almost black) chocolate dog, Marcourt Nardini, by English and American Ch. Chieveley Chump out of English Ch. Chieveley Chess, a very tiny bitch. Nardini was one of the few of this breeding and appears in some of our American pedigrees. Ch. Venda's The Black Imp of Catawba, a grandson of Ch. Chieveley Chump, carried a brown factor and played a part in creating browns at Blakeen. His beautiful son, Ch. Blakeen Eldorado, was from a golden colored bitch, Ch. Venda's Winter Sunshine of Blakeen, by Petit Morceau of Piperscroft out of that lovely orange colored bitch, Ch. Venda's Sunkista of Blakeen. Sunkista was a lovely clear orange right down to her skin, had black eyes and nose, and, aside from her rare color, was a fine Poodle. These two bitches stem back to the old Whippendell brown line. Ch. Blakeen Eldorado, a lovely reddish chestnut brown, was the greatest winner of any dog of this color and sired the black Ch. Blakeen Seabee and Ch. Blakeen Sovereign Gold.

One of the first silvers at Blakeen was Flora of Piperscroft of Blakeen (by the obedience winner, Plata of Eathorpe, out of Pauline), who was to become a founder of strains, as she was the dam of Ch. Platina, foundation bitch at Hollycourt, Ch. Smilestone's Silvern, Ch. Apropos of Cartlane and others, and the grandmother of a number of winners. The English-bred American

143

Ch. Diablotin Danseuse

Ch. Platinum of Eathorpe (Hunningham D'Argent out of Grey Nez of Eathorpe), from Mrs. Twist's old English strain, was also to prove not only a winner but a founder of strains. Ch. Platinum was the sire of Ch. Platina, Ch. Blakeen Heigh Ho Silver, Ch. Blakeen Quicksilver, Ch. Snappy Morn, and others. Another important silver dog at Blakeen was Ch. Blakeen Invincible (by Blakeen High Jinks, in his turn by Platinum out of Pillicoc Elixir). Invincible later went to my own kennels and continued his career in the show ring and as a sire. The winning English bitch, Ch. Lady in Waiting of Misty Isles (by Harpendale John Brown out of Maid in Waiting) was an individual of importance and the dam of Ch. Demon of Misty Isles, Ch. Blakeen Lustre, Ch. Sparkling Lady of Raybrook, and others. Venda's Somebody in Silver, from the old Venda's strain of silvers, was of value at stud.

There is not space in this review to mention all the winning Miniatures at Blakeen, but merely to indicate the various colors and foundation strains in this very rich kennel and to give a partial idea of the very clever fancier, author and judge to whom it belonged.

Although it is no longer in operation, the influence of Blakeen Kennels will be felt for generations to come, for it was of major importance in the foundation and growth of American Miniatures.

144

29

Diablotin Kennels

THE late Mrs. I. Stowell Morse founded her black Miniature strain Diablotin ("little devil") with one bitch, Crowell's Dawn of a New Day. Dawn (by Ch. Venda's The Black Imp of Catawba x Crowell's Mightie Miss) was a full sister of Ch. Blakeen Ace High and Sherwood Hall's Blakeen Chieveley. Dawn was bred back to her grandsire, Ch. Jingle of Piperscroft, to produce Diablotin Devinette and the lovely Ch. Diablotin Danseuse. Danseuse was bred to Ch. Clairwell Him Especially to produce Ch. Diablotin Onyx and Ch. Diablotin Charmeuse. Onyx was the sire of seven champions at Robinsbrook Kennels. Danseuse was bred to Ch. Blakeen Eldorado to produce Ch. Diablotin Demi-Setier and Ch. Diablotin Dentelle. Demi-Setier was the sire of five champions at the Willowbrook Kennels, and Dentelle went to the Hollycourt Kennels where she became the dam of six champions. Devinette, Danseuse's litter sister, bred to Demi-Setier produced the brown Best in Show winner, Ch. Diablotin Forever Amber. Forever Amber was bred to Ch. Smilestone's Sirprise to produce Ch. Diablotin Kahruba and Ch. Diablotin Autumn Leaf, who went to the Beaujeu Kennels where she produced five champions.

From Dawn of a New Day's breeding to Ch. Anthony of Revemir came Ch. Diablotin Dit-On and Diablotin Dryad U.D. Dryad was a brilliant obedience worker with four champion daughters to her credit. Bred to Demi-Setier she produced Ch. Diablotin Dawn Again, Ch. Diablotin Dimity and Ch. Diablotin Firefly. Dryad bred to Onyx produced one of the greatest producing bitches in the annals of the breed, Ch. Diablotin Star of Elblac, who went to Highland Sand where she produced 11 champions.

Ch. Diablotin Forever Amber

Dawn of a New Day was bred to the imported Firebrave Alphonse to produce Diablotin Double Trouble. Double Trouble bred to Onyx produced Ch. Diablotin Prince Charming and Ch. Diablotin Kala Jauhar. Trouble's daughter, Diablotin Ramona, is the dam of three champions.

There have been 16 titleholders bearing the Diablotin prefix. This family is noted for its winning and producing bitches.

Ch. Diablotin Onyx

Produce Class—NCPC, 1949, won by Blakeen Chieveley (with the author, sixth from the left), here pictured with five winning children and three winning grandchildren, handled by friends and club members, and judged by Mr. Trullinger.

Ch. Hollycourt Philippe (by Ch. Barrick Hill Bomber ex Cartlane Pirouette), bred and owned by Hollycourt Kennels.

Ch. Hollycourt Florezel (by Ch. Hollycourt Philippe ex Ch. Hollycourt Fleur Noir) breeder-owner, Hollycourt Kennels.

Ch. Hollycourt Elegant (by Ch. Hollycourt Philippe ex Ch. Hollycourt Fleur Noir) bred by Hollycourt Kennels.

30

Hollycourt Kennels

Miss M. Ruelle Kelchner's Hollycourt Kennels have been most successful, and there are more than 70 titleholders bearing the Hollycourt prefix. The well-known line of silvers was started with the purchase of Platina, who was whelped in 1940. Platina was royally bred. Her sire, Ch. Platinum of Eathorpe of Blakeen, was the sire of four champions. Her dam, Flora of Piperscroft of Blakeen, was also the dam of Ch. Apropos of Cartlane and Ch. Smilestone's Silvern who sired six champions. Ch. Platina was an outstanding show bitch and won a number of Group firsts. Her success as a producer makes her the matriarch of the silver Miniature Poodle in this country. She was wisely used by Miss Kelchner, and her champion descendants number in the hundreds.

Platina was first bred to Bibelot Cadet of Misty Isles to produce the gray Ch. Petit Pierre, who sired nine champions including Ch. Little Ben of Puttencove and Ch. Hollycourt Manicamp. Bred to Ch. Smilestone's Silvern, she produced those three redoubtable full brothers: Ch. Hollycourt Platinum (sire of 13 champions), Am. & Can. Ch. Hollycourt Osmium of Paragon (sire of four champions) and Ch. Hollycourt Light of Star Tavern, who went to the West Coast where he sired 12 champions and did a great deal to further interest in silvers, both in Miniatures and Toys. Light's beautiful son, Ch. Barclay Summer Smoke, was a Best in Show winner and sired 10 champions. A mating of Platina to her grandson Ch. Hollycourt Manicamp resulted in a litter containing Hollycourt Iridium, who had three majors. Iridium was the dam of Ch. Hollycourt Grillon Argente and Ch. Hollycourt Plume Argentee by Hollycourt Chevalier Argente, and of Ch. Hollycourt Vaillant by Ch. Hollycourt Mercure. Vaillant was the sire of Ch. Hollycourt Talent of Silver (sire of ten champions) and Am. & Can. Ch. Touchstone Silversmith (sire of five champions). Plume Argentee was bred to Platinum to give Ch. Hollycourt Blue Ice, who is the sire of several champions. Another Manicamp daughter, Ch. Hollycourt Aure de Montalais, was a remarkable producer with seven champions to her credit. Montalais was the dam of Ch. Hollycourt Mercure, Ch. Hollycourt Melisande and Ch. Hollycourt Miche of Catawba (by Ch. Hollycourt Venture); Ch. Hollycourt Gala and Ch. Hollycourt Merry Spirit (by Hollycourt Breeze of Challendon); Ch. Hollycourt Millamant (by Ch. Hollycourt Grillon Argente); and Ch. Hollycourt Talent of Silver (by Ch. Hollycourt Vaillant). Ch. Hollycourt Venture (by Francois of Mannerhead x Puttencove Tiptoes) was the sire of five champions.

Miss Kelchner, who is the leading authority on the breeding of silvers, considers silver a dilute color and warns against the introduction into a silver line of any other color that could cause mismarking or spoil the lovely light silver color that is so attractive and desired. Her great success in establishing the Hollycourt silver strain is proof of her knowledge and diligence.

The black and brown line at Hollycourt has wisely been kept separate from the silver line, and is successful on its own account. Two bitches are primarily responsible for the records made—Cartlane Pirouette and Ch. Diablotin Dentelle. Cartlane Pirouette (by Cartlane Augustin x Cartlane Colombe) was a fine producer for Hollycourt and for others as well. At Hollycourt she was the dam of Ch. Hollycourt Philippe and Ch. Hollycourt Penelope (by Ch. Barrack Hill Bomber) and of Ch. Hollycourt Patricia (by Ch. Smilestone's Bacarat). Pirouette was also the dam of Ch. Bric A Brac Blithe Spirit (by Bric A Brac Black Pepper), who was the dam of three champions at Lydney Kennels and also produced the untitled Smilestone's Pandora (also by Ch. Smilestone's Bacarat), the dam of three champions. Ch. Diablotin Dentelle (by Ch. Blakeen Eldorado x Ch. Diablotin Danseuse) was bred to the brown Surrey Brazil (by Sirod Tony of Woodend x Blakeen Penny of Woodend) to produce three Group-winning champions: Ch. Hollycourt Brandywine, Ch. Hollycourt Doree and Ch. Hollycourt Fleur Noire. Dentelle was also the dam of Ch. Hollycourt Platon and Can. & Swedish Ch. Hollycourt Pavot by Ch. Hollycourt Philippe, and of Ch. Hollycourt Black Bobbin by Ch. Hollycourt Blackamoor. Ch. Hollycourt Doree was the dam of four champions: Ch. Hollycourt Bronze Knight, Ch. Hollycourt Vichyssoise (both by Ch. Smilestone's Sirprise), Ch. Hollycourt Dalriada (by Ch. Hollycourt Philippe) and Ch. Hollycourt Opale Noire (by Ch. Hollycourt Blackamoor). Ch. Hollycourt Bronze Knight was the sire of ten champions including Ch. Hollycourt Ensign (sire of five) and Ch. Cappoquin Bon Fiston (sire of 17). Ch. Hollycourt Fleur Noire was the dam of Ch. Hollycourt Elegante and Ch. Hollycourt Florezel, by Ch. Hollycourt Philippe, and of Ch. Hollycourt Valentina

150

Ch. Platina at 12 years of age winning Brood Bitch class at 1952 Poodle Club of America Specialty, with her sons: Ch. Petit Pierre (winner of Veterans Class at 10 years), Ch. Hollycourt Platinum, and Am. & Can. Ch. Hollycourt Ozmium of Paragon. Platina is being handled by her owner, Miss M. Ruelle Kelchner.

(by Barrack Hill Troubadour) and Ch. Hollycourt Ganyson (by Ch. Hollycourt Ganymede).

A study of the foregoing illustrates just how successful Hollycourt has been in blending Pirouette and Dentelle bloodlines. A key dog in this program was Ch. Hollycourt Philippe, who was one of the leading black Miniature sires with 20 champions to his credit. Bred to his granddaughter Hollycourt Ellette (by Ch. Hollycourt Elegante ex Ch. Hollycourt Penelope), Phillipe sired Ch. Hollycourt Phillipson, the sire of eight champions. Phillipe also sired Ch. Hollycourt Blackamoor (x Ch. Hollycourt Patricia). Blackamoor in turn sired five champions including Ch. Hollycourt Black Bobbin (x Ch. Diablotin Dentelle), who sired several champions including Ch. Hollycourt Calandra and her famous brown brother Ch. Cappoquin Bon Jongleur (sire of 20 champions).

It would be impossible to list all the champions from this large kennel, but this brief résumé of some of the basic stock may give some idea of their great strength and of the influence of the Hollycourts on American Miniatures.

151

Ch. Fircot L'Ballerine of Maryland

Ch. Bric A Brac Brag About, shown with breeder-owner, Ruth Burnette Sayres.

31

Bric A Brac Kennels

RUTH Burnette Sayres is, of course, well-known as one of America's greatest handlers. But that she also merits distinction as a breeder of outstanding Miniatures, and as a judge that has been honored on both sides of the Atlantic, is not as well known.

One reason why she is not always given the recognition as a breeder she deserves is that many of the dogs bred by her were sold to customers who placed their own prefixes on them. The great winner, Ch. Magic Fate of Blakeen, was bred by Mrs. Sayres, sold to Mrs. Hoyt—who named him, and then sold to Colonel E. E. Ferguson, for whom he made his outstanding show record of 25 Bests in Show. Magic Fate was also an exceptional sire with 13 champions to his credit, including the top winner Ch. Highland Sand Magic Star.

The Miniatures started at Bric A Brac with two sisters, Bric A Brac Ballerina and Bric A Brac Cinderella, by Ch. Venda's The Black Imp of Catawba x Cartlane Noirette. Noirette was by that well-known early sire, Cartlane Augustin out of Ch. Fiddown Floride. Ballerina was the dam of Ch. Magic Fate of Blakeen (by Ch. Black Magic), Ch. Bric A Brac Black Silk (by Ch. Braeval Big Shot), Ch. Bric A Brac Best Man (sire of five champions) and Ch. Bric A Brac Black Velvet, CDX (dam of three champions) by Bric A Brac Barker, an impressive list of winners and producers for any one bitch. Ballerina's sister Cinderella was the dam of Ch. Bric A Brac Blackbird (a Best in Show winner) and Bric A Brac Black Pepper by Ch. Blakeen Tito, Ch. Ensarr Salute (another Best in Show winner) by Bric A Brac Barker and Ch. Blakeen Bubbling Over, by Ch. Black Magic. Bric A Brac Black Pepper was bred to

Ch. Chriscrest Franchonette (by Ch. Sherwood Franchot ex Ch. Qui Vive of King's Point) and her son, Ch. Chriscrest Babaloo, by Ch. Blakeen Bravo, both bred by Mrs. Wakefield. Babaloo owned by Dr. and Mrs. Cranfield.

Cartlane Pirouette (who had left impressive get at Hollycourt) to produce Ch. Bric A Brac Blithe Spirit, dam of three champions.

Mrs. Sayres is also the breeder of the beautiful Ch. Bric A Brac Brag About, who came from the classes to go Best of Breed at the 1962 Poodle Club of America Specialty Show. Brag About has several crosses to Ballerina and Cinderella. Sired by Ch. Bric A Brac Brand New (by Bric A Brac By George x Bric A Brac Black Ruffle) out of Bric A Brac Black Dixiebelle (by Braeval Barley Sugar x Bric A Brac Bouree), Brag About is the sire of seven champions, with more in the making.

One of the great loves of Mrs. Sayres' life was the imported cream Ch. Fircot L'Ballerine of Maryland. Mrs. Sayres piloted "Larry" to top honors at such outstanding events as the Poodle Club of America Specialty in 1955 and Best in Show at the 1957 Morris and Essex Dog Show. Larry had been owned by Mrs. Saunders Meade's Seafren Kennels but was left to Mrs. Sayres when Mrs. Meade passed away. Although used sparingly at stud, Larry has a number of distinguished descendants who have been outstanding winners in the show ring.

Mrs. Sayres also has an interest in breeding Toys. Her lovely imported brown bitch Ch. Montmartre Molecule was Best of Variety at the Poodle Club of America Specialty in 1961.

154

32

Chriscrest Kennels

THIS is the story of what one fancier built from a single pet dog. With comparatively little opportunity, this small kennel made great strides in a short time. Mrs. Wakefield started with one good black bitch as a pet, Ch. Qui Vive of King's Point, who finished her championship with one Group to her credit. Qui Vive was by Napoleon of King's Point (a son of Ch. Sparkling Jet of Misty Isles) out of Pirouette of Misty Isles, a granddaughter of Jet and Ch. Misty Isles Algie of Piperscroft—the classic combination. This, of course, made Qui Vive line-bred to Jet. Qui Vive was whelped in September of 1944, and to her goes the credit of establishing the Chriscrest line.

No other bitch has been purchased from that day to this. And, as Mrs. Wakefield has never owned a stud dog, all the males have been from the outside. But the Chriscrest pedigrees show a certain amount of line breeding, as is right and proper. Aside from the few silvers that came and went, the only adult dogs have been Ch. Qui Vive, her daughters, and, later, her grand-daughters and great-granddaughters, all much loved house pets. From Qui Vive, without exception, descend all the Chriscrest winners. As everybody knows, such breeding requires considerable skill. The classic example of this type of breeding is, of course, that of the late Mrs. Morse's famous Diablotins, who all descended without exception or additional purchases from her bitch Crowell's Dawn of a New Day. The Chriscrests have followed the same pattern.

Ch. Qui Vive was mated to my little Ch. Sherwood Franchot, Mrs. Wakefield's favorite of my Blakeen Chieveley's four champion sons. Ch. Franchot was a grandson of Ch. Venda's The Black Imp of Catawba, and therefore was of Chieveley breeding, so this was a union of two great lines. In the resulting litter were two bitches, Chriscrest Fleurette and Chriscrest Franchonette, both of whom gained their championships. Qui Vive's next litter by Ch. Blakeen Bubbling Over contained Chriscrest Yvonne.

Ch. Chriscrest Fleurette went to Texas as a puppy and was later bred to Ch. Diablotin Onyx to produce Duncount's Dauphin (who was pointed) and Duncount's Dariole. Dariole was bred to the Toy, Georgian Black Magic, to produce the blue Toy, Ch. Ardlussa Gascon, who sired several Toy champions. Fleurette was also bred to Ch. Magic Fate of Blakeen to produce Duncount's Folly, the dam of Ch. Link's Bubbling Over and Ch. Link's Dark Star (both by Ch. Highland Sand Magic Star).

At home, Ch. Chriscrest Franchonette produced four champions: Ch. Chriscrest Babaloo (by Blakeen Bravo), and Best in Show littermates Am. & Can. Ch. Chriscrest Jamboree and Am., Can. & Cuban Ch. Chriscrest Jubilee. Jamboree was the sire of six champions and an important sire in the Chriscrest family. Bred to Ch. Chriscrest Flirtation (Ch. Chriscrest Babaloo x Chriscrest Yvonne) he produced the Best in Show winner Ch. Chriscrest The Fiddler, a sire of 16 champions who has been particularly important on the West Coast. Ch. Chriscrest Jubilee first went to the Midcrest Kennels, where she was the dam of Ch. Midcrest Black Sabre and Ch. Midcrest Sabrina by Ch. Link's Bubbling Over. She later went to the Aizbel Kennels where she became the dam of the Best in Show winner Ch. Aizbel Collector's Item and Ch. Aizbel Imperial Imp by Ch. Chriscrest The Fiddler, and of Cuban Ch. Aizbel Ebony Effigy and Cuban Ch. Aizbel Magic Emblem by Ch. Armenonville Tresor. Franchonette was bred to her son, Ch. Chriscrest Babaloo, to produce Chriscrest Ebony Eve. Ebony Eve, bred to Duncount's Dauphin, gave Chriscrest Madcap Mitzie and Ch. Chriscrest Mambo. Madcap Mitzie was the dam of Ch. Chriscrest Eloise, and Ch. Chriscrest Mambo is the dam of Ch. Beaujeu Black Samba of Melmar (by Ch. Braeval Boomerang) and Ch. Chriscrest Star Dust (by Ch. Gustav de Peche). Star Dust was bred to Ch. Chriscrest Jamboree to produce the outstanding producer Ch. Marclair Gipsy of Midcrest, the dam of six champions at Midcrest Kennels.

Qui Vive's untitled daughter Chriscrest Yvonne was the dam of Ch. Chriscrest Flirtation (by Ch. Chriscrest Babaloo) and of Ch. Chriscrest Rumba and Chriscrest Rhythm (by Ch. Chriscrest Jamboree). Flirtation was the dam of the important Ch. Chriscrest The Fiddler by Ch. Chriscrest Jamboree, and of Ch. Fiddler's Green Lorelei by Fiddler's Green Dance Time. Chriscrest Rhythm is the dam of Ch. Honig's Hurrah, Ch. Gale's Mardi Gras of Melmar and of Can. Ch. Chriscrest Epicure In Brown.

The Chriscrests represent a strong black family which has been carefully interwoven with excellent results. This line has a small gene which has also

156

been used to advantage in breeding black Toys. Considering the small size of this kennel, the accomplishments have been remarkable. Breeding activities ceased with the death of Mrs. Wakefield but the line continues in the hands of others.

Ch. Chriscrest The Fiddler (by Ch. Chriscrest Jamboree ex Ch. Chriscrest Flirtation) bred by Christobel Wakefield and Phyllis Tworuk, owned by Phyllis Tworuk Greer, Fiddler's Green Kennels. Sire of 16 champions.

Dorothy Thompson with her special pet, the homebred Ch. Highland Sand Brown Dream (by Ch. Magic Fate of Blakeen x Ch. Diablotin Star of Elblac) bred by Mrs. Thompson.

33

Highland Sand Kennels

IN the wise choice of Ch. Diablotin Star of Elblac, by Ch. Diablotin Onyx x Diablotin Dryad, Dorothy Thompson had a once-in-a-life-time stroke of good fortune. Her selection was well justified, for this little bitch from such a notable family not only completed her championship but became the greatest producing Miniature bitch of all time. She was mated to two of the greatest sires of her day with extraordinary results. Mated to Ch. Magic Fate of Blakeen (sire of 13 champions) she had a litter of two, which contained the lovely brown Group winner Ch. Highland Sand Brown Dream and Am. & Can. Ch. Highland Sand Magic Star, who finished as a 7½-month-old puppy and later won 35 Groups and 11 Bests in Show. Magic Star became one of the great sires of the breed with 23 champions to his credit.

From England Mrs. Thompson imported Busby of Piperscroft and Phillipa of Piperscroft, both of whom became American champions in short order. Busby became an important sire with 15 champions to his credit, nine of them out of Ch. Diablotin Star of Elblac. The combination of Busby and Phillipa produced the lovely black Ch. Highland Sand Buzzette, dam of ten champions, all of them by Ch. Highland Sand Magic Star. Two sons of this combination, Ch. Highland Sand George and Ch. Highland Sand Star Baby, became top producers. George followed in his sire's footsteps by winning 33 Groups and five Bests in Show at all-breed and specialty shows and is the sire of 16 champions. Star Baby went to the Beaujeu Kennels where he sired six champions. The other eight champions from Magic Star to Buzzette are Chs. Highland Sand's Brown Magic, Magic Star II, Caprice, Kiki, Oh and Ah, Star of the East, Pretty Georgia and Brown Angel.

Ch. Potiphar of Piperscroft (white Miniature) by Firebrave Tito ex Dimple of Piperscroft, bred by Piperscroft Kennels, England and owned by Highland Sand Kennels.

Mrs. Thompson produced several silver champions by her Ch. Holly-court Silverado, including Ch. Highland Sand Silver Comet, Ch. Highland Sand Silver Saint and Ch. Highland Sand Silver Victory. The white English imports Ch. Potiphar of Piperscroft and Caroline of Piperscroft (by Eng. Ch. Blakeen Oscar of the Waldorf x Vikki of Piperscroft) were bred to produce Am. & Can. Ch. Highland Sand Whiten Lad (a Best in Show winner), Ch. Highland Sand White Frost and Ch. Highland Sand Shining Son.

Mrs. Thompson also tried her hand with Toys and again met with success. A black Potiphar daughter, Highland Sand Jessica, was the dam of Ch. Highland Sand Fearless Fredy, Ch. Highland Sand Fearless Annie and Ch. Highland Sand Magic Toy II, all by Ch. Orsie's Mi-Ra-Bi-Le. Another Potiphar daughter, Coif-Feur's White Blossom, was the dam of the white Toys Ch. Highland Sand Beau Geste and Ch. Highland Sand Bon Bon.

This kennel believed in showing its winners very young, and thus many of them finished long before they were a year old, a feat made possible by their unusual coats. Fortunately, expense was no object and the dogs were campaigned successfully by able handlers in every section of the country.

Mrs. Thompson says that the ambition of her youth was to breed good dogs, and certainly she has achieved her girlhood desire and reached the top in a record length of time. It is greatly to her credit that, with the exception of her wisely chosen foundation dogs, all her great winners have been home-breds. And Mrs. Thompson has always generously shared them with other serious breeders.

Although no longer active, Highland Sand has a proud record of 45 home-bred Miniature champions to its credit.

Am. Ch. Busby of Piperscroft (by Ch. Top Hat of Piperscroft ex Grisel of Piperscroft) bred by Mrs. A. L. Boyd of Piperscroft Kennels, England, owned by Highland Sand Kennels.

Int. Ch. Highland Sand Magic Star (by Ch. Magic Fate of Blakeen ex Ch. Diablotin Star of Elblac), a famous sire and Best in Show winner.

Ch. Fontclair Festoon (by Eng. Ch. Rudolph of Piperscroft ex Fontclair Fuchsia), English import, owned and campaigned to a great show career by Dunwalke Kennels. Dam of many champions.

34

Dunwalke Kennels

THE Dunwalke Kennels of Clarence Dillon in New Jersey specialize in black Miniatures. The most famous member of this kennel was the beautiful black bitch Ch. Fontclair Festoon, who was Best in Show at the Westminster Kennel Club Show in 1959.

In establishing the kennel Mr. Dillon selected the best individuals and lines that England had to offer. From Braeval Kennels came Ch. Braeval Baroness (Eng. & Am. Ch. Braeval Boomerang x Hygea Hanora). From Emmrill Kennels came Ch. Emmrill Psyche and Ch. Emmrill Lucky Charm (both x Emmrill Lindabelle, a full sister of Festoon). From Montmartre Kennels came Eng. & Am. Ch. Montmartre Miranda and her daughter, Ch. Montmartre Marcella. Festoon was acquired as a puppy in June of 1955 from Mrs. A. D. Jenkins, who owned her sire, the great Eng. Ch. Rudolph of Piperscroft.

To complement this stellar collection of bitches Mr. Dillon required the best male possible. He found his answer in Montmartre What-A-Boy, but What-A-Boy's owner, Mrs. Conn, felt that he was too valuable to her Montmartre Kennel and would not part with him. What-A-Boy was a Best in Show winner in England, and with his litter sister, Eng. Ch. Montmartre Little Mo, founded the Montmartre line. After breeding a number of litters by What-A-Boy, which included Eng. Ch. Montmartre Marksman (sire of seven champions) and the Toy Eng. Ch. Montmartre Miss Muffet, Mrs. Conn decided he could go to Dunwalke. What-A-Boy has become one of the breed's top sires with 15 champions to his credit.

In 1961, Ch. Dunwalke Lorenzo of Montfleuri (by Eng. Ch. Moensfarm Mascot of Montfleuri) joined the Dunwalke stud force, and he has also become

Ch. Dunwalke Marcellus

a top producer. Ch. Braeval Baroness produced Ch. Dunwalke Heroine (by New Hat of Montfleuri) and Ch. Challendon Gay Deceiver (by What-A-Boy). Ch. Montmartre Marcella produced Ch. Dunwalke Marstella (by Ch. Beaujeu Regal) and Ch. Dunwalke Marcellus (by her own sire What-A-Boy). At Highlane, as he was at Challendon, Marcellus is proving to be an outstanding sire. Ch. Emmrill Lucky Charm, a Best in Show winner, also went to the Highlane Kennels, where she produced two champion daughters.

Dunwalke is proudest of the great show and producing records set by Ch. Fontclair Festoon. Shown 68 times, she won 58 Bests of Variety, 38 Group Firsts, 3 Specialty Bests of Breed and 16 Bests in Show including Westminster. Retired from the show ring after her Westminster triumph, she became one of the breed's greatest producing bitches. In her first litter was the Group winner Ch. Dunwalke Tione (by Ch. Ardian Girlie's Son). From her three litters by What-A-Boy came seven champions: Ch. Dunwalke Carnation (Best in Show winner), Ch. Dunwalke Black Tulip (Best in Show winner), Ch. Dunwalke Garland (Group winner), Ch. Dunwalke Primrose, Ch. Dunwalke Daffodil, Ch. Dunwalke Bouquet and Ch. Dunwalke Boutonniere. Festoon's last litter was whelped in 1963 by Ch. Dunwalke Lorenzo of Montfleuri and produced the group-winning bitch Ch. Dunwalke Sweetbrier and her Best in Show brother, Ch. Dunwalke Sweetwilliam. In 1961, after seeing Festoon's early ability as a producer, it was decided to center all attention on her and her children. Of Festoon's 14 children by three sires, 10 are champions—a remarkable record. With this splendid heritage the future looks bright for the Dunwalke black Miniature line.

164

Ch. Dunwalke Lorenzo
of Montfleuri

Ch. Dunwalke Sweetbrier,
Group winner.

Ch. Dunwalke Black Tulip,
Best in Show winner.

Bric A Brac Bonne Femme, foundation bitch of Cappoquin Kennels.

Ch. Cappoquin Bon Fiston (by Ch. Hollycourt Bronze Knight ex Bric A Brac Bonne Femme). Sire of many champions.

35

Cappoquin Kennels

THE Cappoquin Kennels of Mary Griffin are located in Pennsylvania (the name "Cappoquin" refers to the village of Cappoquin in Ireland, where Mrs. Griffin saw her first Poodle). Cappoquin's success in the show ring is largely due to the selection of the black Miniature puppy Bric A Brac Bonne Femme (Bric A Brac and Braeval breeding) for her foundation. From Bonne Femme's first litter came the sire of 16 champions, Ch. Cappoquin Bon Fiston (by Ch. Hollycourt Bronze Knight). In Bonne Femme's second litter were Ch. Hollycourt Calandra and the famous Am. & Can. Ch. Cappoquin Bon Jongleur.

Jongleur was a great winner with 21 Best in Shows to his credit. Many consider him the finest brown Miniature in the history of the breed. Bon Jongleur, or "Charley Brown" as he is known to his fans, is the sire of 20 champions. Bonne Femme is also the dam of Ch. Cappoquin Bonne Nuit (Winners Bitch at Westminster, 1961) by Ch. Hollycourt Phillipson. Bonne Femme was bred to her grandson, Ch. Cappoquin Guyon (by Ch. Cappoquin Bon Fiston), to produce Cappoquin Bonne Princesse, the dam of Ch. Cappoquin Railsplitter (Best of Winners at Westminster, 1962) and Ch. Cappoquin Honest Abe (Best of Winners at Westminster, 1963), both by Ch. Ardian Girlie's Son. A full sister of Bon Jongleur, Daddy's Girl, was bred to Ch. Cappoquin Bon Fiston to produce the Best in Show winner and top producer Ch. Cappoquin Carriage Trade.

Cappoquin was also the home of the silver-beige Miniature Group winner Ch. Cappoquin Creme de la Creme (by Ch. Hollycourt Platinum x Cappoquin Rikiki). Cappoquin also has the silver Toy Group winner Ch. High

Mrs. Robert Tranchin with a group of her Beaujeu Miniature Poodles.

Heritage Headstudy (by Ch. Silver Sparkle of Sassafras x High Heritage Heather Hue), who sired Ch. Cappoquin Sugar Bun (Best of Winners at Westminster, 1966).

Cappoquin is also known for the black Toy bitch Ch. Cappoquin Little Sister. Mrs. Griffin recognized Little Sister's quality even in a pet trim, purchased her, grew a show coat on her and started her on a fabulous show career. Little Sister was Best of Winners at Westminster in 1959, Best of Variety in 1960 and Best in Show in 1961. After finishing her championship and before her specials career, Little Sister was sold to Florence Michelson in Florida. She was shown throughout her career by Anne Rogers Clark. After her retirement she produced four champions: Ch. Tropicstar Do It Up Brown and Ch. Tropicstar In The Black (by Ch. Carlima's J.D.), Ch. Tropicstar Sister Sue (by Blackabit of Sassafras), and the Best in Show winner Ch. Tropicstar Tequila (by her son Do It Up Brown).

168

36

Beaujeu Kennels

THE Beaujeu Kennels of Mr. and Mrs. Robert Tranchin were started in 1952 with the acquisition, as a six-week-old puppy, of the black Miniature Ch. Diablotin Kala Jauhar (Ch. Diablotin Onyx x Diablotin Double Trouble). They also purchased the brown female Ch. Diablotin Autumn Leaf (Ch. Smilestone's Sirprise x Ch. Diablotin Forever Amber). These two gave Beaujeu's top-producing brown bitch Beaujeu Diablesse (dam of six champions). The black male Ch. Highland Sand Star Baby (Am. & Can. Ch. Highland Sand Magic Star x Ch. Highland Sand Buzzette) also became a top producer with six champions to his credit. Beaujeu also owned the black Best in Show winner Eng., Am. & Can. Ch. Braeval Boomerang, who was the sire of 15 champions.

From these excellent beginnings based on top American and English lines Mrs. Tranchin has bred many champions. Autumn Leaf is the dam of Ch. Beaujeu Bittersweet (by New Hat of Montfleuri), Ch. Beaujeu Solitaire (by Wendoley Wilson), and Chs. Beaujeu Sunrise, Beaujeu Eloise and Beaujeu Playboy, all three by Innisfail Marlon. Bittersweet was sold to the Crikora Kennels where she produced three champions. Autumn Leaf's untitled daughter, Beaujeu Diablesse, is the dam of seven titleholders. Mated to Beaujeu Meteor (Ch. Highland Sand Shooting Star x Ch. Desmoulins Delight of Montfleuri), she produced Ch. Beaujeu Pride, Ch. Beaujeu Prejudice, Ch. Beaujeu Pretty Please and Ch. Beaujeu Burnt Chocolate; with Ch. Braeval Boomerang, she gave Ch. Beaujeu Regal (a Best in Show winner and sire of seven champions), Ch. Beaujeu Royal (a Best in Show winner) and Ch. Beaujeu Pin-Up. Pride went to the Crikora Kennels where she became

Eng. & Am.
Ch. Montmartre Maria Nina

the dam of four champions. Another Beaujeu import, Towhey's Pimpernel Jet Flame, is the dam by Ch. Highland Sand Star Baby of Ch. Beaujeu Jet Star, Ch. Beaujeu Love and Kisses and Ch. Beaujeu Boom Bang.

Beaujeu was also the owner of the white English import Ch. Icarus Duke Otto, the winner of six Bests in Show and sire of nine champions. Otto's daughter, Beaujeu Blanchette Cherie, produced four champions for Mrs. Dwight Lawson.

Mrs. Tranchin has recently added several English imports to her kennel which should continue their impressive winning and producing records. The black male Eng., Am., Can. & Mex. Ch. Montmartre Bartat By Jingo was a top winner in England with 14 Challenge Certificates to his credit, became a Best in Show winner on this side of the Atlantic. He has sired a number of champions here and in England. Beaujeu is also the home of two bitches that have won top honors in England and America, Eng. & Am. Ch. Montmartre Maria Nina, and Eng. & Am. Ch. Aspen Bonne Amie.

Beaujeu has been the home of over 75 champions. More than half of them have been black Miniatures.

170

Eng. Am. & Can. Ch. Montmartre Bartat By Jingo, winning under judge Forest N. Hall. Handled by Maxine Beam.

Eng. & Am. Ch. Aspen Bonne Amie, winning under judge Mrs. Ena Stewart.

Int. Ch. Vichnou de Lamorlaye, winner in Italy, Belgium and France, with small brown Miniature bitch, breeder-owner, Princesse Amedee de Broglie, Lamorlaye Kennels, Paris, France.

37

Poodles in France

By

Princesse Amedee de Broglie

So many American visitors have bought Poodles in France and taken them home with them, that it may be of interest to them, and perhaps to other fanciers, to hear of some of the differences between French and American methods of breeding and showing.

On the Continent, the kennel clubs of the different European countries follow the rules and regulations of the FCI (Federation Canine Internationale). In France, as elsewhere in Europe (with the exception of Great Britain), Poodles must be bred in the fundamental colors: black, brown, and white. No other color was admitted by the Societé Central Canine until recently when silver was, at last, accepted as a regular color. But no mixture whatever is allowed when breeding Poodles, not even black to brown.

In France our Poodles are divided into three classifications of height:

Standards, which measure more than 45 centimeters and must be under 55 centimeters (that is over $17\frac{3}{4}$ inches and under $21\frac{3}{4}$ inches).

Moyens, or mediums, over 35 centimeters and under 45 centimeters (over $13\frac{3}{4}$ inches and under $17\frac{3}{4}$ inches).

Nains, or dwarfs, under 35 centimeters (what corresponds to our Miniatures under $13\frac{3}{4}$ inches).

Confusion often arises when an American inquiry is received for a Standard, a Miniature, or a Toy, because our French definitions of height do not correspond with the American standards.

To be accepted in a French show, Poodles must be in the "lion" clip. This is very much like the English "Saddle" Clip, but the hindquarters are entirely shorn with no pattern left on. There is a pompon left on the end of the tail and ruffles on the hocks. The dog's face is also clipped, but a moustache is retained and the hair on the forehead and top of the head is shortened and evenly shaped.

In France there is a general rule concerning the registration of dogs, no matter what breed. Each year a letter of the alphabet is taken in sequence; therefore the age of the dog can be known according to the initial letter of his pedigreed name. For example, in 1951 we started again at the beginning of the alphabet and the names of all the dogs whelped that year had to begin with "A."

Another rule is that an owner is not permitted, as he is in England and America, to add his kennel name or prefix to that of any dog he has not bred. The dogs retain their original name, and their new owners have no right to change them in any way, even when they happen to have been privately bred and sold and have no prefix or suffix. Registration in the LOF (Livres des Origines Francais) requires four generations of numbered and registered dogs.

Poodles are a very ancient breed in France, and as we search far back into their origin, we find some very famous strains which have followed through to the present time. We like to find in the pedigrees of our browns, "du Barrois," "de la Gage," and "Maritza"; and in the background of our black Poodles, "de Madjige," "de Puy Valador," and "d'Azay." In our whites, "De Samarobrive" and "Du Briois" are of the utmost value. As the owner of a very large kennel with varied colors and sizes, I have exported as well as imported many Poodles, and I have certainly improved my own stock with the "Von Sadowa," "Sirius" (both German), and "Labory" (Swiss), as well as British and American purchases.

Our French standard of beauty is nearly the same, apart from minor variations, as in all the other countries. Our judges, however, are very exacting in regard to length of ear leather and uniformity of color. Unlike both England and America, our dogs are not judged by points but must obtain one of the mentions, "Excellent," "Very Good," "Good." (There are, by the way, no classes for dogs under ten months old.) Only a first prize in "Open Dogs" with the mention "Excellent" qualifies a dog for a championship certificate, or CAC (Certificat D'Apitude au Championnat). To become a French champion, a dog must acquire at least three CAC's, one of which must be won at the Annual International Show in Paris, held under the auspices of the Societe Centrale Canine de France. Since only one Poodle of each sex and color can obtain the title in any one year, few people realize what an achievement it is to make a French champion.

May these few notes bring a better understanding between the Poodle fanciers of different countries. We would all gain by working together to bring about an even greater perfection of this incomparable breed.

174

I'm sure this clearly written description of French rules and regulations and methods of breeding, clipping, naming, and showing Poodles will interest our readers as much as it has me.

Undoubtedly it will clear up a great deal of confusion among the many owners of French-bred Poodles in America. One of the stumbling blocks has been the fact that the "moyen," medium or in-between size, over Miniature height and under Standard qualification, is not recognized in England and America. Unfortunately, it contains many of the best French dogs, but with us it is neither fish, flesh, fowl, nor good red herring, as there is no classification for it in the shows. Also, in France there is no classification for Toys. England has no separate classification either, but a special class of under eleven inches in which they may be entered. Note that whereas our limit in height is ten inches, in England it is eleven.

The present-day official French clip for show Poodles bars even the pompons on the hips in what has always been known as the "Continental" Clip. Today the dog's hindquarters are completely bare of trim except for ruffles at the hocks. This has a strange look to us, but has the definite advantage of exposing all defects of lower back line and hindquarters. Some of our own winners with crooked spines and unsoundness in hindquarter would benefit from just such a public exposé, which would certainly prevent them from winning and passing on their defects to other generations.

Again, the stressing of two points which we consider minor points, namely, purity of color and length of ear leather, should have more importance with us in America than is now accorded them.

The French method of awarding championships differs very little from that practiced in England. The two different requirements are the grading of the dogs as "Excellent," "Very Good," and "Good," and the fact that to qualify as a champion in France the dog must win its final CAC at the big International Show in Paris held only once a year. In England a dog must also win three "Challenge Certificates," or CC's, in order to become a champion of record. But there is no grading of contestants and the certificates may be won at any show where they are offered. These are limited to just a certain number of the largest shows where the classification for Poodles and the entry the year before warrant the offering of challenge certificates. A great many of the smaller shows do not have them. The practice in England, unlike our own of placing champions "For Specials Only," is to show champions for competition in the classes so that a really outstanding dog may win any number of CC's and hold back younger dogs battling for the title.

The rule that an owner who has not bred a dog cannot use his prefix

Am., Fr., It., & Belg., Ch. Vichnou de Lamorlaye (white Standard) breeder-owner, Princesse Amedee de Broglie, Lamorlaye Kennels, Paris.

on its registered name is to my mind an excellent one. In many cases both in England and America, big winners have brought renown to the kennels whose prefix or suffix they bear, whereas their breeders are either unknown or overlooked, and this is not at all as it should be.

I'm sure you will join me in thanking Princesse de Broglie for a clear, straightforward, and generous effort to clear away the cobwebs and establish a better understanding between Poodle lovers on both sides of the water.

LYDIA HOPKINS

Black Miniature owned by Princesse Amedee de Broglie, Lamorlaye Kennels, Paris.

French Ch.
Vulcain d'Ajol

A white champion
of the Lamorlaye Kennels

French Ch.
Katja v. d. Muruisel

38

Outstanding Miniature Sires

Monarch Line

ENGLISH, AMERICAN & CANADIAN
CH. PIXHOLME FIREBRAVE GUSTAV, C.D. INT.

Whelped September 30, 1947   Died August 16, 1959

Bred by Alida Monro, Firebrave Kennels, England
Owned by Poodhall Kennels

```
                    Robin of Piperscroft (blk)
          Firebrave Alphonse (blk)
                    Pegotty of Piperscroft (blk)
    Eng. & Am. Ch. Firebrave Pimpernel (blk)
                    Firebrave Copperfield (brn)
          Eng. Ch. Firebrave Nicolette (blk)
                    Firebrave Mam'selle (blk)
```

ENG., AM. & CAN. CH. PIXHOLME FIREBRAVE GUSTAV, C.D. INT. (blk)

```
                    Monty of Piperscroft (blk)
          Francois of Piperscroft (blk)
                    La Pompadour of Piperscroft (blk)
    Firebrave Mam'selle (blk)
                    Eng. & Am. Ch. Chieveley Chopstick (blk)
          Chieveley Chatty (blk)
                    Eng. Ch. Chieveley Chess (blk)
```

ENG., AM. & CAN. CH. PIXHOLME FIREBRAVE GUSTAV, C.D. INT.

<u>Sire of 23 champions:</u>   <u>Out of:</u>

Am. & Can. Ch. Poodhall Gus
Am. & Can. Ch. Poodhall Black Angus
Ch. Poodhall Merry Minstrel
Ch. Poodhall Lettice
Ch. Poodhall La Pompadour   Yasmin of Montfleuri
Ch. Poodhall Gustavia
Ch. Poodhall Mam'selle
Can. Ch. Poodhall Pompette
Can. Ch. Poodhall Yasmin

Ch. Poodhall Busy Bee
Ch. Poodhall Minuet   Poodhall Sita
Ch. Poodhall Polonaise

Ch. Gustav de Peche   Poodhall Amala
Ch. Yasmin de Peche

Ch. Poodhall Whirlaway   Ch. Poodhall Lettice
Ch. Gaily Go Firebrave   Ch. Chosette of Hockford
Ch. Sunnyheath Maeschele   Ch. Charlotte of Hockford
Eng. Ch. Aultone Pixholme Louis   Eng. Ch. Lorna of Mannerhead
Ch. Winmarleigh Gustavia   Emilie of Hockford
Can. Ch. Poodhall Fidelio
Eng. Ch. Digbycourt Lady Babette
Italian Ch. Pixholme Emlyn
Austrian Ch. Pixholme Jan

ENG. CH. RUDOLPH OF PIPERSCROFT

Whelped January 1951   Died 1964

Bred by Mrs. Grace Boyd, Piperscroft Kennels, England
Owned by Mrs. A. D. Jenkins, Fontclair Kennels, England

```
                              Tip Top of Piperscroft (blk)
                 Voila of Piperscroft (blk)
                              Firebrave Black Beauty (blk)
          Clipper of Piperscroft (blk)
                              Firebrave Andre (blk)
                 Steeplejack Mezali of Piperscroft (blk)
                              Monica of Piperscroft (blk)

ENG. CH. RUDOLPH OF PIPERSCROFT (blk)

                              Eng. Ch. Barty of Piperscroft (blk)
                 Ruffles of Piperscroft (blk)
                              Bijou of the Rigi (blk)
          Show Girl of Piperscroft (blk)
                              Cirrus of Piperscroft (blk)
                 Pants of Piperscroft (blk)
                              Michou of Piperscroft (blk)
```

ENG. CH. RUDOLPH OF PIPERSCROFT

Sire of 28 champions:	Out of:
Swedish Ch. Moensfarm Mikado of Montfleuri	
Ch. Moensfarm Mandarin of Montfleuri	
Eng. & Am. Ch. Moensfarm Marcelle of Montfleuri	Moensfarm Mimi
Eng. Ch. Moensfarm Mascot of Montfleuri	
Eng. Ch. Sibon Sombrero	
Eng. & Am. Ch. Sibon Magic Moment	Sibon Nutbeem Mist
Eng. Ch. Montravia Sibon Lady of Spain	
Ch. Fontclair Festoon	Fontclair Fushia
Eng. Ch. Fontclair Fleur of Burdiesel	
Eng. & Am. Ch. Lucilla of Montfleuri	
Ch. High Kick of Montfleuri	Eng. Ch. Braebeck Jonella of Montfleuri
Swedish Ch. Tarrywood Courtier	
Swedish Ch. Tarrywood Countess	Tarrywood Black Opal
Eng. Ch. Adastra Magic Ace	Adastra Magic Charm
Eng. Ch. Baroque of Montfleuri	Eng. Ch. Trilla of Montfleuri
Ch. Emmrill Lucky Charm	Emmrill Lindabelle
Ch. Frivolity of Montfleuri	Eng. Ch. Valentina of Montfleuri
Ch. Helena of Burdiesel	Jasmine of Sendora
Ch. Icarus Prince de Parma	Eng. Ch. Icarus Toukais Jeanne-Nisette
Ch. Pirouette of Hockford	Pierette of Hockford
Eng. Ch. Rippwood Milord of Eldonwood	Aultone Bonne Bouche of Eldonwood
Eng. Ch. Rippwood Petronella of Eldonwood	Mahopac Chloe of Eldonwood
Eng. Ch. Willowbrae Gavotte of Montfleuri	Willowbrae Sankette of Montfleuri
Ch. Wychwood Black Nero	Fleur of Filozelle
Ch. Montfleuri San Souci of Willowmead	Petitbrun Sweet Maiden
Int. Ch. Bella Donna of Burdiesel	Fontclair Flona
Swedish Ch. Final Fling of Montfleuri	Macushla of Montfleuri
Finnish Ch. Snowdown Rudolph	Snowdown Fifi

Ch. Emmrill Lucky Charm

AM. & CAN. CH. CAPPOQUIN BON JONGLEUR

Whelped July 22, 1956

Bred by Cappoquin Kennels
Owned by Frank T. Sabella

```
                              Ch. Hollycourt Philippe (blk)
                   Ch. Hollycourt Blackamoor (blk)
                              Ch. Hollycourt Patricia (blk)
        Ch. Hollycourt Black Bobbin (blk)
                              Ch. Blakeen Eldorado (brn)
                   Ch. Diablotin Dentelle (blk)
                              Ch. Diablotin Danseuse (blk)


AM. & CAN. CH. CAPPOQUIN BON JONGLEUR (brn)

                              Ch. Braeval Big Shot (brn)
                   Bric A Brac Buster Brown (brn)
                              Bric A Brac Betinka (blk)
        Bric A Brac Bonne Femme (blk)
                              Samarkand Sweet Talk (blk)
                   Samarkand Sweetie Pie (blk)
                              Samarkand Mystic (blk)
```

182

AM. & CAN. CH. CAPPOQUIN BON JONGLEUR

Sire of 22 champions: Out of:

Ch. Boarzell Beaute   Ch. Kendall's Tonette
Can. Ch. Boarzell Bon Jouer

Ch. Canyonwyck Velvet Brown   Mer-Ev-Ell's La Poupee
Ch. Canyonwyck Cricket

Ch. Challendon Tender Trap   Challendon Cheer
Ch. Challendon Tokay

Ch. Challendon Cio-Cio San   Hollycourt Sirena
Ch. Loramar's Arabesque

Ch. Ledahof Ballet Master   Ledahof Brilliance
Ch. Ledahof Brazen Brat

Ch. Leeann's Libation of Thalia   Nigreta's Daicquiri
Ch. Leeann's Mardi Gras

Ch. Baron Crest Black Plume   Baron Crest Muffin of Bon-Zu
Ch. Estid Charlie Brown   Estid Finale
Ch. Canito's Wendy   Ch. Jais Luisant of Trent
Ch. Denbur's Enola Gay   Petite Caniche Joli Tiki
Ch. Logan's Ebony Star   La Gai Juliette
Ch. Meridian's Abundance   Meridian Calais
Ch. Phidelan's Echo of Surrey   Ch. Surrey La Belle Jeune Fille
Ch. Stillfair Silhouette   Ch. Melissa of Meisen
Ch. Terudon's Gay Lover   Terudon's Charm Bracelet
Ch. Cypress Hill The Saracen   Cypress Hill's Circe

Ch. Estid Charlie Brown

ENGLISH, AMERICAN & CANADIAN
CH. BRAEVAL BOOMERANG

Whelped August 7, 1953   Deceased

Bred by Mrs. P. Austin-Smith, England
Owned by Mrs. Robert Tranchin, Beaujeu Kennels

```
                                  The Elfin Boy of Toytown (blk)
                    Eng. Ch. Toy Boy of Toytown (blk)
                                  Seething Duchess (blk)
          Eng. Ch. Braeval Bobo (blk)
                                  Firebrave Andre (blk)
                    La Poupee of Heatherton (blk)
                                  Festive of Heatherton (blk)

ENG., AM. & CAN. CH. BRAEVAL BOOMERANG (blk)

                                  Eng. Ch. Braeval Bobo (blk)
                    Eng. Ch. Braeval Bolero (blk)
                                  Braeval Brighteyes (blk)
          Braeval Burnt Grass (brn)
                                  Eng. Ch. Braeval Bobo (blk)
                    Braeval Bubble Gum (blk)
                                  Braeval Black Orchid (blk)
```

184

ENG., AM. & CAN. CH. BRAEVAL BOOMERANG

Sire of 15 champions: Out of:

Ch. Beaujeu Regal
Ch. Beaujeu Royal   Beaujeu Diablesse
Ch. Beaujeu Pin-Up

Ch. Beaujeu Hot Coffee   Ch. Crikora Chocolate Chip
Ch. Belle Thais

Ch. Crikora Cantata   Ch. Beaujeu Pride
Ch. Crikora Castanet

Ch. Braeval Baroness   Hygea Hanora
Eng. Ch. Braeval Big Apple   Braeval Bonnetta
Ch. Beaujeu Black Samba of Melmar   Ch. Chriscrest Mambo
Ch. Beaujeu Black Taffeta   Beaujeu Suzee
Ch. Beaujeu Mr. Bobby   Ch. Beaujeu Prejudice
Ch. Beaujeu Marjeau   Ch. Desmoulin's Delight of Montfleuri
Ch. Hilador Chocolate Souffle   Ch. Highland Sand Dark 'N Sweet
Ch. Kate's Black Satin   Ch. Bric A Brac Black Silk

Eng. Ch. Braeval Bobo

Eng. Ch. Braeval Bolero

CH. HOLLYCOURT PLATINUM

Whelped September 15, 1947   Deceased

Bred and owned by
Miss M. Ruelle Kelchner, Hollycourt Kennels

```
                              Ch. Talon's d'Argent of Meredick (si)
                   Ch. Aucassin (gr)
                              Ch. Marcourt Josephine (gr)
          Ch. Smilestone's Silvern (si)
                              Plata of Eathorpe (si)
                   Flora of Piperscroft of Blakeen (si)
                              Pauline (si)

CH. HOLLYCOURT PLATINUM (si)

                              Hunningham d'Argent (si)
                   Ch. Platinum of Eathorpe of Blakeen (si)
                              Griz Nez of Eathorpe (si)
          Ch. Platina (si)
                              Plata of Eathorpe (si)
                   Flora of Piperscroft of Blakeen (si)
                              Pauline (si)
```

186

CH. HOLLYCOURT PLATINUM

<u>Sire of 13 champions:</u>   Out of:

Ch. Cappoquin Creme de la Creme   Cappoquin Rikiki
Ch. Gamique D'Argent of Meridick   Petite Mimi of Meridick
Ch. Hollycourt Blue Ice   Ch. Hollycourt Plume Argente
Can. Ch. Hollycourt Gray Morn   Round Table's Silver Gleam
Ch. Hollycourt La Vedette   Hollycourt Ma Cherie
Ch. Hollycourt Rosetta   Hollycourt Lady Rosemary
Ch. Hollycourt Starbright   Hollycourt Nicole
Ch. Hollycourt Toison D'Or   Seyberne's Majolica
Ch. Parigon Finesse (Toy)   Paragon Dorinda

Ch. Perrevan Coupon
Ch. Perrevan Pioneer   Ch. Silverette of Ledahof
Ch. Perrevan Premium
Ch. Perrevan Tinsel

Ch. Hollycourt Light of Star Tavern, an important West Coast sire, owned by Marie Medley. Litter brother of Ch. Hollycourt Platinum.

ENGLISH, AMERICAN & CANADIAN
CH. ADASTRA MAGIC FAME

Whelped October 3, 1951   Deceased

Bred by Mr. and Mrs. L. H. Coventon, England
Owned by Maxine Beam

```
                              Harwee of Mannerhead (blk)
                  Ch. Snow Boy of Fircot (wh)
                              Solitaire of Piperscroft (gr)
          Eng. Ch. Blakeen Oscar of the Waldorf (wh)
                              Ch. Blakeen Minnikin (wh)
                  Ch. Blakeen Christable (wh)
                              Blakeen Alba (wh)

ENG., AM. & CAN. CH. ADASTRA MAGIC FAME (wh)

                              Eng. Ch. Adastra Magic Beau (blu)
                  Adastra Magic Gold (wh)
                              Adastra Cocotte (si)
          Adastra Magic Glitter (wh)
                              Eng. Ch. Adastra Magic Beau (blu)
                  Adastra Magic Snow (wh)
                              Popipoupa (wh)
```

ENG., AM. & CAN. CH. ADASTRA MAGIC FAME

Sire of 14 champions:

Ch. Furore Little Princess
Ch. Terudon Dilly Devine

Ch. Silhou-Jette's Ice Cream
Ch. Silhou-Jette's Snow Flurry

Ch. Winelist Brillante
Ch. Winelist Solera

Ch. Calico Puff of Westford Ho
Ch. Della's Pamper Me
Ch. Marney's Nougat
Ch. Freeland's Study in White
Ch. Lorac's Magic Gay Blade
Can. Ch. Wedgedale's Happy Bachelor
Ch. Woodland Snow Fall, C.D.
Can. Ch. Robinsbrook Diamond Chip

Out of:

Miss Blarney of Lime Crest

Ch. Blakeen Snow Flurry

Winelist Pousse Cafe

Pompadour P. K. of Westford Ho
Winters White Magic De Bo-Mi
Ivardon Lucia
Estid Nesta
Lime Crest Jezebel
Can. Ch. Fancy Fame's Dresden Doll
Burlingame Golden Flurry, C.D.

Ch. Woodland Snow Storm (by Silhou-Jette's Magic Fame ex Ch. Woodland Snow Fall, C.D.), sire of several champions. Snow Storm is a double grandson of Ch. Adastra Magic Fame.

AMERICAN & CANADIAN
CH. SUMMERCOURT SQUARE DANCER OF FIRCOT

Whelped March 7, 1956

Bred by Miss S. A. Williams, England
Owned by Jewel Garlick, Gaylen Poodles

```
                        Eng. Ch. Cremola of Swanhill (crm)
            Victor of Fircot (apr)
                        Cream Puff of Fircot (crm)
    Spotlight of Summercourt (blu)
                        Vendas Zante (gr)
            Vendas Falaise (brn)
                        Vendas Madame Bovary (blk)

AM. & CAN. CH. SUMMERCOURT SQUARE DANCER OF FIRCOT (crm)

                        Eng. Ch. Toomai of Montfleuri (blk)
            Pippo of Montfleuri (blk)
                        Eng. Ch. Philippa of Montfleuri (blk)
    Mistress of Pipers Lane (blk)
                        Mandarin of Mannerhead (blk)
            Mangeur of Bushill (blk)
                        Fifi of Swale (crm)
```

190

AM. & CAN. CH. SUMMERCOURT SQUARE DANCER OF FIRCOT

Sire of 61 champions: Out of:

Ch. Poodanne's Dancing Lady
Can. Ch. Poodanne's N-Vee-Me
Ch. Poodanne's Snow Dancer
Ch. Poodanne's Snow Mickey   Int. Ch. Simloch Ice de la Fontaine
Ch. Poodanne's Whip Cream
Ch. Poodanne's White Cloud
Ch. Poodanne's White Iceing
Ch. Tropicstar Poodanne Ingenue

Ch. Lawson's High Flyer
Ch. Lawson's Lancer   Beaujeu Blanchette Chere
Ch. Lawson's Muffin L
Ch. Lawson's Nosey John

Ch. Estid Ballet Dancer
Ch. Estid Gala Dancer   Estid Anitu
Ch. Estid Noble Dancer

Ch. Midcrest Cleopatra
Ch. Midcrest The Cameo   Ch. Midcrest The Vamp
Ch. Midcrest The Cosmopolitan

Can. Ch. Sunlock Snow Dancer II
Can. Ch. Sunlock Star Dancer   Int. Ch. Midcrest Ice-A-Rama
Can. Ch. Sunlock Swinging Sweetheart

Ch. Bluehevn's Tamara Dancer   Ch. Moss Oaks Sugar Plum
Ch. Starfire Dancing Master

Ch. Challendon Zippety Doo-Dah   Challendon Madonna
Ch. Challendon Zircon

Ch. Della's Pamper Me-Too   Ch. Della's Pamper Me
Ch. Della's Pamper Mee-Tutu

Ch. Jermel's Dancing Dorinda   Cardave's Sphanx
Ch. Jermel's Petite Etoile

Ch. Sandsturm-Baby Ruffles Pixie   Sandsturm Baby Ruffles
Ch. Square Dancer's Annie

Ch. Tedwin's Top Billing   Tedwin's Small Talk
Ch. Tedwin's Two Step

Ch. Woodland Lovely Light   Ch. Woodland Snow Fall
Ch. Woodland Love Affair

Ch. Round Table Danseuse Noel   Round Table Eloise
Ch. Round Table Fan Dancer

Ch. Alladin's Meringue   Beaufresne Crystal
Ch. Avron's Square Dancer   Avron Pirouette
Ch. Barbree Razzle Dazzle   Meryl's Moonbeam of Barbree

                                        - continued

Out of:

Ch. Barbree Round Dancer	Ch. Meryl's Snowflake of Barbree
Ch. Gaylen's Native Dancer	Edelair Snow Queen
Ch. Gaylen Square Dancer's Ginny	Loabelo Bonnie
Ch. Jarshay's Bis Baloo	Ch. Tricot Lamour of Markee
Ch. Linncrest Peggy's Prince	Winter's Awakening
Can. Ch. Manderlay's Snowflake	Champagne De La Fontaine II
Ch. Mullfaire's Square Dancer	Mullfaire's Diamond Lisa
Can. Ch. Pavlova De La Fontaine	Can. Ch. Simloch Yena de la Fontaine
Ch. Pixiecroft Swan Lake	Dawn of Pixiecroft
Ch. Plaza-Toro Sugarberry	Ch. Plaza-Toro Sugar Plum Fairy
Ch. Round Table Bal de Noel	Blue Bell Dancing Girl
Ch. Step A Long Exotic Dancer	Freeland's Lucie
Ch. The Colonel of Westford-Ho	Penelope of Westford-Ho
Ch. Top Brass of Gladgay	Pompadour Jessica
Ch. Woodland Burning Bright	Woodland Paprika, U.D.
Ch. Beaufresne Gilded Lily	Ch. Pixiecroft Sunbeam
Ch. Challendon Primrose	Challendon Roulette
Ch. Madrigal's Musette	Ch. Glendoune Patachou
Can. Ch. Cum Laude's Dancing Moonlight	Barbree Colleen Baughn
Can. Ch. Madrigal's Snowflake	
Vez. Ch. McColl's For Ever Amber	

Ch. Midcrest The Cosmopolitan

Ch. Lawson's Nosey John

Ch. Tedwins Top Billing

A trio of Toy puppies from Meisen Kennels.

The Toy Poodle

Portrait of a child with small white Poodle, German, circa 1620.

39

The Toy Poodle

EARLY HISTORY

THE original small white Poodle is perhaps the oldest member of the three Poodle varieties—so old in fact, that his origins are somewhat of a mystery. There are little Poodles represented on monuments at the time of the Emperor Augustus about 30 A.D. Much later, we have evidence of a small white Poodle affectionately looking up at a child in a German painting, circa 1620.

In early illustrations the small Poodles are captioned "Petit Bouffon" or "Barbet." The small Poodle was used as a "truffle dog" on the Continent and in England. Most were white or white with markings that made them easier to see at night, which was considered the proper time for hunting truffles (a small globular rootless and leafless fungus prized by gourmets). One line of truffle hunters in England is traceable back to its Spanish origins 300 years ago. From paintings these earlier dogs do not seem to have been very tiny, but rather about the size of the smaller Miniatures of today. Their heads were similar to the larger Poodles of their era with broad skulls, round eyes and ear leathers which were short and high set.

One theory on the origin of the very small Toy credits the French with having introduced the Maltese and a very tiny white Cuban dog called the Havanese in order to produce the very tiny size which was so highly desired. There are paintings in the Louvre in Paris showing tiny white Poodles as elegant drawing room pets in the early 1800's where they were great favorites at the French court. The Maltese characteristics are known to be among the most dominant and persistent in dogdom, and the Toy Poodle even today is plagued with the short legs, long bodies, round eyes with pink rims, short wide heads and soft silky coats which resulted from the initial cross. That these specimens were regarded as Toy Poodles at all was due more to the manner in which they were trimmed than their type. A pair of Continental whites were imported by the Piperscroft Kennels in England, and laid the foundation for the white Miniature and white Toy there. The small white Continental Poodles were also the foundations for the white Toy Poodle in America.

THE TOY POODLE IN AMERICA

Muriel Sanderson Clark and her mother, Mrs. Charles Clark of the famous white Muriclar Toy Poodles, who are now regarded as pioneers in the variety, wrote of their introduction to the white Toy Poodle: "Our memory and records take us as far back as 1917 and the personal acquaintance of two Toy Poodle breeders, now dead, who were breeding true Toys as far back as 1896. These breeders were Mrs. Sinclair of Orkney Kennels, and Mrs. Kronholm who used the prefix Kay's. Both lived in San Francisco. When we visited the Orkney Kennels in 1917, there were some twenty mature Toy Poodles. Several were very tiny, and under five pounds. Ch. Some Boy Boy, whom we saw, weighed three and a quarter pounds. Others, principally bitches, were larger, but none as recollected exceeded the present breed standard of ten inches at the shoulder. It should be remembered that the breed standard at that time only required that a Toy Poodle be under 12 pounds with no stipulation as to height at the shoulder. In the early 1930's we became acquainted with Mrs. Kronholm who was then an elderly woman in her 80's. She reported that she had bred Toys for fifty years and had never owned a Miniature. The trophies that line the walls of the homes of these women indicated their success in the show ring.

Their bloodlines are still in existence today but way, way back in the pedigrees. As a comparison on type in Toy Poodles of the original lines mentioned, the Orkney and Kronholm lines were very tiny, and quite faulty according to modern judgment; the more recent Orsie and Peaster lines had much better confirmation and better heads. The eyes on the old lines were much too round.

In 1952, Mrs. Clark admitted that although the crossing of Toys and Miniatures had brought about much needed improvement, she felt that there was a danger of the Toy becoming too large and of the old pure Toy line becoming extinct. She felt that the ideal size for the Toy Poodle should be between seven and eight inches at the shoulder, and that the weight should be between four and six pounds.

In the East, Mr. Thomas Hartmann of Philadelphia whose prefix was "Little Wonder" had started breeding white Toys in 1911, and by 1928 claimed to have finished 48 white Toy champions. Since records in those days were not as complete nor as detailed as today, we can only guess as to the ac-

198

Ch. Tinker Tim of Carlsgate, first silver Toy Poodle in the world to win a Toy Group— LAKC, 1941, owner-breeder, Florence Applegate, judge, Frank Foster Davis.

curacy of this statement. In 1929, Mrs. Lucy Kingsland finished a female named Sasin. Mrs. Bertha Peaster of the La Rex Doll Kennels in Philadelphia, Mrs. Winfield S. Pruden and Mrs. Minnie Lafferty were all early breeders in the East.

CH. HAPPY CHAPPY

An important development in the history of the Toy Poodle was the birth on December 30, 1932 of Ch. Happy Chappy. Happy Chappy was bred by Florence Orsie of Burbank, California. Happy Chappy, who finished his title with a Group win, was a definite improvement on the Toys that had been bred up to that time, and early Toy breeders were quick to recognize and take advantage of his superior quality. Fortunately he proved to be a great sire, and most American-bred Toy Poodles trace back to him in tail male line. Happy Chappy's son Ch. Beau Beau of Muriclar (bred by Mrs. Charles Clark)

Ch. Orsie's Chan Son, first silver Toy Poodle to become a champion—July 9, 1943, owned by Florence Orsie, handled by Violet Boucher.

carried his valuable lines to Eastern breeders, and he sired six champions. To Happy Chappy also goes the honor of having sired the first colored Toy champions. Bred to a gray Miniature, Chee Chee of Carlsgate, he produced a litter whelped May 19, 1940 containing Orsie's Chan-Son and Tinker Tim of Carlsgate. Both were silver and both finished their titles. After Tinker Tim won a Group, a protest was sent to the American Kennel Club stating that he was not of pure ancestry since he was from the pure white Toy strain, which some thought did not spring from the same source as the Miniature strain. The registration papers were revoked by the A.K.C. from this first Toy to Miniature breeding and other litters similarly bred.

After a great deal of research, data was presented to the A.K.C. by Col. E. E. Ferguson, which influenced them to accept the colored Toy as purebred. In 1943, the A.K.C. Gazette announced that henceforth Toy Poodles would be considered Poodles, and would be judged as a variety of the breed instead of as a separate breed. The breed standard for the first time was the same for all three varieties, the only difference being in size. Up to this time the Toy Poodles were judged mostly by Toy judges, who placed great emphasis on tiny size and compared the Toy Poodle with the other members of the Toy Group. With the new status and the new breed standard, the Toy enthusiasts set about trying to make the Toy Poodle more closely resemble his larger counterparts.

The Poodle Breed Standard states that the Toy Poodle must be a "solid color" and "10 inches or under at the withers." These are the two biggest problems in producing show quality Toys. The quickest way of improving quality was to breed the white Toy males to colored Miniature females, hoping to attain the superior Poodle type and color from the Miniature while retaining the small Toy size. (Breeders felt that breeding a Miniature male to a smaller Toy female might well present a real whelping hazard for the Toy bitch due to the increase in size coming from the Miniature and the small pelvis of the Toy bitch). From literally thousands of Toy-Miniature crosses comparatively few small well-balanced Toys resulted. Actually the first generation crossed seemed amazingly successful because the Miniature head and eye and overall quality was dominant, but so were the short Toy legs. All too often it was necessary to grow huge coats on these short-legged Miniatures (who only qualified as Toys because they were under 10 inches due to their short legs) to make them look like balanced Poodles. Some even became big winners (and still today), but when the coat was pressed down at the shoulder or cut off, far too few had the overall balance that is so important to the essential elegance of the Poodle. In the second and subsequent generations there were even greater problems with size and color.

The consistent breeding of under-10-inch Toys is still a serious problem, and will probably be for some time to come. There were many Toys resulting from the first generation of the Toy-Miniature cross but the larger genes did not just disappear; they were just waiting for a chance to exert their influence and often represented a hazard to the breeder. When these crossbreds were bred to similar crossbreds (doubling up closely on the Miniature genes), the puppies were often too large for the Toy size dam to whelp normally, resulting in Caesarian sections, and sometimes in the death of the dam or puppies or both.

Several breeders who were greatly disappointed in oversized puppies set on a course of action that would solve the problem once and for all. The plan was very simple—why not breed several generations of all under-10-inch Poodles, discarding everything that went oversize? Surely these would be pure for their small genes and prepotent for their small size. Again Mother Nature asserted herself, for by the third and fourth generation many of the bitches were much too small to be bred at all. Toy breeders have also learned that in breeding Toys it is an almost invariable truth that the bigger the puppy in a litter, the better it is in quality. The larger puppies seem to revert to their Miniature ancestry in size and quality, while the smaller puppies tend to resemble their old-fashioned Toy ancestry. Also, if there is a testicle problem in a litter it seems more apt to affect the smaller males than the larger males.

These problems are recognized by the serious Toy breeders, and they are striving to overcome them. It has been found that the oversized Toy males, even with superior quality, rarely get the chance to exert their potential because many of the females to be bred already have a size problem, and their breeders are hoping to achieve the small size through the selection of a small male. However, the oversized Toy females have proven to be very valuable for breeding. Not only are they usually better in quality than their undersized sisters, and therefore possessing superior type to transmit, but they are also apt to produce larger numbers of puppies in a litter and thus give the breeder a larger choice of selection. The opportunity of selection is the keynote for breed improvement. If the small bitch has only one or two puppies, and faults are present (as they invariably are), such as a size problem, a color problem, or a bite problem, then the entire litter may be a complete failure. Hopefully, if there are four or more puppies in the litter, there may be at least one or more that have show possibilities. This is where the Standard breeder with litters of ten or more has a far greater opportunity for improving his variety. Even the Miniature breeder with five or six has an easier time, for he can exert more control through selection from one generation to the next.

The Toy breeder has to make every puppy count, so he has to breed much more carefully to try to control the variables. In other Toy breeds, it was learned long ago that an oversized quality bitch that carried a small gene (usually through her sire) bred to a small male (with a Toy background) would produce a good proportion of within-size Toy get.

COLOR BREEDING

Of equal importance to size in the breeding of Toy Poodles is the problem of color. When white Miniatures are bred to white Toys there are no color problems since all the puppies will be white, for white is a recessive. In the breeding of white Toys to colored Miniatures there were many problems for future generations. Usually in the first generation of the Toy-Miniature cross all of the puppies were solid, as the dominant Miniature colored genes succeeded in covering the white recessive genes. However these hybrids presented special breeding problems. The white genes which were so easily covered in the first generation often reappeared in the second and subsequent generations in the form of white chest marks, white toes, and sometimes out-and-out particolors (basically a white dog with colored spots, sometimes called harlequins).

There are three forms of mismarkings in Poodles, and all are disqualifications: 1. the white spots, mentioned above, on what would otherwise be a solid dog; 2. particolors; and 3. the two-tone (sometimes called "phantoms" or "dobe" markings because the pattern is the same as that of the tan spots on the Doberman Pinscher). This pattern can be brown markings on a black, silver markings on a black, or any number of weird combinations and all wrong. Perhaps the most dangerous form of this is the two-tone silver which quite often will blend so that it is very hard to distinguish. The pattern on all is a simple recessive and is inheritable. The sure sign in the new-born puppy is the light triangle under the tail. As the puppy matures the lighter color develops on the feet and legs, a bar across the chest, and dots over the eyes.

Three forms of mismarked Poodles: left, White Spots; center, Particolor; right, Two-tone or "Phantom."

Toy breeders have learned from experience that the small amounts of white on the chest and toes occur less frequently as the white Toy is pushed into the background on their pedigrees, and more and more solid genes are added. Toy breeders have also found that the particolor genes and the two-tone genes are simple recessives and although they can be covered up in the first generation (with luck), they will reappear later. For this reason many breeders withhold papers when selling particolors or two-tones. Even with several generations of all black and brown breeding it is difficult to get a good black who stays black. With one white (or silver) parent or grandparent, it is almost impossible. Silver should never be introduced into a black or brown line because of the continual coat color fading which results from the introduction of the dilution factor. The silver cross to the white Toy was even less fortunate than the blacks—the white did not dilute the silver to platinum. The usual results were dark greys or ugly blues with grave danger of mismarks.

As the short legs of the Maltese cross were dominant, so were the short legs in the Miniature-Toy cross, and we are still coping with this problem today. The best results of the cross were obtained when the Miniature bitches were of high quality with short bodies and lots of leg under them, and had a good color background. But too many breeders in their haste used poorer quality Miniature bitches and this has often only compounded the problems. Now almost 25 years later certain color-bred Toy lines are beginning to emerge, and their breeders are due great credit for having succeeded in the face of almost overwhelming obstacles and numerous disappointments. Virtually any Toy breeder who has bred for a time has had the great disappointment of having that dream puppy turn up with a spot of white, or go just over the measure. The Toy breeder has all the problems of the Miniature and Standard breeders, plus those of size and color.

There have been certain lines in Miniatures that have exhibited a tendency to produce exceptionally small puppies in a litter with normal size litter-mates. The white Ch. Snow Boy of Fircot line had this small gene, as did the old Chieveley black line. The black Firebrave line (which has a strong Chieveley foundation) also has a small gene. In England the Braeval and Montmartre Miniature lines have a small gene, as do others. The high quality which is present in these lines is also apparent in its smaller specimens and it is to the smaller specimens from these lines to which Toy breeders are turning for quality and small size. The English Toy Poodle is founded on these small Miniature specimens bred together for a number of generations. England furnished a great number of basic lines for this country in both Standards and Miniatures, and their influence is beginning to make itself felt in the Toy variety. Since the American Toy has had problems with both color and size, the small solid-bred English Toy should be of service.

The Toy Poodle has benefited enormously from the introduction of the Miniature cross, but the day of breeding just any Miniature bitch of any size in order to have Toy puppies is fading into the past. Toy breeders have learned through experience that the fastest way is not always the most worthwhile, and they have learned that patience is a most important asset. There is no one line in Toy Poodles tht has all of the virtues and none of the faults. If this were true, all the other lines would be discarded in favor of that one. Toy breeders have learned that the safest course to follow is to breed color to color, i.e. black to black or brown, apricot to apricot, silver to silver, and white to white. There are certain lines that are beginning to emerge that can be counted on to reproduce their color with a fair degree of consistency. These will be the lines to which to adhere. There is no purpose to be served in the further mixing of colors.

Show quality puppies do not appear in every litter. It isn't that easy. But the quality of Toy Poodles has improved through the years, and it is easier to breed good puppies now than it was twenty, or even ten years ago. There are a number of sires and dams which not only have won high honors in the show ring, but also have demonstrated their ability to reproduce quality in their offspring. Two Toy Poodles achieved the highest honors in this country by winning Best in Show at the Wesminster Kennel Club. Ch. Wilber White Swan, who won in 1956, was the sire of 38 champion get. Ch. Cappoquin Little Sister, who took top honors in 1961, is the dam of four champions. All Toy Poodle breeders can look to their accomplishments with pride.

Silver Toy Poodle puppies of the DeGillen Kennels.

Ch. Mitor of Muriclar

Ch. Le Petit Seigneur de Muriclar

Ch. Beau Beau of Muriclar

Ch. Pruden's Little Skipper

Ch. Barnes Edmund

Andre Boy

Ch. Happy Chappy

40

"Happy Chappy" Line
Ch. Happy Chappy

Despite the hundreds and hundreds of old-fashioned pure white Toy Poodles that had been bred, it was not until the advent of Ch. Happy Chappy that the variety even remotely began to look like a Poodle. Until his presence began to make itself felt, the Toy Poodle seemed more closely akin to the Maltese, with all of its faults.

Happy Chappy appeared with Billie Burke in the great Ziegfeld Follies. He was a very sound little dog with a longer, leaner head than the Toys of his time. He also carried a profuse stiff coat, which was rare in those days, as was his short back. Because Toy Poodles were comparatively rare then, he did not finish his title until he was five years old in 1937, and this was with a Group win.

Happy Chappy also sired the first litter out of a Miniature bitch, and this litter produced two champions—Orsie's Chan-Son and Tinker Tim of Carls-gate (the first colored Toy Poodle to win a Toy Group). In all, Ch. Happy Chappy sired a total of six champions. His most famous son was Ch. Beau Beau of Muriclar who went to the East Coast. Beau Beau's son Ch. Gremlin (ex a Miniature dam) was the first brown Toy champion, and Gremlin's daughter Ch. Cherin was the first black Toy champion. Ch. Gremlin sired the highly influential sire Ch. Leicester's Peaches and Cream. Peaches and Cream in turn sired Fieldstreams Kennels' blue Ch. Leicester's Eudoron (sire of nine champions) and Ch. Leicester's I'll Take Vanilla (sire of four champions). Eudoron was the sire of the black Fieldstreams Topflight, who was the sire of five champions. Eudoron and Topflight were both effective size reducers.

Another Gremlin son Barnell's Tres Joli, a gray, sired Voltaire II, also gray, who sired the black Baron de Gladville. Baron bred to the 10½ inch pure Miniature black, Puttencove Dot, produced two Best in Show sons. One of these, Ch. Blakeen King Doodles was a great winner with 50 Bests in Show to his credit, and was the sire of 13 champions. Blakeen King Doodles was the sire of the black Ch. J. C. King Doodles who is the leading black Toy sire with 38 champions. The two Doodles, father and son, represent one of the strongest influences in black Toy Poodles. Another son of Ch. Gremlin, Ski Mo, sired Ch. Pulaski's Masterpiece, who produced Pulaski's Master D.C., who in turn sired Ch. Frere Jacques of Crestwood. Frere Jacques produced Betz' Beau Jacques Silverpiece, who sired the brown Betz' Chocolate Bon Bon (sire of five champions).

Ch. Beau Beau of Muriclar also sired Ch. Pruden's Little Skipper, who in turn sired the great Ch. Leicester's Bonbon. Bonbon became the next great step forward in Toy Poodle breeding. Although he only lived to the age of three years, he sired 12 champions. Bonbon's blue son Ch. Leicester's Bonbon's Swan Song sired the famous Am. and Can. Ch. Wilber White Swan and Ch. Leicester's Silver Boots. White Swan brought a great deal of attention to the Toy Poodle with his Best in Show victory at the 1956 Westminster show. He has been a leading influence in white Toys throughout the country. White Swan was the sire of 38 champions including Ch. Plath's White Wilber (sire of five champions); Ch. MacAulay's White Cygnet (sire of four champions); Ch. Pixdown Little Bit (sire of eight champions); and Ch. Wayne Valley Sir Galahad (sire of five champions). Sir Galahad's litter brother, Ch. Wayne Valley Prince Valliant, sired the non-titled Wayne Valley Skippy (sire of five champions). Sir Galahad and Prince Valliant are both Best in Show winners. White Swan also sired the silver Ch. Alltrin Adonis of Cartlane, who in turn sired Ch. Shiran Citation (sire of six champions).

White Swan's half brother, Ch. Leicester's Silver Boots (also by Bonbon's Swan Song), founded the greatest silver Toy line in the history of the breed. Silver Boots had a beautiful long lean head, long neck, well-developed body, a clear harsh silver coat, and well-muscled and angulated hindquarters. Silver Boots sired the champagne-silver Ch. Leicester's Golden Slippers, who sired seven champions including the Best in Show winner, Ch. Thornlea Silver Souvenir.

Souvenir combines the best of the East and West Coast lines, and has proved a dominant sire. He has a beautiful head, and is well up on his legs with beautiful balance and type. Because Souvenir was one of the first outstanding silver Toy males with an excellent silver-bred, Toy-bred background, he has been widely used on bitches of varying colors, types and backgrounds. Even with these obstacles, his puppies have shown a striking similarity of type. He heads a large winning and producing family.

Souvenir is the sire of two Best in Show winning silver sons who are top producers, Ch. Silver Sparkle of Sassafras and Ch. High Heritage Heirloom. Sparkle is the leading Toy sire of all time with 54 champion get. Heirloom is the sire of six champions and of the non-titled top producer, Jo-Field Silver Heirloom, who is the sire of five champions to date.

Ch. Leicester's Silver Boots also sired the Group winner Ch. Nizet's Mr. Antoine D'Argent who has a Best in Show winning son, Ch. De TeTrault Bitzie's Beau, (sire of five champions).

Ch. Leicester's Bonbon's Swan Song was also sire of the white Best in Show winner Ch. Leicester's Angelo, who in turn was the sire of the silver Group winner, Ch. Renrew's Star Dust. Star Dust is the sire of eight champions. An untitled brother of Star Dust, Renrew's Fandango, sired the black Ch. Tar Baby of Whitehall who was a big winner with 45 Group firsts and 11 Bests in Show. Tar Baby is the sire of several champions including the Best in Show winner, Ch. De Caplette Tar of Roblyn, who too has several champions to his credit.

Another son of Ch. Leicester's Bonbon was Leicester's Bonny Bit of Nibroc, who sired the silver Nibroc The Imp. The Imp sired four champions including the blue Ch. Blakeen Candyman (sire of five champions). A son of Candyman, Ch. Challendon Ivy League, is the sire of the brown Ch. Loramar's I'm A Dandee, who has 85 Best in Show wins, the all time record for all Poodles, all varieties. Ch. Leicester's Bonbon also sired Ch. Georgian Don, whose son Ch. Gregoire's Davie Dumpling is the sire of five champions.

On the West Coast, Ch. Happy Chappy sired Ch. Mitor of Muriclar, who in turn sired Officieux de Muriclar (sire of four champions) and Ch. Petit Magistrate de Muriclar. Magistrate bred to the black Miniature, Ch. Blakeen Nyx de Muriclar, sired the black Aether de Muriclar. Aether bred to the black Mannerhead Belle de Muriclar (a daughter of Beau Beau x the small black English import Highlight of Mannerhead), sired the black Ch. Eurus de Muriclar, whelped in January of 1947. Eurus, one of the early colored Toy champions, was a combination of the best existing Toy and Miniature lines of his day. He sired two highly influential sons, Ch. Orsie's Mi-Ra-Bi-Le and Orsie's Son Sa Ses. Mi-Ra-Bi-Le, a black, sired five champions. Bred to his own daughter, he sired the prepotent Orsie's Petit Drole, who has sired eight champions—all of whom have in turn produced champions. Petit Drole's black son, Ch. Moissonner O'Millhurst, is the sire of five champions. A son of Moissonner, Swanson's Tar Baby, bred to a Moissonner daughter, Swanson's Jetta of O'Millhurst, produced Am. and Can. Ch. Suchan's Little Black Sheikh. Little Black Sheikh was a Best in Show winner at all-breed and specialty shows, won 10 Group firsts and had 61 Bests of Variety. Little Black Sheikh has been a prepotent sire in the Mid-West, and has 11 champions to his credit. His nontitled son, Suchan's Little Napoleon, is the sire of four champions. Another son of Ch. Orsie's Mi-Ra-Bi-Le, Bijou X, has sired two champions including the Best in Show winner, Ch. Fieldstreams Bojangles. Bojangles bred to Ch. Chaman Grouse, a brown Toy from England, produced Ch. Fieldstreams Valentine, an outstanding beautiful Best in Show winner. Valentine is considered one of the best black Toys ever bred. Bred to Chrisward Tambourine (a half American Toy, half English small Miniature combination) he produced the black Ch. Carlima's J.D., a great winner with 82 Bests of Variety, 38 Group firsts, 8 all-breed Bests in Show and 4 Specialty Bests in Show. J.D. is the sire of 11 champions to date. His brown son Ch. Carnival Idle Chatter, who won two Groups on his way to the title, is the sire of several champions.

From Ch. Eurus de Muriclar's breeding to Orsie's Chere-Ami (by Ch. Marmaduke of Meisen x Ch. Orsie's Chan-Son—two of the earliest colored Toy champions) came the small gray Orsie's Son Sa Ses. Although Son Sa Ses was not a champion, he represented a blending of excellent Toy and Miniature lines, and has exerted a wide range of influence. He was particularly successful when bred to Miniature bitches. His son, Ch. Medley's Silver Demon, was one of the first Toys to win Bests in Show at specialty and all-breed shows, and he promoted a great deal of interest in the breeding of show-quality Toys.

Strangely enough, perhaps due to lack of opportunity of suitable bitches, Silver Demon produced only two champions, but his sons have been much more successful as sires. One, Ch. Poquito Perro La Nudo, is the sire of six champions. Another, the blue Panorama Hideho, sired six champions including the Best in Show winning Am., Mexican, and Can. Ch. Mariman Silver Beau, who has 10 champion get. Hideho is also the sire of Blackaboy of Sassafras who has seven champion get. An untitled son of Blackaboy, Blackabit of Sassafras, who unfortunately lost a foot due to an injury which ruined a promising show career, was the sire of 14 champions. Blackaboy of Sassafras is also the sire of Ch. Black Bijou of Sassafras, whose brown son Sarsaparilla of Sassafras is the sire of five champions.

A full brother of Ch. Medley's Silver Demon, Medley Boy de Gladville, a blue Toy with 14 points, was the sire of Ch. Silver Dynamo de Gladville. Dynamo was a pretty-headed, short-bodied, gay, heavily-coated little silver. Although not much used at stud, Dynamo did make a useful contribution to silver Toys. From a type and breeding standpoint, Dynamo represented the best of the early silver Toys from the West, as did Silver Boots in the East. The combination of these two dogs was to bring an enormous improvement in silver Toys perhaps best represented by Souvenir and his descendants. Dynamo's son, Sylvideo de Gladville, sired Ch. Miss Sylvideo de Gladville (dam of Souvenir) and the top producer, Ch. Bon Chance de Sassafras. Bon Chance was the foundation sire of the silvers at Sassafras Kennels. He sired nine champions including Ch. Silver Swank of Sassafras (sire of seven

210

champions), Ch. Silver Fleece of Sassafras (sire of 12 champions) and Ch. The Infanta of Sassafras. The Infanta of Sassafras was the dam of Ch. Silver Sparkle of Sassafras (by Souvenir). Silver Fleece's Best in Show winning son, Ch. Silver Strike of Sassafras, is the sire of several champions to date.

Another son of Orsie's Son Sa Ses, Roi de L'Argent, was an important sire at the de Gladville Kennels in California. His best known son was the white Group winner, Ch. Sir Lancelot de Gladville, who is generally conceded to have been years ahead of his time. Lancelot sired Silhou-Jette's Minute Man (x Silhou-Jette's Pip Squeak, an 11-inch Miniature). Minute Man is the sire of five champions. Bred back to his dam, he produced the outstanding litter brothers, Ch. Silhou-Jette's Snow Sprite and Ch. Silhou-Jette's Cream Topping, both Best in Show winners and top producers.

Orsie's Son Sa Ses also sired the gray Lohn's Petit Fils D'Anatole (sire of five champions) and Ch. La Gai Happy Go Lucky. Lucky's son, Bric A Brac Bonney Lad, sired two champions including the Group-winning top producer Ch. Valzac's Tiny Tim (sire of five champions).

Back to the pure white line, we find that Homme du Monde de Muriclar, a son of Ch. Petit Magistrate de Muriclar, sired Int. Ch. Le Monde Chic de Larson (sire of two champions) and Andre Boy. Andre Boy is the sire of 10 champions including Ch. Barnes Edmund (sire of five champions). Another son of Homme du Monde was Ch. Jacobs Le Mondes Marquis who sired four champions including the Best in Show winner, Ch. Marquis Show Boy of Glade (sire of five champions).

It is interesting that with the hundreds and hundreds of Toy-Miniature crosses, even today most of the top producers in Toys trace directly back to Ch. Happy Chappy in tail male line. It has become increasingly difficult for the old fashioned white Toy to compete with the superior Toy-Miniature rival. Indeed there are few pure white Toy lines still in existence. A second look at the chart points up the fact that the greats of yesterday produced the greats of today and of tomorrow. In the history of any breed a handful of dogs stand out as superior individuals who influence the future of the breed. Usually these dogs prove themselves in the ring, or at stud, or both. Wise breeders recognize these specimens, benefit from their use, and try to improve on their quality. Often these dogs are so ahead of their time that it is not an easy task to duplicate or improve upon them—this is the challenge of breeding. Ch. Happy Chappy and Ch. Leicester's Bonbon were the best of the pure white Toys and laid the foundation for the future. Now certain lines and families are emerging from the early necessary mixtures of colors and sizes and making their influence felt. The two King Doodles and Valentine and his son J.D. seem destined to play a part in the future of the black Toy. In silvers, Souvenir and his son Sparkle are playing leading roles. In whites, Sir Galahad and Little Bit have extended the White Swan influence in the East.

Ch. Pixdown Little Bit

Ch. Leicester's Golden Slippers

Ch. MacAulay's White Cygnet

Ch. Nizet's Mr. Antoine D'Argent

Ch. Wayne Valley Sir Galahad

Ch. Renrew's Stardust

CH. HAPPY CHAPPY
   Ch. Beau Beau of Muriclar (wh) 6
     Ch. Gremlin (brn) 4
       Ch. Leicester's Peaches and Cream (crm) 4
         Ch. Leicester's Eudoron (blu) 9
           Fieldstreams Topflight (blk) 6
       Ski Mo (gr) 1
         Ch. Pulaski's Masterpiece (si) 5
           Pulaski's Master D.C. (gr)
             Ch. Frere Jacques of Crestwood (si)
               Betz' Beau Jacques Silverpiece (si)
                 Betz' Chocolate Bon Bon (brn) 5
       Barnell's Tres Joli (gr)
         Voltaire II (gr)
           Baron de Gladville (blk) 2
             Ch. Blakeen King Doodles (blk) 13
               Ch. J. C. King Doodles (blk) 38
   Ch. Pruden's Little Skipper (wh) 2
     Ch. Leicester's Bon Bon (wh) 12
       Ch. Leicester's Bonbon's Swan Song (blu) 9
         Ch. Wilber White Swan (wh) 38
           Ch. Plath's White Wilbur (wh) 5
           Ch. Wayne Valley Sir Galahad (wh)
           Ch. Wayne Valley Prince Valiant (wh) 2
           Wayne Valley Skippy (wh) 5
           Ch. Pixdown Little Bit (wh) 8
           Ch. MacAulay's White Cygnet (wh) 4
           Ch. Alltrin Adonis of Cartlane (si) 1
             Ch. Shiran Citation (si) 6
         Ch. Leicester's Silver Boots (si) 8
           Ch. Leicester's Golden Slippers (chpn--si) 7
             Int. Ch. Thornlea Silver Souvenir (si) 33
               Ch. Silver Sparkle of Sassafras (si) 55
               Ch. High Heritage Heirloom (si) 6
                 Jo-Field Silver Heirloom (si) 5
           Ch. Nizet's Mr. Antoine D'Argent (si) 5
             Int. Ch. DeTetrault's Bitzie's Beau (blu) 5
         Ch. Leicester's Angelo (wh) 3
           Ch. Renrew's Stardust (si) 8
           Renrew's Fandango (blk)
             Ch. Tar Baby of Whitehall (blk) 3
               Ch. DeCaplette Tar of Roblyn (blk) 3
      Leicester's Bonny Bit of Nibroc (wh)
        Nibroc The Imp (si) 4
          Ch. Blakeen Candyman (blu) 5
            Ch. Challendon Ivy League (gr) 1
             Ch. Loramar's I'm A Dandee (brn) 2
     Ch. Georgian Don (wh)
       Ch. Gregoire's Davie Dumpling (wh) 5

Ch. Moissoner O'Millhurst

Medley Boy de Gladville

Ch. Suchan's Little Black Sheikh

Ch. Silver Dynamo de Gladville

Ch. Valzac's Tiny Tim

Ch. Silver Strike of Sassafras

CH. HAPPY CHAPPY
    Ch. Mitor of Muriclar (wh) 4
        Officieux de Muriclar (wh) 4
        Ch. Petit Magistrate de Muriclar (wh) 1
            Homme du Monde de Muriclar (wh) 1
                Int. Ch. Le Monde Chic de Larson (wh) 2
                    Andre Boy (wh) 10
                        Ch. Barnes Edmund (wh) 5
                    Ch. Jacobs' Le Mondes Marquis (wh) 4
                        Ch. Marquis Show Boy of Glade (wh) 5
        Aether de Muriclar (blk) 1
            Ch. Eurus de Muriclar (blk) 1
                Ch. Orsie's Mi-Ra-Bi-Le (blk) 5
                    Bijou X (blk) 2
                        Ch. Fieldstreams Bojangles (blk) 1
                            Ch. Fieldstreams Valentine (blk) 13
                                Ch. Carlima's J.D. (blk) 11
                                    Ch. Carnival Idle Chatter (brn) 3
                                    Ch. Tropicstar Do It Up Brown (brn) 3
                                Ch. Starfire My Funny Valentine (blk) 3
                    Orsie's Petit Drole (blk) 8
                        Ch. Moissoner O'Millhurst (blk) 5
                            Swanson's Tar Baby (blk) 1
                                Ch. Suchan's Little Black Sheikh (blk) 11
                                Suchan's Little Napoleon (brn) 4
                Orsie's Son Sa Ses (gr) 7
                    Ch. La Gai Happy Go Lucky (blk)
                        Bric A Brac Bonney Lad (blk) 2
                            Ch. Valzac's Tiny Tim (blk) 6
                    Lohn's Petit Fils D'Anatole (blu) 5
                    Ch. Medley's Silver Demon (si) 2
                        Ch. Poquito Perro La Nudo (si) 6
                    Panorama Hideho (gr) 7
                        Int. Ch. Mariman Silver Beau (si) 10
                        Blackaboy of Sassafras (blk) 7
                            Blackabit of Sassafras (blk) 14
                            Ch. Black Scamp II of Sassafras (blk) 5
                            Ch. Black Bijou of Sassafras (blk)
                            Sarsaparilla of Sassafras (brn) 5
                Medley Boy de Gladville (blu) 2
                    Ch. Silver Dynamo de Gladville (si) 1
                        Sylvideo de Gladville (si) 2
                            Ch. Bon Chance de Sassafras (si) 9
                                Ch. Silver Swank of Sassafras (si) 7
                                Ch. Silver Fleece of Sassafras (si) 12
                                    Ch. Silver Strike of Sassafras (si) 3
                Roi de l'Argent (si) 5
                    Ch. Sir Lancelot de Gladville (wh) 3
                        Silhou-Jette's Minute Man (wh) 5
                            Int. Ch. Silhou-Jette's Snow Sprite (wh) 10
                            Int. Ch. Silhou-Jette's Cream Topping (crm) 13

GEORGIAN BLACK MAGIC

Whelped August 8, 1950   Died November 5, 1966

Bred and owned by Georgie Shepperd

```
                              Zoulou-Labory (blk)
                    Pinochio-Labory (blk)
                              Bouboule-Nice-Labory (blk)
          Vichnou-Labory of Blakeen and Nibroc (blk)
                              Zoulou-Labory (blk)
                    Cloe-Labory (blk)
                              Janyre-Labory (blk)

GEORGIAN BLACK MAGIC (blk)

                              Ch. Pruden's Little Skipper (wh)
                    Ch. Leicester's Bonbon (wh)
                              Ch. Leicester's Fidele de Lafferty (wh)
          Nibroc Silver Star (si)
                              Beau's Black Racquet (blk)
                    Mistinguette (gr)
                              Smilestone's Letty (gr)
```

216

41

"Black Magic" Line
Georgian Black Magic

ALTHOUGH the Georgian Black Magic sire line is considerably smaller in influence than that of the Ch. Happy Chappy line, and
more recent, dating from the early fifties, it is nevertheless an important one.
Actually it is an offshoot of the other line since Black Magic's dam was a
daughter of Ch. Leicester's Bonbon. The Happy Chappy line was of pure
white origin and the colored Toys that came from it were developed through
the introduction of colored Miniature bitches. The introduction of the Black
Magic line offered breeders an opportunity to obtain a concentration of
black bloodlines and small size—both of which were sorely needed.

The story of Georgian Black Magic begins with the importation of his sire,
Vichnou-Labory of Blakeen and Nibroc, to this country. Mrs. Sherman Hoyt
brought him from Switzerland and sold him to Mrs. C. K. Corbin of the
Nibroc Toy Poodles. Vichnou was of all-black Continental Toy breeding. He
was described as a very nice little jet-black dog, well under 10 inches, a real
Toy. He had a beautiful, heavy thick coat and was short-bodied and stylish.
He was Winners Dog at the 1950 Interstate Poodle Club Specialty Show, but
his early death prevented finish of his championship. From his few breedings
came Ch. Nibroc Adoreable, Ch. Smilestone's Mascot, and Ch. Smilestone's
Fancy Fee. Fancy Fee, a Best in Show winner, was also Best of Variety at
Westminster for four consecutive years—1952, 1953, 1954 and 1955.

Bred to Nibroc Silver Star, a daughter of Ch. Leicester's Bonbon, Vichnou
sired Georgian Black Magic. Black Magic, whelped August 1950, was bred
and owned through his long life by Mrs. Georgie Shepperd. Black Magic was
about nine inches tall, with an outstandingly beautiful head, very heavy coat,

217

Ch. Ardlussa Gascon

good legs and hindquarters. His back could have been shorter but he was not long-bodied. Black Magic was shown only twice and won his class both times. Several handlers were interested in showing him but he did not care for the ring. He was, however, much in demand at stud. Black Magic was one of the first good black Toys and he founded a large family of winning and producing descendants. He was outstanding for producing beautiful heads, good coats, and sturdy, cobby puppies. He was a consistent size reducer and produced puppies that were extremely small and refined. Black Magic sired

Ch. Nibroc Pixie

blacks for the most part, with occasional browns, silvers, and beautifully pigmented whites. He never sired a particolor.

Georgian Black Magic bred to his half sister, Ch. Nibroc Adoreable, produced Ch. Nibroc Comet II, Ch. Nibroc Marla and Nibroc White Shadow. White Shadow sired Ch. Nibroc Gary who was Best of Breed at the Poodle Club of America Specialty in 1956. Bred to another half sister through Vichnou, Black Magic sired the small blue Ch. Nibroc Pixie, who was the sire of four champions, and the foundation of the Renea Kennels. Black Magic was bred to Burlingame Mimi II (of English breeding) to produce the black Toy Ch. Barcwyn Etienne. Etienne in turn sired the 11¼ inch blue Group winner Ch. Turner's New Adventure. New Adventure sired three black champion Toy daughters: Ch. Avron's Cha Cha Cha, Can. Ch. Harlane Black Adventuress and Ch. Douai Unity. A litter brother of Ch. Douai Unity, Douai Ulysses, was the sire of the black Group winner Ch. Douai Fantasy (sire of five champions). Fantasy, bred to Ch. Douai Atlanta, produced Ch. Douai Mixmaster who was Winners Dog at Westminster in 1963. Mixmaster, a group winner from the classes, is the sire of several champions to date.

Another son of Georgian Black Magic was the black Group winner, Ch. Escapade of Exton. Escapade sired four champions including the gray Ch. Escapades Echo of Exton, who was the sire of 12 champions and founder of the Raines Ranch Kennels. Ch. Escapade of Exton also sired the small black Group winner, Ch. Peapacton's Rackarock. Rackarock sired one of the smallest Poodles to ever win its championship, the 6½ inch Ch. Wee Wee Martini. Martini sired the 7½ inch black Twinbark Farfadet A Tout Petit who had seven points including one major. Tout Petit is the sire of the 8½ inch black Ch. High Heritage Hellzapoppin who was Best Toy Puppy and Best Junior Puppy, All Varieties at the William Penn Puppy Futurity. Hellzapoppin is the sire of two champions to date. An untitled son of Hellzapoppin, Renea's Raven Rook, sired Ch. Dassin's David who had a sensational puppy career and finished his title with five majors by going Winners Dog at the Poodle Club of America Specialty in 1967 at just eight months of age.

Another son of Georgian Black Magic, Ch. Ardlussa Gascon, was the sire of Ch. Applewood Cider and the famous Ch. Cappoquin Little Sister. Little Sister was Best in Show at Westminster 1961, and Best of Breed at the Poodle Club of America Specialty in 1960. After her sensational show career Little Sister was retired for maternal duties. She produced four champions: Ch. Tropicstar Do It Up Brown and Ch. Tropicstar In The Black (by Ch. Carlima's J.D.), Ch. Tropicstar Sister Sue (by Blackabit of Sassafras), and the Best in Show winner Ch. Tropicstar Tequila (by her son Do It Up Brown).

Ch. Peapacton's Rackarock

Ch. High Heritage Hellzapoppin

Ch. Wee Wee Martini

Renea's Raven Rook

Twinbrook Farfadet A Tout Petit

Ch. Dassin's David

GEORGIAN BLACK MAGIC
    Ch. Nibroc Pixie (blu) 4
    Ch. Barcwyn Etienne (blk) 1
        Ch. Turner's New Adventure (blu) 3
            Douai Ulysses (blk) 2
                Ch. Douai Fantasy (blk) 5
                    Ch. Douai Mixmaster (blk) 3
    Ch. Escapade of Exton (blk) 4
        Ch. Escapades Echo of Exton (gr) 12
        Ch. Peapacton's Rackarock (blk) 1
            Ch. Wee Wee Martini (blk) 1
                Twinbark Farfadet A Tout Petit (blk) 1
                    Ch. High Heritage Hellzapoppin (blk) 2
                        Renea's Raven Rook (blk) 1
                            Ch. Dassin's David (blk)
    Ch. Ardlussa Gascon (blk) 3

Ch. Douai Mixmaster

Ch. Douai Fantasy

Ch. Cappoquin Little Sister (by Ch. Ardlussa Gascon ex Ardlussa Jou Jou) Best in Show at 1961 Westminster Kennel Club show. Dam of four champions. Owned by Florence Michelson, Tropicstar Poodles.

Mademoiselle MiMi II (by Ch. Emsie's Black Knight ex Westwood's Lady Pamela), dam of eight champions for the Whitehall Kennels.

42

Leading Toy Dams

THE number of Top Producing Bitches (those that have been the dam of three or more champions) in Toys is considerably less than in either Miniatures or Standards, which is understandable in view of the comparatively few puppies a Toy bitch is capable of producing during her lifetime.

The problem of size adds a further difficulty to making a production record. The Toy is less established as a variety than either the Miniature or Standard due to the influx of Miniature breeding, which—although improving type—has presented a continuing size problem. Only recently have certain lines and families been created that can be depended upon to produce Toy quality in generation after generation.

The leading Toy dam of champions is the black Mademoiselle MiMi II, who produced eight champions for the Whitehall Kennels.

The leading cream bitch has been Ch. Petite Susette, with seven champions to her credit.

Special salute should be paid to Ch. Cappoquin Little Sister, who did not begin her maternal duties until after her outstanding show career. In her first litter, at almost five years of age, this Westminster Best in Show winner produced Ch. Tropicstar Sister Sue (by Blackabit of Sassafras). In Little Sister's second and third litters (both by Ch. Carlima's J. D.) were Ch. Tropicstar Do It Up Brown and Ch. Tropicstar In The Black. Little Sister was then bred to her son, Do It Up Brown, to produce the Best in Show winner, Ch. Tropicstar Tequila. Both Do It Up Brown and In The Black are sires of champions.

Of the 35 Toy bitches that have produced three or more champions to rate as Top Producers, 12 have been champions.

223

Ch. Tropicstar Do It Up Brown (by Ch. Carlima's J.D. ex Ch. Cappoquin Little Sister), brown Toy, sire of champions. Bred and owned by Florence Michelson, Tropicstar Poodles.

Ch. DeCaplette Tar of Roblyn (by Ch. Tar Baby of Whitehall ex DeCaplette Merrybell), black Toy, Best in Show winner and sire of champions. Owned by Dixie Caplette and Olive Kelperis.

Mrs. Helen Kincaid and Sherwood Renaissance (black Toy) sired by Sherwood The Black Bandit ex Bryellen's Cream Cup.

Ch. Leicester's Bonbon shown going Best of Variety at the Poodle Club of America Specialty 1947, handled by his breeder-owner Mrs. Leicester Harrison.

Ch. Leicester's Peaches and Cream

Ch. Leicester's Fidele de Lafferty

43

Leicester's Kennels

LEICESTER HARRISON owned her first Toy Poodle in 1916, but it wasn't until 1942 that she started her present line. The Leicester's Toy Poodles have played a large role in the development of the Toy Poodle as we know it today. Mrs. Harrison started with the pure old-fashioned white Toy, and it is a tribute to her ability as a breeder that this line has come so far in such a comparatively short period of time. As Toy Poodles were scarce in 1942, Mrs. Harrison searched for some time before locating a six-weeks-old puppy bitch, Leicester's Fidele de Lafferty, who was to found the Leicester's line. Fidele was sired by Ch. Beau Beau of Muriclar (from the West Coast) x Lafferty's Dimples. Prior to finishing her championship Fidele was bred to her half brother Ch. Pruden's Little Skipper (also by Beau Beau) to produce the famous little Ch. Leicester's Bonbon.

Bonbon, whelped January 3, 1945, was 8½ inches tall and weighed 4½ pounds. He represented a great stride forward in Toy development as he did not possess many of the faults that were then prevalent in Toy Poodles. Bonbon's outstanding features were his squareness of body, lovely almond eyes with flat cheeks, jet-black pigmentation, high tail set and correct rear-quarters. His merry disposition and outstanding showmanship attracted attention not only to himself but to the Toy variety as well. When the Poodle Club of America first admitted the Toy variety as a participant at its annual specialty show in 1947, Bonbon was awarded Best of Variety. He had a successful show career and was never beaten except by his half brother Ch. Leicester's Peaches and Cream. Peaches and Cream was by the brown Ch. Gremlin (also by Beau Beau) and also out of Fidele. Bonbon died when he was only three years old but he sired 12 champions, and left a legacy of winning and producing descendants.

Mrs. Harrison was one of the first Toy breeders to realize the value of breeding small Miniature bitches to Toy sires to improve the quality in Toys. She insisted that the Miniature bitches be of excellent quality with good backgrounds. Bonbon was bred several times to the small blue Miniature, Leicester's Alouette (by Ch. Robin Goodfellow), to produce five Toy champions: Ch. Leicester's Bonbon's Swan Song, Ch. Leicester's Bon Ami, Ch. Leicester's Ouida, Ch. Leicester's Frolic and Ch. Leicester's Valentine Nibroc. Three of these were Group winners. Frolic was bred to Peaches and Cream to produce Ch. Leicester's Eudoron. Valentine Nibroc was bred to Leicester's Bonny Bit of Nibroc (a son of Bonbon) to produce the silver Nibroc The Imp (sire of four champions). Bonbon sired Nibroc Silver Star whose son Georgian Black Magic founded another sire line. Bonbon's daughter Ch. Cartlane Once (x a white Miniature) attracted much attention to the variety. She was Best of Variety at the parent specialty in 1949, 1950 and was Best of Breed there in 1951. She also won three Bests of Variety at Westminster and won the Toy Group there in 1950 and 1951.

Bonbon's most important son was the blue Ch. Leicester's Bonbon's Swan Song (ex Leicester's Alouette). Swan Song was the sire of eight champions including Am. and Can. Ch. Wilber White Swan, Ch. Leicester's Silver Boots (silver), Ch. Leicester's Swan Song's Legacy (black), Ch. Leicester's Angelo (white) and Ch. Leicester's Little Eva (cream). Ch. Wilber White Swan was a great winner with 16 Bests in Show including Westminster 1956. White Swan exerted a tremendous influence on white Toys and sired 38 champions. Ch. Leicester's Silver Boots was one of the foundation sires in silver Toys. Silver Boots with limited opportunity sired eight champions. His son, Ch. Leicester's Golden Slippers, was the sire of Ch. Thornlea Silver Souvenir. Another son of Silver Boots, the Group winner Ch. Nizet's Mr. Antoine D'Argent, was the sire of five champions. Ch. Leicester's Swan Song's Legacy was the sire of three champions. Ch. Leicester's Little Eva was the dam of Ch. Renrew's Yvette by Ch. Leicester's Angelo and of Ch. Renrew's Risque and Ch. Renrew's Apricot Brandy by Ch. Wilber White Swan. Risque was bred to Ch. Leicester's Angelo (a Best in Show winner) to produce the Group-winning silver Ch. Renrew's Star Dust (sire of eight champions).

Ch. Leicester's Peaches and Cream was the sire of four champions. Bred to the blue Ch. Leicester's Frolic (Bonbon x Alouette) he produced Field streams Kennels' blue Ch. Leicester's Eudoron. Eudoron sired nine champions including the beige Ch. Blakeen Penny Wise (dam of four champions at Lime Crest) and the white Ch. Pixdown Loabelo Blanchette (dam of four champions and founder of the Pixdown Kennels). Eudoron was also the sire of the black Fieldstreams Topflight (sire of five champions). Peaches and

Ch. Leicester's Silver Boots

Ch. Leicester's Bonbon's Swan Song

Cream was bred to Lafferty's Ma Chere to produce Ch. Leicester's I'll Take Vanilla (sire of four champions), and the top producing sisters Leicester's Saint Barbara and Leicester's Peach Melba. Saint Barbara was bred to Ch. Leicester's Bonbon's Swan Song to produce Ch. Leicester's Angelo, Ch. Leicester's Flirt In Silver and Can. Ch. Leicester's Raven Beauty. Peach Melba bred to her sire, Peaches and Cream, produced Ch. Leicester's Peach Charlotte and Leicester's Peach Parfait. Peach Parfait is the sire of the black Ch. Hollyday Cuddles. Peach Melba bred to Bonbon's Swan Song produced the black Ch. Leicester's Soprano Solo. Peach Melba was bred to Ch. Leicester's Silver Boots to give her third champion Ch. Leicester's Golden Slippers (sire of seven champions).

There are over 25 Leicester champions, in all colors. Many of these were handled by their owner. The Leicester's influence, starting in the East, has spread over the entire country for the betterment of Toy Poodles. The only two Toy Poodles to go Best in Show at Westminster, Ch. Wilber White Swan and Ch. Cappoquin Little Sister, are both descended from this line.

229

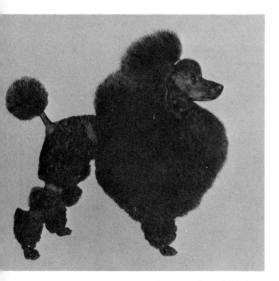

Little Sir Echo of Meisen

Ch. Meisen Golden Gaiete
(Miniature)

Ch. Meisen Bit O'Gold

Meisen Bit O'Golden Glow

44

Meisen Kennels

HOW many Poodle breeders have started out to breed one color, and have ended up becoming more famous for another? Certainly, the Meisen Kennels of Hilda Meisenzahl, must be one of the best known, for it is world famous for its apricots. Miss Meisenzahl's original plan was to breed black Toys, but nature in the form of recessive apricot genes asserted itself, and Miss Meisenzahl was wise enough to utilize her good fortune.

The start was in 1941 with the cross of the white Toy Ch. Orsie's Kumsi to the gray Miniature Maree Ang. A year later, an accidental mating from two of this litter produced the black Toy Ch. Marmaduke of Meisen. As there were no color-bred Toy lines then available, and as Miss Meisenzahl did not wish to introduce more white Toy breeding for fear of mismarking and poor type, she imported a small black Miniature male, Giovanni of Toytown, from one of England's smallest Miniature lines. She was not aware at the time that Giovanni's dam, Etroite of Toytown, was an 8½ inch apricot. Since apricot is recessive and needs an apricot gene from each parent to make its appearance, Giovanni did not sire any apricots himself (none of the bitches he was bred to carried an apricot gene). However in subsequent generations, when linebreeding to Giovanni occurred, beautiful golden apricot puppies appeared from time to time. Apricots were very rare in those days and these were not only good in color, but also good in type. While she was carefully establishing her black Toy line, Miss Meisenzahl was at the same time creating a good background for her apricots. In line with her plan for breeding blacks she bred Giovanni to Meisen's Meri-Tot (by Ch. Marmaduke of Meisen) to produce the black Meisen's Bright Knight. More small black

231

breeding was added with the purchase of the 12-inch black Ch. Sherwood Petite Poupee. Petite Poupee was by the 10½ inch black Ch. Sherwood Pocket Edition, who finished undefeated as a Miniature. Pocket Edition sired two black Toy champions at Sherwood Hall. Petite Poupee was bred to Bright Knight to give Meisen's Little Bit O'Black C.D. Little Bit O'Black was bred to the black Susan's Mademoiselle GiGi (by Giovanni of Toytown) to produce the 10½-inch black Little Sir Echo of Meison. Although himself black, Little Sir Echo (from a grandson to daughter of Giovanni) fortunately inherited the ability to produce apricots.

Little Sir Echo has played a key role at Meisen. He was the sire of black champions and apricot champions, Toy champions and Miniature champions. Little Sir Echo was bred to Peg O' My Heart of Meisen to produce three champions: Mex. Ch. Meisen Marcella (black Toy), Ch. Meisen Mademoiselle Zsa Zsa (apricot Miniature) and Ch. Meisen Golden Gaiete (apricot Miniature). Golden Gaiete has been an exceptional sire and has produced six apricot champions. Gaiete is the sire of the Group winner, Ch. Meisen Golden Gamin.

Gamin is the sire of three champions including the beautiful Miniature, Ch. Pixiecroft Sunbeam. Sunbeam finished her championship with a Group win as a puppy. Sunbeam has been the greatest winning apricot in the history of the breed in this country. Winner of many Bests in Show, she won the Non-Sporting Group at Westminster in 1965.

Little Sir Echo also sired two black Toy champions, Ch. Sequoia's Iron Duke and Ch. Meisen Robert Rascal. Robert Rascal finished his championship by going Winners Dog at the Westminster Show in 1960. He had a lovely head, and was short in body and high on leg. Many Toy breeders felt he had a great deal to offer to the Toy variety. Miss Meisenzahl seemed close to her goal in black Toys but unfortunately Rascal died too early to leave his mark as a stud dog. More recently, a grandson to a granddaughter of Little Sir Echo were bred to produce the lovely black Meisen Little Black Bear. Black Bear is a promising sire and one of his get, Meisen Inky Idol, was Best Puppy, All Varieties at the 1965 William Penn Puppy Futurity. Another Black Bear son, Meisen Bing Boy In Black, was Best Toy Puppy Male at the 1966 Wm. Penn Futurity.

Little Sir Echo of Meisen also sired the cream Toy, Meisen Ecru Elf. Elf was bred to the Group-winning white Ch. Meisen Paper Doll (by the Best in Show winning Miniature, Ch. Paper Boy of Toytown, who had an apricot gene) to produce the beautiful tiny Ch. Meisen Bit O'Gold. Bit O'Gold was bred to a dark apricot daughter of Ch. Meisen Golden Gaiete to produce Ch. Meisen Flaming Fella and Meisen Bit O'Golden Glow. Golden Glow has proven to be an exceptional sire with six apricot Toy champions to his credit. Of these, four are Group winners.

Ch. Meisen Robert Rascal

Miss Meisenzahl's apricots have furnished the background for most of the apricot Miniatures and Toys in this country. Her accomplishments have made the breeding of apricots easier for those who have followed her lead.

Ch. Meisen Golden Gamin, Miniature male, and a notable example of apricot coloring. A specialty Best in Show winner and Group winner, Gamin was bred and owned by Miss Hilda Meisenzahl, (later sold), and handled by Frank T. Sabella. This dog is of particular interest because of Miss Meisenzahl's early interest and pioneering in Toy and Miniature apricots.

Ch. Silver Fleece of Sassafras

Ch. Silver Sparkle of Sassafras

45

Sassafras Kennels

THE Sassafras Kennels of Pamela Ingram of California is one of the largest Poodle kennels in the world, and one of the most successful.

Mrs. Ingram first saw a gray Toy Poodle at a dog show in 1952 and became determined to breed silver Toys herself. She leased a bitch from the de Gladville kennels, and in the resultant litter was a silver Toy male who founded the Sassafras silver Toy line. This male, Ch. Bon Chance de Sassafras, became a Top Producer with seven champions to his credit including Ch. Silver Fleece of Sassafras (Best in Show winner, sire of 12 champions), Ch. Silver Swank of Sassafras (sire of seven champions) and Ch. The Infanta of Sassafras (dam of three champions). The Infanta, a lovely headed little bitch, was bred to Ch. Thornlea Silver Souvenir to produce the littermates Ch. Silver Spark of Sassafras and Ch. Silver Sparkle of Sassafras.

Silver Sparkle, a Best in Show winner, is a refined, high-on-leg, short-bodied type. He is the Top Producing Toy sire with 54 champions to his credit. There are several reasons for Sparkle's great success at stud. Mrs. Ingram states that he has never sired a two-tone or particolor. Since many Toy bitches are low on leg and long in body, Sparkle has been especially useful in breeding to them to shorten bodies and add length of leg. He is also an excellent size reducer. There were a great number of daughters of Bon Chance, Swank and Fleece in Sparkle's home area and he was bred to these with outstanding success. Sparkle has produced silvers, silver-beiges, blues, grays, creams and whites. Most of the Sassafras whites and creams are based on Sparkle's ability to produce these colors.

Ch. Silver Swank of Sassafras

Ch. Bon Chance de Sassafras

Mrs. Ingram has also had success with her black Toys. Ch. Lime Crest Mr. Chips (by Ch. Blakeen King Doodles) has sired four champions including Ch. Black Scamp II of Sassafras, who has five champion get. From a different line, Blackaboy of Sassafras was the sire of seven champions. An untitled son of Blackaboy of Sassafras, Blackabit of Sassafras, had the start of a promising career with a Best of Variety win over Best in Show specials, but due to an accident was unable to complete his championship. Blackabit was a handsome little dog and a prepotent sire. He was the sire of 14 champions.

Mrs. Ingram has a marked ability to select promising puppies and many Sassafras champions are choice-of-litter puppies. There are over 100 title-holders bearing the Sassafras name, with more in the making.

Ch. Black Scamp II of Sassafras

Blackabit of Sassafras

Ch. Medley's Silver Demon (Orsie's Son Sa Ses ex Blakeen Huba Huba, Miniature), bred and owned by Marie Medley, shown winning Best in Show at Santa Ana Valley Kennel Club Show.

Eng. Ch. Sudbrook Sunday Suit

Wychwood Gatesgarth Monarch

Eng. Ch. Sudbrook Sunday Best

Eng. Ch. Tophill Toyboy

·Eng. Ch. Sudbrook Sunday Special

Eng. Ch. Wemrose Newboy

46

Toy Poodles In England

ALTHOUGH the Toy Poodle in England was not recognized as a separate variety by the English Kennel Club until 1957, there have been Toy-sized Poodles in England for many, many years. The English standard is the same for all three varieties except that the Toy must be under 11 inches at the shoulder.

The white Toy and the white Miniature in England both trace back to the small white Miniature which was imported from the Continent. They both had the same faults of large round eyes, short legs and general lack of Poodle elegance. With but a few exceptions the white Miniature in England was unable to compete in the show ring with the superior blacks and browns until the advent of Ch. Snow Boy of Fircot (who was from a colored background) and his son Eng. Ch. Blakeen Oscar of the Waldorf. A few breeders were captivated by the smaller whites, and by the introduction of selected Miniature bloodlines improved the quality and established the white Toy. Lady Stanier's small Seahorses white Toys are known all over the world.

There have been certain colored Miniature strains which from the beginning have produced an occasional smaller specimen in a litter of normal sized Miniatures. The Chieveley strain produced tinies measuring as small as 9 inches at maturity. Ch. Chieveley Chess, was only 12 inches and because she figures so importantly in certain lines the small genes have persisted in appearing. Eng. Ch. Toyboy of Toytown was on the small side and carried a small gene. The great producer Bonny Forget-Me-Not (dam of four champions) was only 11½ inches, and her descendants have also carried the small genes. Her grandson, Harwee of Mannerhead, sired some small ones, and his two sons Ch. Snow Boy of Fircot and Eng. Ch. Toomai of Montfleuri (out of a 12-inch French import Ch. Tresor de Madjige) figure importantly in Toy pedigrees in England and America. Snow Boy's in-bred Miniature daughter, Blakeen Solitaire, was the dam of seven Toy champions. Toomai's 10-inch black son, Ravenslea Black Ace, sired Emmrill Le Petit Czicko, the foundation sire of the Emmrill Toys. A son of Toomai bred to a Toyboy daughter produced Jervis of Rosvic. Jervis, combined with some colored breeding going back to the Seahorses, produced England's first great Toy sire, Wychwood Gatesgarth Monarch.

Monarch was a very handsome dog with an exaggeration of Poodle quality. He was a good black with a long, lean head, small eyes, low-set ears, well-developed body, good tailset and extreme angulation. He won well in the Under-11 inch classes in the days when the Toys still had to compete with the Miniatures. Monarch was used extensively to improve quality and reduce size. His owner, Anne Hall, said that he consistently reduced size to under 11 inches, even when bred to full-sized Miniatures. Monarch sired a total of eight champions. His lovely daughter Ch. Merrymorn Lita came to the States, where she was the first English-bred Toy Poodle to go Best in Show. Monarch's influence was so great that at every Crufts Show (the equivalent of our Westminster) from 1959 through 1967 (with one exception, 1964) a direct descendant of Monarch was either Best of Breed or Best of Opposite Sex: Monarch's son, Eng. Ch. Tammy of Manapouri (out of a small daughter of Eng. Ch. Rudolph of Piperscroft), was Best of Breed at Crufts in 1961, and his son Eng. Ch. Raphael of Manapouri was Best of Breed there in 1966. Tammy was the first big winning Toy Poodle, with 12 challenge certificates to his credit. Monarch's son, the late Eng. Ch. Tophill Toyboy, is still England's leading black Toy sire with 10 champions. Toyboy (out of a double granddaughter of Rudolph) was a lovely little dog who was small enough to have won here. He had a beautiful head, short body, was high on leg and with a good rear—a tiny in perfect balance. Toyboy's son, Eng. Ch. Wemrose Newsboy, is the third in a line of outstanding sires. He has produced five champions including the beautiful Eng. Ch. Barsbrae Branslake Harriet who was Best of Breed at Crufts in 1966 and 1967. Harriet is one of England's greatest winning Toy Poodle bitches with 11 c.c.'s to her credit.

The Montmartre Miniature strain also has a small gene, and Mrs. Conn has used this to create the Montmartre Toys. Montmartre What-A-Boy, who was on the small side for a Miniature, had seven crosses to Ch. Toyboy of Toytown plus small genes through the Braevals and Firebraves, both of which lines go back to the Chieveleys. What-A-Boy's small daughter, Montmartre Marietta, was the dam of three Toy champions. Marietta bred back to What-A-Boy gave the black Toy, Eng. Ch. Montmartre Miss Muffet, who was also the dam of three Toy champions. Miss Muffet was bred to Australian

Montmartre Ring-Master

Montmartre Minute Man

Ch. Montmartre Mighty Tiny (by Eng. Ch. Montmartre Marksman, a What-A-Boy son out of Eng. Ch. Montmartre Little Mo, a sister of What-A-Boy) to produce the lovely brown Am. Ch. Montmartre Molecule (Best of Variety at the Poodle Club of America Specialty in 1961) and her brother Montmartre Louis Miguel. Louis Miguel bred to his dam, Miss Muffet, produced the black Eng. Ch. Montmartre Master Singer, sire of 3 champions, and now in this country. Master Singer bred to Montmartre Minute (also by Louis Miguel) produced the 9-inch black Montmartre Ring-Master. Ring-Master was the sire of four imports which finished their titles in the States during 1967. Two of these, Eng. and Am. Ch. Montmartre Minouche and her sister Ch. Montmartre Marlaine, are Best in Show winners. Ring-Master's son, Montmartre Minute Man, has joined the Beaujeu Kennels, but he left behind Eng. Ch. Montmartre Carmen Miranda and Eng. Ch. Montmartre Mint-Master.

Mrs. Conn, starting with excellent Miniature stock, has carefully selected the smaller specimens and interbred them to produce English-sized Toys, and she has further reduced some to the American standard of under 10 inches. This line is pure Miniature in origin with no introduction of the white Toy size for size reduction. Other breeders have attempted to breed Toys down from a pure Miniature line, but to date no one has been as successful as Mrs. Conn.

The Petitbrun Kennels of Les and Mick Watson have also benefited from the small gene in their successful Bidabo-Petitbrun Miniature line. They bred Braeval Bonbon to their small Black Rhapsody of Petitbrun to produce the handsome little brown Ch. Petitbrun Screwball. Screwball is the most successful brown Toy sire in England with five champions to his credit. Bred to Snippet of Petitbrun (by Eng. Ch. Wemrose Newsboy), he produced Eng. Ch. Tea Tray of Petitbrun and her lovely sister Eng. Ch. Tea Cup of Petitbrun. Tea Cup is one of the top-winning Toy Poodle bitches in England with 11 c.c.'s and 8 reserve c.c.'s to her credit.

Since the Toy Poodle has been recognized in England, one line has almost completely dominated the winning and producing records in whites, and this is Sudbrook. The first c.c. won by a Toy bitch in England went to Mrs.

Harold Cox's lovely-headed Sudbrook Sunday Morning. Sunday Morning was bred to The Cherub of Braxted (Seahorses breeding) to produce Sudbrook Sunday Knight, who also did some nice winning. Mrs. Cox then bred Knight to his full sister, Sudbrook Sunday Eve, to produce the Best in Show winner, Ch. Sudbrook Sunday Suit. Sunday Suit produced five champions including Ch. Sudbrook Sunday Best. Sunday Best was also a Best in Show winner, and sired five champions. Mrs. Cox considers him the best that she ever bred.

Mrs. Cox had the great misfortune to lose both of these dogs in a kennel accident, but she was fortunate in having the third generation to continue the line. This is her 9½-inch Ch. Sudbrook Sunday Special, who is the winner of 8 c.c.'s, a Best in Show, and the sire of 12 champions to date. Sunday Special is a very impressive little dog with a Miniature type head and eye. He has a beautiful combination of balance and size of bone. Two of Sunday Special's sons have finished here, Harmo Kennels' Ch. Sudbrook Sunday Go T'Meeting and Mrs. Richard Stevens' Ch. Piccoli Little Peppermint.

When it is realized that the only three white Toys in England to gain the top producer ranks (sire of five or more champions) are the three successive generations of Sudbrook males—Sunday Suit, Sunday Best and Sunday Special—the achievement becomes all the more remarkable. The American Toy, and especially the white American Toy, has shown a distressing tendency to revert to their old apple-headed, pop-eyed, pure white Toy ancestry. It may well be that the English Sudbrook line which excels in head will be of great use to American breeders.

The silver Toy in England, still in the developing stage, has been based on the initial cross of the silver Miniature with the white Toy and this has brought about problems in both size and color. The initial cross is receding into the background and through selection certain lines are just beginning to emerge. Doris Turner has done pioneering work in this color with her small Andavian silver Toys. The most successful silver Toy to date has been Donald Wicken's handsome Ch. Silcresta Silver Sprat who was the top winning male Toy Poodle in England for 1966 with 11 c.c.'s to his credit. Sprat is a popular stud and should figure in the future of the silver Toy in England.

The apricot Toy Poodle in England is still in the process of being created. Mrs. Edwards' Greatcoats and Mrs. Dobson's Puckshill Miniatures have been of great value. The apricot Toy in England received a great boost with the sensational win of Eng. Ch. Oakington Puckshill Ambersunblush's great victory of Best in Show at the Crufts' Show in 1966. Ambersunblush's owner, Mrs. Claire Perry, is specializing in apricot Toys and is founding the Tio Pepi line on Ambersunblush. The first apricot Toy to finish her championship in England was Mrs. Price-Jones' Eng. Ch. Frenches Golden Jewel. The

Eng. Ch. Silcresta
Silver Sprat

Eng. Ch. De'Regis
Silver Diamite

most successful apricot Toy male in England has been Eng. Ch. Rhosbridge Golden Shred, who has won 11 c.c.'s. There have been very few apricot Toy champions to date in England as it is difficult for them to compete with the blacks, but progress is being made.

During the formative period in the development of the English Toy Poodle, the Kennel Club in England allowed the interbreeding of the Toy Poodle and the Miniature, and the progeny that were under 11-inches at maturity could be registered as Toy. Even the smallest members of all Miniature litters with all-Miniature breeding could be registered as Toys as long as they were under 11 inches at maturity. Now being considered is a ruling that in the future both parents must be registered as Toys in order to qualify for a Class I registration. The Toy Poodle has become enormously popular in England and they closely rival the Miniatures in numbers. For example, in 1966 there were 8514 Toys registered as compared to the 8716 total for Miniatures. The Kennel Club feels that there have been enough Toys now registered to allow the variety to be developed within its own framework. This ruling will of course be a great help in stabilizing size when eventually there will be pedigrees of three, four and more generations of all under 11 inch background.

The English Miniature has been a continuing source of supply for American Miniature breeders since the very beginning, and many of their top winners and producers, or their sons, have been brought to this country for the utilization of these breeders. The English Toy at its best is a lovely animal and as breeders continue to reduce size, they will also be a source of supply for American Toy breeders. It is of course safer to breed an English Toy bitch to an American male in hopes of reducing size. When breeding an American Toy bitch to an English Toy male, his pedigree should be carefully studied to make sure that his background is sufficiently small so that there will be no whelping difficulties. Every year for the past several years there has been a slight increase in the number of English imports that have come to this country and gained their titles. Properly used, these little dogs can benefit the future of the American Toy.

47

Outstanding Toy Sires

CH. LEICESTER'S BONBON

Whelped January 3, 1945   Died March 25, 1948

Bred and owned by Leicester Harrison

```
                        Ch. Happy Chappy (wh)
              Ch. Beau Beau of Muriclar (wh)
                     Fluffy of Muriclar (wh)
        Ch. Pruden's Little Skipper (wh)
                        Ch. Mitor of Muriclar (wh)
              Justine de Muriclar (wh)
                     Dena of Muriclar (wh)
```

CH. LEICESTER'S BONBON (wh)

```
                        Ch. Happy Chappy (wh)
              Ch. Beau Beau of Muriclar (wh)
                     Fluffy of Muriclar (wh)
        Ch. Leicester's Fidele de Lafferty (wh)
                     Rowdy (wh)
              Lafferty's Dimples (wh)
                     Lafferty's Dream Girl (wh)
```

CH. LEICESTER'S BONBON

Sire of 12 champions: Out of:

Ch. Leicester's Bonbon's Swan Song
Ch. Leicester's Bon Ami
Ch. Leicester's Frolic   Leicester's Alouette
Ch. Leicester's Ouida
Ch. Leicester's Valentine Nibroc

Ch. Leicester's Sweet Stuff   Lafferty's Ma Chere
Ch. Leicester's Bonny Boy of Nibroc

Ch. Princess Snow White
Ch. Roger The Lodger   La Belle Helene Bonsoir

Ch. Cartlane Once   Cartlane Odette
Ch. Georgian Don   Nibroc Primadonna
Ch. Leicester's Moon Mist   Mistinguette

Ch. Cartlane Once, the first Toy Poodle to win an all-breed Best in Show.

AM. & CAN. CH. WILBER WHITE SWAN

Whelped December 11, 1951   Died January 21, 1966

Bred and owned by Mrs. Bertha Smith

```
                              Ch. Pruden's Little Skipper (wh)
                    Ch. Leicester's Bonbon (wh)
                              Ch. Leicester's Fidele de Lafferty (wh)
          Ch. Leicester's Bonbon's Swan Song (blu)
                              Ch. Robin Goodfellow (blu)
                    Leicester's Alouette (blu)
                              Minette (blk)

AM. & CAN. CH. WILBER WHITE SWAN (wh)

                              Gamin Greenleaf (si)
                    Wil-Ber Valentin (si)
                              Dorem Gaminette (gr)
          Wil-Ber Victoire (si)
                              Ch. Barrack Hill Bomber (blk)
                    Barrack Hill Truffle (blk)
                              Barrack Hill Mince Ruissaune (blk)
```

246

AM. & CAN. CH. WILBER WHITE SWAN

Sire of 38 champions: Out of:

Ch. Poivre of Trent
Ch. Blakeen Ding Ding
Ch. Blakeen Hubba Hubba II
Ch. Loabelo Snow Flake   Blakeen Solitaire
Ch. Loabelo Cygnet
Ch. Loabelo Carbon Copy
Ch. White Magic of Trent

Ch. Wayne Valley Sir Galahad
Ch. Wayne Valley Prince Valiant   Wayne Valley Ducharme Silhou
Ch. Wayne Valley Rhapsody in Blue
Ch. Wayne Valley Ducharme Jack

Ch. Ty-Del's Dancing Girl
Ch. Ty-Del's Fancy Girl   Seahorses Marquisette
Ch. Ty-Del's Lady Bird
Ch. Ty-Del's Jelly Bean

Ch. Bermyth Lola
Ch. Bermyth White Monarch   Bermyth Surprise
Ch. Bermyth White Swan's Replica

Ch. Renrew's Apricot Brandy   Ch. Leicester's Little Eva
Ch. Renrew's Risque

Ch. Smilestone's Delight   Georgian Patti
Ch. Smilestone's Wee Mite

Ch. Alltrin Adonis of Cartlane   Cartlane Oomph
Ch. Bermyth Gardez Bien   Bermyth Juliette
Ch. Bermyth Poudrette Blanche   Loabelo Joan
Ch. Bermyth Snow Drop   Bermyth Little Mite
Ch. Bermyth Whisper   Bermyth Loabelo Joan
Ch. Frosty Boy of Carribrook   Bric A Brac Powder Puff
Ch. Gran-Ellen Snow Breath   Daikar Frivol
Ch. Jay's Mr. Wonderful   Sangaree's Folly
Ch. MacAulay's White Cygnet   Ch. Bermyth Snow Drop
Ch. Pixdown Little Bit   Ch. Pixdown Loabello Blanchette
Ch. Taylor's Merry Mimi   Bermyth Sonia
Ch. Ty-Del's A.M.   Ty-Del's Call Me Madame
Ch. Ty-Del's Dorene   Leicester's Call Me Madame
Ch. White Swan's Cygnet of Vista   Bond Hill Beautique
Ch. Plath's White Wilber   Ch. Petite Susette
Can. Ch. St. Aubrey's Charm

Ch. Bermyth White Swan's Replica   **Ch. Blakeen Ding Ding**

Am. & Can. Ch. Silhou-Jette's Snow Sprite. Bred and owned by Miss Martha Jane Ablett, Silhou-Jette Kennels.

AM. & CAN. CH. SILHOU-JETTE SNOW SPRITE
AM. & CAN. CH. SILHOU-JETTE'S CREAM TOPPING

Whelped March 13, 1956   Both deceased

Bred by Martha Jane Ablett


```
                          Roi de l'Argent (si)
              Ch. Sir Lancelot de Gladville (wh)
                          Barnes' Little Gay Fluffball (wh)
       Silhou-Jette's Minute Man (crm-wh)
                          Bubbles of Piperscroft and Blakeen (wh)
              Silhou-Jette Pip Squeak (wh)
                          Ch. Blakeen Snow Flurry (wh)

AM. & CAN. CH. SILHOU-JETTE SNOW SPRITE (wh)

AM. & CAN. CH. SILHOU-JETTE CREAM TOPPING (crm)

                          Michel of Piperscroft (wh)
              Bubbles of Piperscroft and Blakeen (wh)
                          Dimple of Piperscroft (wh)
       Silhou-Jette's Pip Squeak (wh)
                          Ch. Snow Boy of Fircot (wh)
              Ch. Blakeen Snow Flurry (wh)
                          Ch. Blakeen Flurry (wh)
```

248

Am. & Can. Ch. Silhou-Jette's Cream Topping. Owned by Challendon Kennels.

AM. & CAN. CH. SILHOU-JETTE'S CREAM TOPPING

<u>Sire of 13 champions:</u>   Out of:

Ch. Bel Tor Plath's Sugar Lump
Ch. Bel Tor Plath's Sure Thing
Ch. Bel Tor Plath's Sweet Success   Ch. Petite Susette
Ch. Plath's Miss Plath
Ch. Plath's The Doctor

Ch. Calvinelle Tipsy Trifle   Lilli Liante of Trent
Ch. Calvinelle Dancing Deacon

Ch. Palmares Challendon Glitter   Palmares Frosted Mittens
Ch. Palmares Mr. Doodle Bug

Ch. Magic Choice of Rafter O   Ch. Adastra Magic Choice
Ch. Petite Herkimer Be Gay   Forzando Linda Lisa
Ch. Sylvester's Cream Puff   Zsa's Cherie of Abon Hassan
Ch. Wymarsch's Sorority Girl   Wymarsch's Son Sa Star Kista

AM. & CAN. CH. SILHOU-JETTE'S SNOW SPRITE

<u>Sire of 10 champions:</u>   Out of:

Ch. Hampton House High Society   Ch. Hampton House Heidi
Ch. Collette's Snow Avalancher (Min.)   Collette's Phalene de la Neige
Ch. Silhou-Jette's Cream Tart   Ch. Silhou-Jette's Sais Si Bon
Ch. Silhou-Jette's Ice Fairy   Silhou-Jette's Mamselle Puff
Ch. Silhou-Jette's Icerama   Silhou-Jette's Cookie Oh
Ch. Silhou-Jette Melodie D'Amour   Silhou-Jette's Milady Belle
Ch. Silhou-Jette's Sweet Talk   Silhou-Jette's Cream Fluff
Ch. Silhou-Jette's Take Me Along   Silhou-Jette's Sachet
Ch. Xvenska's Susie Snowflake   Carousel's My Fancy Folly
Ch. Silhou-Jette's Sugar Babe   Silhou-Jette's Sugar Cookie

AM. & CAN. CH. THORNLEA SILVER SOUVENIR

Whelped April 2, 1956

Bred and owned by Mrs. George Dow

```
                          Ch. Leicester's Bonbon's Swan Song (blu)
              Ch. Leicester's Silver Boots (si)
                          Leicester's Silver Shoon (si)
    Ch. Leicester's Golden Slippers (chpn-si)
                          Ch. Leicester's Peaches and Cream (crm)
              Leicester's Peach Melba (crm)
                          Lafferty's Ma Chere (wh)


AM. & CAN. CH. THORNLEA SILVER SOUVENIR (si)

                          Ch. Silver Dynamo de Gladville (si)
              Sylvideo de Gladville (si)
                          Bonnie Marie de Gladville (gr)
    Ch. Miss Sylvideo de Gladville (si)
                          Orsie's Son Sa Ses (gr)
              Susie of Pickwick Manor (gr)
                          Belle of Pickwick Manor (gr)
```

250

AM. &· CAN. CH. THORNLEA SILVER SOUVENIR

Sire of 34 champions:	Out of:

Ch. Elfin's Wish Upon A Star
Ch. Kell-Mar Topper
Ch. Kenbrook Forest Vodka   B.G. of Yew Tree
Ch. Lady Bug of Yew Tree
Can. Ch. Sirhan's Something Special
Ch. Thornlea Silver Signature

Ch. Encore Rose Marie
Ch. Encore Silver Showman   Ch. Rothara Carbaric Silvia
Ch. Encore Star Dancer

Ch. Silver Spark of Sassafras   Ch. The Infanta of Sassafras
Ch. Silver Sparkle of Sassafras

Ch. High Heritage Heirloom   High Heritage Heather
Can. Ch. High Heritage Heiress

Ch. Pood-I-Man Golden Girl   Pood-I-Man Silver Rosemary
Ch. Pood-I-Man Silver Fortune

Ch. Bayou D'Argent Larry   Bayou D'Argent Larissa
Ch. Belle Fleur Silver Satan   Belle Fleur Silver Flirt
Ch. Glenwood Pom Pom   Mariton's Lana
Ch. Haldacar's Silver Dream   Ch. Silver Song of Sassafras
Can. Ch. High Heritage Highland   High Heritage Heather Hue
Ch. Lochmanor's Silver Galaxy   Fieldstreams Silver Spangle
Ch. Shanelle's Golden Trinket   Gigi's Cherie of Seascott
Ch. Pala Rora's Silver Silhouette   Ch. Sharazad's Silver Mirage
Ch. Souvenir's Silver Sensation   Petite Penny of San Souci
Ch. Thornlea Silver Mint   Ramaco Swansdown
Ch. Thornlea Silver Cricket   Ch. Thornlea Silver Trinket
Ch. Thornlea Silver Siren   Ch. Silver Gleam of Aurillac
Ch. Thornlea Silver Dollar   Puttencove Trilby
Ch. Gilkey's Top Dollar   Ch. Thornlea Silver Dollar
Ch. Twinkle Star of Brandt's   Quietcorner Gabriella
Can. Ch. Dan-La-Mar Mister-In-Between Merrymorn Princess Pretty
Italian Ch. Parrish Souvenir Sue   Silver Jacquie K
Swedish Ch. Thornlea Silver Traveller Ch. Thornlea Silver Siren
Can. Ch. Northlight's Mr. Armand

Ch. High Heritage Heirloom

CH. SILVER SPARKLE OF SASSAFRAS

Whelped September 5, 1957

Bred and owned by Pamela A. P. Ingram

```
                        Ch. Leicester's Silver Boots (si)
             Ch. Leicester's Golden Slippers (chpn-si)
                      Leicester's Peach Melba (crm)
    Am. & Can. Ch. Thornlea Silver Souvenir (si)
                          Sylvideo de Gladville (si)
             Ch. Miss Sylvideo de Gladville (si)
                       Susie of Pickwick Manor (gr)

CH. SILVER SPARKLE OF SASSAFRAS (si)

                          Sylvideo de Gladville (si)
              Ch. Bon Chance de Sassafras (si)
                        Sunny Sue de Gladville (si)
      Ch. The Infanta of Sassafras (si)
                       Quietcorner Gille Gorm (si)
              Quietcorner Susie Fry (si)
                       Quietcorner Brunette (brn)
```

252

CH. SILVER SPARKLE OF SASSAFRAS

Sire of 54 champions: Out of:

Ch. Sassafras Silver Sparklette
Ch. Silver Moon of Sassafras
Ch. Mister Sassafras of HyTides   Sassy Lass of Sassafras
Can. Ch. Sterling Silver of Sassafras

Ch. Silver Lotus of Sassafras
Ch. Silver Sauce of Sassafras   Ch. Silverango of Sassafras

Ch. Neldic's Silver Mimi
Ch. Neldic's Silver Nappy   Miss Sassafras of Hopi Hollow

Ch. Sassafras Silver Poppins
Ch. Silverado of Sassafras   Viola of Sassafras

Ch. Blue Boy of Sassafras II   Bellafontine of Sassafras
Ch. Challendon Gadget   Challendon Nipperkin
Ch. Cutler's Platina of Sassafras   Ann's Silver Doll
Jap. Ch. Du Moi Pulani of Sassafras   Ch. Silver Coquette du Moi
Ch. Edrita's Phull-O-Sass   Edrita's Phull-O-Pholly
Ch. Gentry Silver Serena   Gentry's Silver Snowflake
Can. Ch. Grenoble's Angel of Sassafras   Mon Petite D'Argent
Ch. High Heritage Headstudy   High Heritage Heather Hue
Ch. Little Noel of Sassafras   Silver Lady of Sassafras
Can. Ch. Marborough Miss of Sassafras   Bon Cafe de Sassafras
Am. & Can. Ch. Marborough Mist of Sassafras   Silver Jewel of Sassafras
Can. Ch. Misty Angelique of Sassafras   Brunotti's Gigi Angelique
Jap. Ch. Mona Lisa of Sassafras   Toyon's Mona Lisa
Ch. Onno Nay's Toyopet   Onno Nay's Dinah-Might
Ch. Sassaboy of Sassafras   Sassabelle of Bettrich
Am. & Can. Ch. Sassafras Starfire   Skyline Cloudwisp
Can. Ch. Sassafras The Sunflower   Bo Bo La Bleu
Ch. Sassafras The Snowball   Silver Sante of Sassafras
Ch. Silverchips Sassy Patachou   Mistinguette Missy
Jap. Ch. Silver Bonnet of Sassafras   Nell's D'Argent Sans Souci
Ch. Silver Coquette du Moi   Yot Club Jamais Eclair
Ch. Silver Dusty of Sassafras   Petite Silver Tinkerbell
Ch. Silver Mittens of Sassafras   Agee's Jeanine
Ch. Silver Muff of Sassafras II   La Gai Wee Silver Muffet
Swedish Ch. Silver Selsendy of Sassafras   Du Moy Angel of Sassafras
Can. Ch. Silver Sayonara of Grenhall   Silver Sharizade of Grenhall
Ch. Silver Shrimp of Sassafras   Linda's April in Paris
Am. & Can. Ch. Silver Sibling of Sassafras   Silver Shadow Mitzie
Ch. Silver Sinner of Sassafras   Bittersweet of Sassafras
Ch. Silver Smoke of Sassafras   Silver Sally of Sassafras
Jap. Ch. Silver Sparkle Jr. of Sassafras   Barclay Tu-Tu
Ch. Silver Splash of Sassafras   Gribouille, C.D.
Ch. Silver Soda of Sassafras   Ellen's Silver Tina
Am. & Can. Ch. Silver Spice of Sassafras   Bon Blanche of Sassafras
Am. & Can. Ch. Silver Stinker of Sassafras   Flurette of Hopi Hollow
Am. & Can. Ch. Silver Sunday of Sassafras   Difrey's DiDi of Sassafras
Brazilian Ch. Silver Starlette of Sassafras   Shooting Star of Star Dew
Can. Ch. Silver Strutter of Sassafras   Mademoiselle de Radford
Can. Ch. Soutache of Sassafras   Bien Aimee Nanette
Ch. Spotlight of Sassafras   Honeybit Hoppit of Sassafras

Out of:

Can. Ch. Tres Chic of Morrow
Ch. Very Fancy of Sassafras
Ch. Virlen's Silver Surprise
Tri-Int. Ch. Marvel's Mouse of Sassafras

Morrow's Silver Simone
Fran-Del's Fancy of Sassafras
Brunotti's Gigi Angelique
Cheri Marie Bernardi

Ch. Very Fancy of Sassafras

Am. & Can. Ch. Silver Spice of Sassafras

Ch. Christal Silver Typhoon (by Christal Silver Cosmeau ex Sonia's Susette), silver Toy Group winner and champion producer. Owned by Mr. and Mrs. A. C. Pearson, Florian Poodles.

Ch. J. C. Fabulous Fanny (by Ch. J. C. King Doodles ex Glo-Bill's Gigi Bell), black Toy Best in Show winner. Owned by Mr. and Mrs. A. C. Pearson.

CH. J. C. KING DOODLES

Whelped November 16, 1955

Bred by Juanita M. Argo
Owned by Mr. and Mrs. J. Stokes Smith

```
                          Voltaire II (gr)
               Baron de Gladville (blk)
                          Barnes Mimi (wh)
        Ch. Blakeen King Doodles (blk)
                          Ch. Puttencove Antonio (blk)
               Puttencove Dot (blk)
                          Sirod Doris of Blakeen (blk)

CH. J. C. KING DOODLES (blk)

                          Ch. Busby of Piperscroft (blk)
               Ch. Winelist Cognac (blk)
                          Ch. Lotus of Piperscroft (blk)
        Sansterre Living Doll (blk)
                          Ch. Puttencove Antonio (blk)
               Puttencove Prissy (blk)
                          The Rani of Poodhall (blk)
```

256

CH. J. C. KING DOODLES

Sire of 32 champions: Out of:

Ch. J. C. Lucki Ann
Ch. J. C. Mister Lucki   Ch. J. C. Doodles Penny
Ch. J. C. Snow White
Ch. J. C. King Tar

Ch. J. C. Darktown Strutter   Midnight Bijou
Ch. J. C. Hello Dolly Bobbet's

Ch. Wappoo Weatherman   Ch. Wappoo Whirlydoodle
Ch. Wappoo Whirling Dervish

Can. Ch. Cybelia's Vandee   Cybelia
Ch. J. C. Big Spender   Brigette Poqueito Evans
Ch. J. C. Diamond Jim   Souffle's Suzette
Ch. J. C. Black Fashion   Luce's Petite LaNette
Ch. J. C. Gentleman Jim   J. C. Marguerite
Ch. J. C. Fluff Ruff   J. C. Dorothy's Dot
Ch. J. C. Hi Lillie   Cherie Femme Kegonsa
Ch. J. C. Meridian Amedee   J. C. Black Cherry
Ch. J. C. Midnight Madam   Webb's Crepes Suzette
Ch. J. C. Mister Completely (Min.)   J. C. Tammy of Meridian
Ch. J. C. Pat's Little Number   Francene II
Can. Ch. J. C. Petite Bo Peep   Baba's Souffle
Ch. J. C. Sally Rand   Ryan's Littlest Angel
Ch. J. C. Readi Teadi   Serrina
Ch. Railey's Doodle Doll   Princess Nina de Babess
Ch. Ro Mo Little Prince   Poodtowne Ritzy
Can. Ch. Joyel's Jigelo Jack   J. C. Tippin Jammik
Ch. J. C. Fabulous Fanny   Glo-Bill's Gigi Bell
Can. Ch. Bibelot's Small, Dark,   J. C. Little Lorraine
    and Handsome
Can. Ch. J. C. Minstrel Man
Ch. J. C. Gunslinger   Westons Pennsy Pamper
Ch. J. C. King Pin   J. C. Many Many
Can. Ch. J. C. Miss Fairweather
Can. Ch. J. C. Little Doc

Ch. J. C. Readi Teadi

CH. FIELDSTREAMS VALENTINE

Whelped February 14, 1957   Died February 14, 1968

Bred and owned by Audrey Watts Kelch

```
                          Ch. Orsie's Mi-Ra-Bi-Le (blk)
              Bijou X (blk)
                          Mona Lisa III (blk)
    Ch. Fieldstreams Bojangles (blk)
                          Barrack Hill Beau Geste (blk)
              Marcelle Bon Bon (blk)
                          Simon Bon Bon (blk)

CH. FIELDSTREAMS VALENTINE (blk)

                          Braebeck Tino of Montfleuri (blk)
              Adam of Evesgarden (blk)
                          Marie-Lou of Montfleuri (blk)
    Ch. Chaman Grouse (brn)
                          Hollyhill Desmoulin Dalmahoy (blk)
              Camille (blk)
                          Hollyhill Janice of Gatton (blk)
```

CH. FIELDSTREAMS VALENTINE

Sire of 12 champions:

Ch. Carlima's Bridget
Ch. Carlima's Gus

Ch. Carlima's J.D.
Ch. Starfire My Funny Valentine

Can. Ch. Weejet's First Lady
Can. Ch. Weejet's Standing Ovation

Ch. Alltrin Holiday Greetings
Ch. Baliwick Blackbird
Ch. Starfire Early Morn
Ch. Crestwood's Tippy Top
Ch. Mike Mar's Dream Come True
Ch. Or-Ra's Valentina

Out of:

Ch. Black Orchid of Wembley Downs

Chrisward Tambourine

Ch. Mur-Villa's Black Pearl

Alltrin Berenice
Ch. Baliwick Begin
Fieldstreams Gamine
Fieldstreams Mona Lisa
Denbur's Wendy
Or-Ra's Black Jangles

Ch. Chaman Grouse

Ch. Fieldstreams Bojangles

Ch. Starfire My Funny Valentine

Ch. Baliwick Blackbird

Ch. Blakeen Luzon with her three-months-old puppies.

The Standard Poodle

Int. Ch. Nunsoe Duc de la Terrace of Blakeen, owned by Blakeen Kennels, Best in Show, Westminster, 1935, first Poodle to win this award.

Foreword to
Standard Male Lines

THERE are four important male lines in the Standard variety. Two of these, the "Prinz Alexander" line and the "Anderl" line, had their origins on the Continent. Some of the intervening generations came by way of England where they were influenced by the English stock with which they were combined. The English "Whippendell Carillon" line was on the small side but offered a needed elegance to the Continental lines. The fourth sire line is headed by Ch. Blakeen Cyrano, who is of course an American-bred dog. This line is more recent than the others, as Cyrano was whelped in 1934, and this coupled with the fact that this line was particularly rich in the strength of the bitches it produced (rather than producing males) makes it appear less widespread than the others, but it is no less important in its impact on the variety.

The Standard sire lines from the previous edition have been consolidated in this revision and greatly lengthened to bring them up-to-date. In the last ten years 851 Standard Poodles have completed their championships. A commentary hitting the highlights of each line precedes the charts. The charts note the male line of descent from father to son featuring those dogs which are top producers (sire of five or more champions). These charts also give the colors, and the number in parentheses at the end of each name indicates the number of champions produced.

263

Int. Ch. Prinz Alexander von Rodelheim

Group of Salmagundi white Standards. Dog on
left is Int. Ch. Prinz Alexander von Rodelheim.

49

"Prinz Alexander" Line
Ch. Prinz Alexander
von Rodelheim

THE fountainhead of all the most famous Standard whites was under the snow-clad mountains of Switzerland in the Labory Kennels of Mme. Reichenbach, where could be seen the strains from the famous German kennels, such as Schneeflocke and Rodelheim, as well as La Terrace. The great Poodles gathered together there were later to be distributed to English and American kennels.

These large and handsome dogs were originally of German origin, there is no doubt. They are, as their records show quite clearly, far superior in size, type, and showiness to the English white Standards exhibited in England before their arrival. The English dogs were, in many cases, small and snipey, inclined to weakness of hindquarters, or, if of another type, with coarse heads, wide skulls, and with wide and loose fronts.

The Labory dogs are noted for the combination of size without coarseness, extreme elegance of type and pride of carriage, combined with good bone, black eyes, and exquisite refinement and beauty of expression. Their skin is of silver, not pink, pigmentation and they carry immense snowy coats of perfect texture. Many have heads that are truly superb and are flawless in construction, putting to shame even the best heads among blacks. Notable examples of Poodles with perfect heads were Ch. Blakeen Eiger, Ch. Blakeen Luzon, and Ch. Broadrun Cherry.

The faults, and, alas, even the best families have them, are shortness of ear leather and wide fronts, which are characteristics descended from the Schneeflocke line. These shortcomings have been largely overcome in the hands of our cleverest breeders, to whom we owe so much for their rare manipulation and interweaving of the white bloodlines obtained from

265

Mme. Reichenbach, and for their own pluck and perseverance. America has reason to be proud of her white Standard Poodle fanciers and their really great achievements.

The greatest winning and producing white Standard line is not only numerically large, but has also steadily held top place generation after generation. This can, I believe, be accounted for by the fact that the foundation dogs were all of exceptional quality—famous on both sides of the water, and winners in all the Continental countries as well as their native Germany and their adopted Switzerland. Nor were the bitches any less excellent than the dogs, as the records will prove. Therefore, there is every reason for the continued success of this white bloodline. Perhaps no other strain has had a more splendid beginning, and present day breeders are wisely preserving this valuable heritage. Most probably, the royal titles used so liberally in the beginnings of this family were chosen because of the regal bearing of its members. However, they did prove to be canine royalty, with every right to their titles.

The founder of this dynasty was Continental Ch. Prinz Alexander von Rodelheim. Prinz Alexander produced two noted daughters, Ch. Edelweis du Labory of Salmagundi and Ch. Princess du Labory of Salmagundi, and four influential sons: His Excellency of Salmagundi, Int. Ch. Salmagundi's Choice, Int. Ch. Nunsoe Duc de la Terrace of Blakeen and Piperscroft Pippo de la Terrace.

My first love among the gleaming white Standard Poodles was Prinz Alexander's lovely daughter, Ch. Edelweis du Labory of Salmagundi, who took my breath away when I saw her for the first time in Mrs. Justin Greiss' home at Salmagundi. Edelweis was a beautiful Poodle and a charming one. Mrs. Greiss told me that she bought her as a puppy from Mme. Reichenbach in Switzerland and that she was her constant companion from then on. Her American owner was so fond of the beautiful bitch that it was very reluctantly that she consented to her show career, which proved so brilliant with, I believe, thirty-five Group firsts and eight Bests in Show. Edelweis' dam was Ch. Nelly von der Schneeflocke of Blakeen whom Mrs. Sherman Hoyt later brought to America.

Prinz Alexander joined his famous daughter at Salmagundi where his greatness was properly appreciated, and he lived to a ripe old age. Prinz Alexander was bred to Edelweis to produce her best two children, Int. Ch. Salmagundi's Choice (who after completing his American title, was sent to England, where he promptly gained an English championship) and His Excellency of Salmagundi. Prinz Alexander, bred in Switzerland to his daughter Alba de la Terrace (litter sister of the famous Duc), produced Am. Ch. Princess du Labory of Salmagundi, whom Mrs. Greiss also imported. Princess bred to her three-quarter brother, His Excellency, gave six champions: Ch. Salmagundi Perhaps So Wise and Ch. Knight Errant, Ch. His Highness, Ch. Happy Choice, Ch. Dame Choice and Ch. Chosen Dame—all of Salmagundi. Princess was also bred to Ch. Salmagundi's Choice (His Excellency's full brother) to produce Ch. White Cocade of Salmagundi and Ch. Lucite of Salmagundi.

White Cocade, a Best in Show winner, went to Cartlane where he was greatly loved and retained his regal bearing to the end of his long life. White Cocade sired eleven champions, including Ch. Cartlane Laurent. Laurent was the sire of Ch. Tour d'Argent Christopher, who sired seven champions. White Cocade was bred to the black Ch. Carillon Colline to produce the great obedience winner Ch. Carillon Jester U.D.T., who was black like his dam. Jester sired the cream Petitcote Baron Chico C.D., who was the sire of Am. and Can. Ch. Petitcote Domino (sire of nine champions). Domino sired Wencair's Frere Jacque (sire of six champions) as well as the greatest producing bitch in the history of the breed, Am. and Can. Ch. Wycliffe Jacqueline U.D. (dam of 21 champions).

Now to return to Cocade's litter brother, Ch. Lucite of Salmagundi. Lucite was bred to Ch. Pillicoc Pearl to produce the magnificent headed Ch. Ensarr Glace. Glace was an outstanding winner with two Bests in Show to his credit. He sired eight champions including Davdon Kennels' Best in Show winner Ch. Hillandale C'Est Vrais (ex Ch. Cartlane Hillandale Cadenza—a daughter of Ch. White Cocade of Salmagundi). C'Est Vrais bred to his Best in Show daughter Ch. Davdon Miss Demeanor produced Ch. Davdon Captivation (dam of four Alekai champions). C'Est Vrais's son Ch. Valeway Temptation of Davdon sired three champions including Ch. Davdon Summa Cum Laude (dam of six Alekai champions). An unshown brother of Glace, Pillicoc Courier, was bred to Blakeen Surrey Romance to produce Ch. Pillicoc Barrister. Courier and Romance were both out of Ch. Pillicoc Pearl (three crosses to the Duc). Courier's sire, Ch. Lucite of Salmagundi, was by Ch. Salmagundi's Choice ex Ch. Princess du Labory of Salmagundi. Both were sired by Prinz Alexander ex daughters of Prinz Alexander. Surrey Romance was sired by Ch. Knight Errant of Salmagundi. Both of Knight Errant's parents, His Excellency of Salmagundi and Ch. Princess du Labory of Salmagundi, were by Prinz Alexander ex daughters of Prinz Alexander.

Barrister therefore represents strong intensification of these lines. A close study of his pedigree reveals a dozen crosses to the originator of the line, Ch. Prinz Alexander von Rodelheim. There are few bloodlines that can be put to such a close test of breeding and come through with flying colors, but Barrister's ancestors had been carefully selected for generation after generation. Barrister is the grandsire of two of the greatest members which this family has produced, Ch. Puttencove Promise and Ch. Paloma's Bon Vivant. But to return to Barrister, he sired six champions including two important sons, Ch. Blakeen Bali Hài and Ch. Blakeen Sorcerer's Apprentice. Bali Hài, a Best in Show winner, went to Puttencove Kennels. Bali Hai's son Ch. Loabelo Jonny sired one of the breed's greatest winners and producers, the magnificent Ch. Puttencove Promise (ex a Barrister daughter). Promise with his great tail-wagging showmanship was a favorite with the ringsiders and with the judges too. He climaxed his great career with his Best in Show win at Westminster in 1958. Promise sired a total of 27 champions, including Ch. Puttencove Moonshine (sire of four champions), Can. Ch. Calvados de la Fontaine (sire of five champions) and Ch. Alekai Nohea (sire of six champions). Ch. Pillicoc Barrister's other most important producing son, Ch. Blakeen Sorcerer's Apprentice, went to the Forzando Kennels in California. Apprentice sired six champions, including the small but handsome Ch. Paloma's Bon Vivant. Bon Vivant, a Best in Show winner, sired 26 champions including the Best in Show winner Ch. Hallmark Harmony O'Windridge (sire of six champions) and Ch. Forzando Bergamasque (sire of five champions). Sorcerer's Apprentice also produced Windridge Savoir Vivre (14 points), who in turn sired Windridge Christopher (sire of five champions).

An even greater thrill than Edelweis was meeting the Emperor of them all, Int. Ch. Nunsoe Duc de la Terrace of Blakeen, and his two gorgeous children, Ch. Blakeen Jung Frau and her litter brother Ch. Blakeen Eiger, the latter two being one of the most magnificent braces of all time. No one could fail to see in the Duc dignity, pride and true nobility of character. There was something awe-inspiring and impressive about him, which I have never seen before or since in any Poodle. He was choice of a litter bred by Mme. Emile Warney at La Terrace from a bitch bred by Mme. Reichenbach by Int. Ch. Prinz Alexander von Rodelheim. The Duc gained his titles in France and Switzerland, was imported into England by Miss Jane Lane of Nunsoe fame, gained his English championship without turning a hair, and was purchased as a magnificent gift by Mrs. Whitney Blake for her daughter, Mrs. Sherman Hoyt. In America, shown eighteen times, he was undefeated in his breed, and won 16 Groups, including three at Westminster, and was nine times Best in Show including Westminster 1935. The Duc was a magnificent specimen of the breed. Though taller and heavier-boned than the English Poodles, he was not coarse. His beautiful proportions and elegant appearance changed the opinions of British breeders on size and substance. He had an outstanding show career in the fiercest competition, and permanently improved the white Standard in England and America.

Fortunately for the breed, the Duc proved to be as great a sire as a show dog. His two most famous get were Ch. Blakeen Jung Frau and Ch. Blakeen Eiger mentioned above. Jung Frau won 40 Groups and 19 Bests in Show, including the 1940 Morris and Essex Show. She was the dam of Ch. Blakeen Miss Puff and Ch. Blakeen Radiance by Lucas du Brios of Blakeen. Eiger won

57 Groups and 17 Bests in Show. Eiger and Jung Frau were out of Ch. Nelly von der Schneeflocke of Blakeen (mentioned earlier as the dam of Ch. Edelweis du Labory of Salmagundi), as were Ch. Blakeen The Ghost (three Bests in Show), Can. Ch. Blakeen Monch (Best in Show), Can. Ch. Blakeen Schatzy (Best in Show) and Ch. Blakeen Schneeflocke. In addition to these six champions, an untitled full sister, Blakeen Nelly, proved an excellent producer. Bred to Lucas du Brios of Blakeen she produced Ch. Broadrun Cherry and Ch. Broadrun Cheerio. Then bred to her son Cheerio she produced Ch. Barrack Hill Just Charles and Ch. Blakeen Luzon. The Duc was also the sire of the Best in Show winner Ch. Blakeen Cafe Parfait. Prior to leaving for the States the Duc had produced six litters in England. Two sons from these litters also came to America, Ch. Nunsoe Con Amour of Salmagundi and Ch. Knight of Piperscroft and Blakeen (Best in Show winner). Of the Duc's nine champion get, seven were Best in Show winners—an amazing record.

Interestingly, it is through an untitled son of the Duc, sired in England, that the Duc tail male line comes down today. This son, Marechal of Piperscroft, sired the brothers Ch. Rettat's Slick and Rettat's Spinner. Slick was bred to Pillicoc Alabaster (a granddaughter of the Duc and Ch. Pillicoc Rumpelstilskin) to produce Ch. Pillicoc Pegasus and Ch. Pillicoc Pearl. Pearl was the dam of Ch. Ensarr Glace. Ch. Pillicoc Pegasus sired five champions including the silver Ch. Astron Silver Star (dam of three champions). An untitled Pegasus son, Southland Swagger, produced Ch. Sultan de San Souci (sire of seven champions). In England, Rettat's Spinner sired the blue Berkham Hansel of Rettats, who in turn sired the silver Mist of Piperscroft. Mist sired three champions including Eng. Ch. Frenches Blue Peter. Blue Peter impressed me very much when I saw him in England, for he was a sound, short-backed dog with a refined head and an immense, clear-colored blue coat. Blue Peter was one of England's greatest Standard sires with 14 English champions to his credit. Blue Peter was bred to White Lady of Burgois (dam of five champions) who was also a granddaughter of Berkham Hansel of Rettats, to produce Eng. and Am. Ch. Frenches Blue Marvel. Blue Marvel completed his English title undefeated in three consecutive shows. He was then imported by the Clarion Kennels. He made his American debut at the Poodle Club of America Specialty in 1952 where he went straight through to Best of Breed. Blue Marvel sired 12 champions including the Best in Show winning cream Ch. Algonquin of Champaign. Algonquin is the sire of Ch. Kickapoo of Champaign who has five titled get. Blue Marvel, whelped in 1949, was the last English Standard import to have any effect on the breed here.

A full brother of the great Duc, Piperscroft Pippo de la Terrace, went to England where he sired Ch. Scallawag of Piperscroft of Blakeen. Scallawag

269

Int. Ch. Nunsoe Duc de la Terrace
of Blakeen

Marechal of Piperscroft

imported to America was bred to the black Ch. Torchlight Dunkerque to produce the black Ch. Torchlight St. Pierre Eglise (sire of six champions).

The Ch. Prinz Alexander von Rodelheim line is without a doubt one of the greatest winning and producing strains in the history of dogdom. It also represents one of the closest bred families in the history of the breed. We have reduced the many complicated relationships to their simplest terms so that the sire line could be more easily followed. The only two Standard Poodles to ever win Best in Show at Westminster were members of this family, and Ch. Puttencove Promise is a linebred descendant of Ch. Nunsoe Duc de la Terrace of Blakeen with many crosses to Ch. Prinz Alexander von Rodelheim, the founder of the line.

Ch. Pillicoc Barrister

Ch. Blakeen Bali Ha'i

CH. PRINZ ALEXANDER VON RODELHEIM
   Int. Ch. Nunsoe Duc de la Terrace of Blakeen (wh) 9
      Marechal of Piperscroft (wh) 1
         Ch. Rettat's Slick (wh) 3
            Ch. Pillicoc Pegasus (wh) 5
               Southland Swagger (wh) 1
                  Ch. Sultan de San Souci (wh) 13
         Rettat's Spinner (wh)
            Berkham Hansel of Rettats (blu)
               Mist of Piperscroft (blu)
                  Eng. Ch. Frenches Blue Peter (blu) 14
                     Eng. & Am. Ch. Frenches Blue Marvel (blu) 12
                        Ch. Kickapoo of Champaign (crm) 5
                           Ch. Algonquin of Champaign (wh) 5
   Piperscroft Pippo de la Terrace (wh) 2
      Ch. Scallawag of Piperscroft of Blakeen (wh) 1
         Ch. Torchlight St. Pierre Eglise (blk) 6
His Excellency of Salmagundi (wh) 6
Ch. Salmagundi's Choice (wh) 2
   Ch. White Cocade of Salmagundi (wh) 11
      Ch. Cartlane Laurent (wh)
         Ch. Tour D'Argent Christopher (wh) 7
      Ch. Carillon Jester U.D. (blk) 1
         Petitcote Baron Chico C.D. (crm)
            Am. & Can. Ch. Petitcote Domino C.D. (blk) 9
               Wencair's Frere Jacques (blk) 6
   Ch. Lucite of Salmagundi (wh) 2
      Ch. Ensarr Glace (wh) 8
         Ch. Hillandale C'Est Vrais (wh) 11
      Pillicoc Courier (wh) 1
         Ch. Pillicoc Barrister (wh) 6
            Ch. Blakeen Bali H'ai (wh) 3
               Ch. Loabelo Jonny (wh) 2
                  Ch. Puttencove Promise (wh) 27
                     Ch. Alekai Nohea (wh) 6
                     Can. Ch. Calvados de la Fontaine (wh) 5
                     Ch. Ivardon Sheraton (wh)
                        Ivardon Kenilworth of Ensarr (wh) 2
                           Ch. Alekai Kila (wh) 6
            Ch. Blakeen Sorcerer's Apprentice (wh) 6
               Ch. Paloma's Bon Vivant (wh) 26
                  Ch. Forzando Bergamasque (wh) 5
                  Ch. Hallmark Harmony O'Windridge (wh) 6
               Windridge Savoir Vivre (wh) 14 pts.
                  Windridge Christopher (wh) 5

Eng. & Am. Ch. Frenches
Blue Marvel

Ch. White Cocade
of Salmagundi

50

Black and Brown
Standards

THE American Poodles popular at the end of the nineteenth century were undersized Standards of French origin. The French called them "Caniche," which still remains the French designation for the breed we call the Poodle. This term is presumed to have been derived from an early employment of the Poodle in the hunting of ducks and the retrieving of game from water, just as our current word Poodle, of German derivation, describes a "puddle dog." The nomenclature removes any doubts that Poodles were originally a sporting breed.

These Caniche were nondescript in type, too small for our present concepts of a Standard and much too big for a Miniature, thick and short in head, not too well made in the other parts of their anatomies, and deficient in length of coat. They were frequently barbered in an elaborate manner with the owner's monogram or even his coat of arms embossed on their flanks. Readily taught little clowns, they were instinctive exhibitionists, avid for applause, for which they would go to any length. They were especially responsive to children, as children were to Poodle antics.

But they have melted into the distance, these Caniche, gone the way of the Victorian era of which they were a part, beloved little ghosts in the nostalgia of those of us to whose childhood they afforded so much of amusement and affection. None of their blood appears to have come down the years to flow in the veins of our winning Standard Poodles of the present day. Perhaps it does in fact. Perhaps we hesitate to trace modern pedigrees back to these early Caniche lest we might find them, commoners among the progenitors of a race that we consider to be aristocratic.

With the renaissance of the popularity of the Poodle in America in the early 1930's or thereabouts came a revision of the concept of Poodle type and structure. Along with increase of stature in the Standard Poodle, we came to demand more gorgeous and spectacular coats, longer and leaner heads, longer and better set ears, better structured shoulders and hindquarters, shorter bodies, adequate feet, and refinements all around. Other breeds had bettered through the years; and without some overhauling of our Poodle ideals, a renewal of public interest in the long abandoned variety could never have been brought about.

Carillon Epreuve, UDT, first dog of any breed to gain all obedience degrees, owned by Carillon Kennels, trained and handled by Blanche Saunders.

Int. Ch. Anderl von Hugelberg

Eric Labory of Misty Isles

Continental Int. Ch. Mousse Labory

51

The "Anderl" Line
Ch. Anderl von Hugelberg

THE breeders of black and brown Standard Poodles, like the breeders of white Standards, owe a great debt of gratitude to the Labory Kennels of Mme. Lucienne Reichenbach in Switzerland. Not only was she responsible for recognizing and establishing the great Ch. Prinz Alexander von Rodelheim line in white Standards, but she was also responsible for popularizing and spreading the influence of the most successful colored line in Standard Poodles, that of Int. Ch. Anderl von Hugelberg. Continental championships are not easily attained, so the individuals holding them have to be of outstanding merit. Mme. Reichenbach deserves credit not only for her uncanny ability to recognize the best individual specimens and lines, but also for knowing what to do with them once she found them. There is no doubt that she is one of the greatest breeders of all time. She often resorted to very close breedings, and although she undoubtedly had disappointments, she also had great successes.

The Int. Ch. Anderl von Hugelberg line was purely Germanic in origin and strongly black-bred. Anderl's great influence in England and America comes to us through his Labory descendants. Anderl was bred to Bella v Zwisse to produce the great producing bitch Swiss and French Ch. Mira Labory (dam of five champions). Mira was bred back to her sire, Anderl, to produce European Ch. Nunsoe Chevalier Labory who went to the Nunsoe Kennel. In England, Chevalier sired Eng. Ch. Nunsoe Brown Bess.

Anderl was also bred to Cont. Int. Ch. Lidia von Feuerbachtal to produce three important brothers: Eric Labory of Misty Isles, Mousse Labory and Petit.Poucet Labory. On a trip to Switzerland Mrs. Byron Rogers selected

Eric Labory as a mate for her Anita von Lutterspring. Eric was a rather large dog compared with his English contemporaries but he gave the impression of great refinement and grace. He was a dense black. Eric was one of the most influential of the early day sires and produced 12 champions. His son, Ch. Auccassin of Pommel Rock, produced Ch. Cartlane Causeur. Causeur is the sire of the black Cartlane Alcindor (sire of five champions). Doubling up on Anderl, Mousse was bred to his half-sister Ch. Mira Labory to produce Ilka Mignonne Labory (dam of three champions), Gamine du Rond Point of Misty Isles (dam of three champions) and the foundation bitch of Carillon—Ch. Pierette Labory of Carillon, who heads the largest black Standard bitch family in this country.

Mousse's full brother, Petit Poucet Labory, was also bred to Mira Labory and this produced Eng. Ch. Amour Labory of Piperscroft, Ensarr Kennels' Ch. Manon Labory of Blakeen (dam of three champions), and the famous gray Ch. Griseley Labory of Piperscroft C. D. Amour's daughter, Dream of Piperscroft of Pillicoc, came to America, where she produced four champions. Griseley was a handsome, well-balanced Poodle. He first went to the Piperscroft Kennel in England, and then to the Blakeen Kennels in America. Griseley was a great influence on the breed. In England, Griseley had sired the black Ch. Kaffir of Piperscroft who was imported by the Carillon Kennels. Kaffir in turn sired Ch. Puttencove Impetuous, who sired 11 champions including Ch. Torchlight Piperheidsieck and the great Ch. Carillon Colin of Puttencove. Piperheidsieck's son Ch. Torchlight Jackanapes produced Bel Tor Salad Days, sire of 19 champions.

Mrs. George Putnam wrote of Ch. Carillon Colin of Puttencove: "Every so often a Poodle grows up that seems to embody qualities a serious breeder is striving to produce. To many, Colin had the elegance coupled with strength they had been searching for, as well as faultless disposition, beautiful clean-cut head and sound body, and that very masculine something so desirable in a sire. Colin won six Bests in Show, and sired 21 champions, and left a permanent influence on the breed." Colin sired Ch. Puttencove Halla's Hugo (sire of six champions), who in turn sired the Best in Show winner, Ch. Rimskittle Black Pirate (sire of eight champions). Colin also sired the white Fanfaron Impressario, who was the sire of five champions.

Without a doubt, Colin's most important son was the black Best in Show winner, Ch. Annsown Sir Gay. Sir Gay sired the impressive total of 22 champions, but more importantly his sons and grandsons have become the single most important influence for winning and producing in black Standards today. Sir Gay sired four great producing sons: Ch. Carillon Dilemma U.D. (sire of 32 champions), Ch. Bel Tor Gigadibs (sire of 28 champions), Ch. Bel Tor Morceau Choisi (sire of 18 champions) and Ch. Annsown Gay Knight of Arhill (sire of 12 champions). Ch. Bel Tor Gigadibs and Ch. Bel Tor Morceau Choisi have been great producers at Bel Tor Kennels. Morceau

Ch. Carillon Dilemma, U.D.

Choisi's son, Ch. Bel Tor McCreery, was the sire of 32 champions including Ch. Bel Tor St Ay Better Mousetrap, who was the sire of 19 champions. Gay Knight was bred to Am. and Can. Ch. Wycliffe Jacqueline to produce the brothers Am. and Can. Ch. Wycliffe Thomas and Am. and Can. Ch. Wycliffe Timothy. Thomas, winner of nine Bests in Show, is the leading sire in the variety with 50 champions to his credit and his get are still being shown. Thomas is recognized as a truly great sire and his get have been winners and producers from coast to coast. Thomas' brother, Timothy, bred back to his dam Ch. Wycliffe Jacqueline, produced Ch. Wycliffe Virgil, who is located in the Mid-West. Virgil has been a prepotent stud and has sired 24 champions. Virgil is the sire of Eng., Amer. and Can. Ch. Bibelot's Tall Dark and Handsome. Tall Dark and Handsome went through the six-months quarantine in England and came out to create a sensation in the English show ring, where he won 13 Bests in Show, Reserve Best in Show all-breeds at Crufts 1967, and was England's Dog of the Year for 1966. He then returned to his home in Canada to continue his winning and producing career. He is the sire of 10 champions to date.

277

Ch. Kaffir of Piperscroft

Ch. Griseley Labory of Piperscroft

Ch. Puttencove Impetuous

Ch. Wycliffe Timothy

Ch. Wycliffe Dudley

Ch. Bel Tor Chance Of A Lifetime

INT. CH. ANDERL VON HUGELBERG
    Petit Poucet Labory (blk)
        Ch. Griseley Labory of Piperscroft (gr) 12
            Ch. Pillicoc Aplomb (blk) 4
            Ch. Kaffir of Piperscroft (blk) 4
                Ch. Puttencove Impetuous (blk) 11
                    Ch. Carillon Colin of Puttencove (blk) 21
                        Ch. Annsown Sir Gay (blk) 22
                            Ch. Annsown Gay Knight of Arhill (blk) 12
                                Ch. Wycliffe Thomas (blk) 50
                                    Ch. Black Rogue of Belle Glen (blk) 5
                                    Ch. Prince Philip of Belle Glen (blk) 5
                                    Ch. Wycliffe Leroy (blk) 5
                                    Ch. Wycliffe Ian (blk) 9
                                    Ch. Wycliffe Kenneth (blk) 9
                                    Ch. Jacques Le Noir of Belle Glen (blk) 7
                                Ch. Wycliffe Timothy (blk) 12
                                    Ch. Wycliffe Virgil (blk) 24
                                        Int. Ch. Bibelot's Tall Dark and Handsome (blk) 10
                                    Ch. Wycliffe Dudley (blk) 5
                            Ch. Bel Tor Gigadibs (blk) 28
                            Ch. Bel Tor Morceau Choisi (blk) 18
                                Ch. Bel Tor McCreery (brn) 32
                                    Ch. Bel Tor Vintage Wine (brn) 5
                                    Ch. Bel Tor St. Ay Better Mousetrap (brn) 19
                                        Ch. Bel Tor Chance of a Lifetime (brn) 5
                            Ch. Carillon Dilemma U.D. (blk) 32
                        Ch. Puttencove Halla's Hugo (blk) 6
                        Ch. Rimskittle Black Pirate (blk) 8
                    Fanfaron Impressario (wh) 5
                Ch. Torchlight Piperheidsieck (apr) 1
                    Ch. Torchlight Jackanapes (blk)
                    Bel Tor Salad Days (blk) 19
    Eric Labory of Misty Isles (blk) 12
        Ch. Aucassin of Pommel Rock (blk)
            Ch. Cartlane Causeur (brn) 2
                Cartlane Alcindor (blk) 5

Ch. Rimskittle Black Pirate

Eng. Ch. Whippendell Carillon

Ch. Whippendell Poli of Carillon, black English import, first Poodle to win Group at Westminster (1933).

52

The "Whippendell
Carillon" Line
Eng. Ch. Whippendell Carillon

THE black Eng. Ch. Whippendell Carillon was the cream of
Miss Millie Brunker's breeding, and a top dog in England, both as a winner
and as a sire. He was described as a magnificent dog with lovely deportment
and carriage, a most elegant and graceful Poodle who stood out in the show
ring whenever he appeared. The Whippendell Standards were never more
than from medium to small in size, and were of extreme elegance and refinement of type. Whippendell Carillon's grandsire was Chieveley Grumps from
the black Miniature line. The best of the Labory dogs were much larger but
lost nothing in refinement, for it must not be thought that they were clumsy,
big-footed, heavy-headed, heavy-boned dogs that very large Standards can
sometimes be today. The Labory bitches were naturally smaller than the dogs
and the combination of the two diverse lines seems to have been ideal.

On a trip to England in 1931, Mrs. Byron Rogers of the Misty Isles Poodles
had seen and admired two sons of Eng. Ch. Whippendell Carillon, Ch.
Nymphaea Jason and Ch. Whippendell Poli of Carillon, and recommended
their purchase to Mrs. Whitehouse Walker of Carillon Kennels. Both dogs
became American champions and influential sires. I remember Ch. Nymphaea Jason as a very impressive, compact Poodle with a refined head and
an immense, sound colored brown coat. At Carillon, Jason sired seven
champions—five of these were out of Carillon Pivoine (by Ch. Whippendell
Poli of Carillon ex Ch. Pierette Labory of Carillon). One of these brown

sons, Ch. Carillon Joyeux, sired the brown Ch. Puttencove Peachstone. Peachstone in turn sired Ch. Puttencove Vim U.D., who sired four champions including Ch. Lowmont d'Artagnon (sire of nine champions). A full brother of Ch. Carillon Joyeux, Carillon Reveur, sired Ch. Carillon Rene. At Puttencove, Rene sired four champions including Ch. Puttencove Grenadier and Ch. Puttencove Reveille. Grenadier produced three sons that extended the sire line: Ch. Puttencove Midshipman, Ch. Puttencove Gauntlet and Ch. Puttencove Indian. Midshipman sired 11 champions including Ch. Puttencove Minuteman (sire of 11 champions). Gauntlet sired the brown Caledonia Grizzly Bear, who in turn sired Ch. Hornpipe Congo (sire of five champions). Ch. Puttencove Indian sired Ch. Perrevan Prince Phillip who in turn produced the black Ch. Tory Hollow Coriander (sire of six champions). Now to return to Ch. Puttencove Reveille who sired Ch. Chloe Tonnerre (sire of four champions). Tonnerre sired Rimskittle Furbelow who sired Ch. Rimskittle Rear Guard (sire of five champions). Ch. Nymphaea Jason also sired two important daughters, Ch. Carillon Celeste (dam of Ch. Carillon Colline) and Blakeen Vigee le Brun (dam of the famous Ch. Blakeen Cyrano).

Ch. Whippendell Carillon's black son Ch. Whippendell Poli of Carillon made breed history by winning the Non-Sporting Group at Westminster in 1931. Poli sired three champions including Ch. Carillon Corbeau (sire of five champions). An English son of Poli, Polichinelle, produced Berkham Eustace, who in turn sired Ch. Piperscroft Berkham Wilfred. Wilfred sired Sunstorm's Snuff who was presented to the Lowmont Kennels. Snuff sired five champions including the Best in Show winner Ch. Robin Hood (sire of five champions).

The third important son of Ch. Whippendell Carillon for us to consider was the English dog Tricotine. His sons, the full brothers Stillington Claus O'Carillon and Stillington Christmas O'Carillon, were imported by the Carillon Kennels. Claus finished his championship here and sired Ch. Carillon Courage C.D.X. I remember Courage very well because he appealed to me so much. He was rather a small dog compared with the German-bred dogs of his day—or perhaps his extreme refinement of type only made him seem so. He had an exaggeratedly narrow skull and long foreface, with dark oval eyes, and a perfect Poodle expression. He was short in back and carried an abundance of inky black coat. He was one of the first Poodles trained for obedience at Carillon, and the day I visited there he was being put through his paces. Perhaps the one best descriptive word for him was "exquisite." Courage was the sire of five champions. Stillington Christmas O'Carillon sired two important sons Ch. Cadeau de Noel C.D.X. and Far Away Moor. Cadeau was Mrs. Erlanger's first Standard, a Christmas present, hence his name. He was a rather small, compact, light brown dog, and as I remember him, rather on the dainty side. He had a brilliant brain and was one of the great obedience stars of his day. He was the first dog to win the C.D.X. title in this country. I remember his showing off by balancing on command—all four feet on a small overturned bowl about eight inches in diameter, the way circus animals balance.

His great son, the star of the kennel, Ch. Pillicoc Rumpelstilskin C.D., was as unlike his sire as it was possible to be. Rumpelstilskin was from a beautiful mother, Ch. Giroflee of Misty Isles (a daughter of Eric Labory of Misty Isles). He was up to size, an extremely well-balanced dog of the massive type and most impressive. Perhaps the most extraordinary thing about him was his immense jet-black coat, which I have never seen equaled—before or since. It was Henry Stoecker's pride, and Rumpelstilskin's sleeping quarters and yard were carefully padded least a single hair of his magnificent jacket be split or broken. Rumpelstilskin had a great show career with six Bests in Show to his credit. He sired 11 champions including the black bitch Ch. Torchlight Ruffled Sealskin (dam of three champions). Rumpelstilskin's untitled sons, Pillicoc Rigolo and Bojangles of Hollybourne, were champion producers. Rigolo sired three champions, and Bojangles sired two champions in addition to Pillicoc Black Knight, who sired four champions. Rumpelstilskin's granddaughter, Pillicoc Alabaster, is the dam of the well-known whites, Ch. Pillicoc Pegasus and Ch. Pillicoc Pearl, who each head important families of their own. Ch. Cadeau de Noel also sired the black Far Away Moor. Moor's son, Danny, sired the black Poli Krat Bizet. Bizet sired the influential West Coast sire Ch. Claudel Rene (sire of eight champions). Rene was the sire of two top producing sons, Ch. Claudel Capitaine (sire of five champions) and the Best in Show winner Ch. Bon Mar Baron Rouge (sire of seven champions).

Ch. Pillicoc Rumpelstilskin, C.D.   Ch. Nymphaea Jason

Ch. Puttencove Grenadier

Ch. Carillon Corbeau, a splendid example of a Poodle in the Continental clip, owned by Ensarr Kennels.

Ch. Puttencove Reveille (black Standard) by Ch. Carillon Rene ex Puttencove Candida, breed-owner, Puttencove Kennels.

```
ENG. CH. WHIPPENDELL CARILLON
   Ch. Nymphaea Jason (brn) 7
      Ch. Carillon Joyeux (brn) 2
         Ch. Puttencove Peachstone (brn)
            Ch. Puttencove Vim U.D. (brn) 4
               Ch. Lowmont d'Artagnon (brn) 9
      Carillon Reveur (blk)
         Ch. Carillon Rene (blk) 4
            Ch. Puttencove Grenadier (blk) 4
               Ch. Puttencove Midshipman (blk) 11
                  Ch. Puttencove Minuteman (blk) 11
                  Avron's Salute (blk)
                     Avron's Toby (blk) 4
                        Ch. Jolipal Fabulous Fellow (blk) 2
                           Ch. Alekai Conquistador (blk) 8
               Ch. Puttencove Gauntlet (brn)
                  Caledonia Grizzly Bear (brn)
                     Ch. Hornpipe Congo (brn) 5
               Ch. Puttencove Indian (brn)
                     Ch. Perrevan Prince Phillip (blk)
                        Ch. Tory Hollow Coriander (blk) 6
            Ch. Puttencove Reveille (blk) 1
               Ch. Chloe Tonnerre (blk) 4
                  Rimskittle Furbelow (blk)
                     Ch. Rimskittle Rear Guard (blk) 5
   Ch. Whippendell Poli of Carillon (blk) 3
      Ch. Carillon Corbeau (blk) 5
      Polichinelle (blk)
         Berkham Eustace (brn)
            Ch. Piperscroft Berkham Wilfred (brn)
               Sunstorm's Snuff (brn) 5
                  Ch. Robin Hood (brn) 6
   Tricotine (blk)
      Ch. Stillington Claus O'Carillon (blk)
         Ch. Carillon Courage C.D.X. (blk) 5
      Stillington Christmas O'Carillon (brn)
         Ch. Cadeau de Noel C.D.X. (brn) 3
            Ch. Pillicoc Rumpelstilskin C.D. (blk) 11
               Pillicoc Rigolo (blk) 3
               Bojangles of Hollybourne (blk) 2
                  Pillicoc Black Knight (blk) 4
            Far Away Moor (blk)
               Danny (blk)
                  Poli Krat Bizet (blk) 2
                     Ch. Claudel Rene (brn) 8
                        Ch. Bon-Mar Baron Rouge (brn) 7
                        Ch. Claudel Capitaine (brn) 5
```

CH. BLAKEEN CYRANO

Whelped July 28, 1934   Deceased

Bred by Blakeen Kennels
Owned by Lowmont Kennels

```
                          Windsfield Joyful Joe (brn)
                 Nunsoe Aurelius (brn)
                          Nunsoe Hazel (brn)
        Ch. Nunsoe David Darling of Blakeen (brn)
                          Eng. Ch. Tom (blk)
                 Nunsoe Mary Ann (brn)
                          Nunsoe Hazel (brn)

CH. BLAKEEN CYRANO (brn)

                          Eng. Ch. Whippendell Carillon (blk)
                 Ch. Nymphaea Jason (brn)
                          Eng. Ch. Nymphaea Juliette (brn)
        Blakeen Vigee le Brun (brn)
                          Maupassant (blk)
                 Sophie (blk)
                          Madam Bella (blk)
```

286

53

The "Blakeen Cyrano" Line
Ch. Blakeen Cyrano

THE magnificent brown, Ch. Blakeen Cyrano, was the only one of the establishing dogs of the four great Standard sire lines that was an American-bred. Cyrano, or "Cy" as he was called, did more to make browns popular than any other Poodle before or since. Many authorities still consider him to be the best brown Standard ever seen and feel that he could still win today. He was the first brown Poodle to win a Best in Show. He was widely shown, and scored 106 Bests of Variety, 46 Group firsts, and six Bests in Show.

Cyrano was whelped in 1934, and in 1940 went to head the Lowmont Kennels. Never was a dog more loved or appreciated. Lowmont based their entire breeding operation on Cyrano with great success. Cyrano was a prepotent sire. His record of 10 champion get is only a small indication of his tremendous influence. His daughters and granddaughters were outstanding producers. One of these, Puttencove Candida, produced five champions and heads a large and important family at Puttencove. Through Candida's grandson, Ch. Carillon Colin of Puttencove, Cyrano's influence comes down through the Bel Tor, Carillon and Wycliffe Standards of today. Mrs. Mason's Bel Tor Kennels is rich in Cyrano breeding and offers the strongest concentration of this line currently available. Her Ch. Bel Tor McCreery (named in honor of Miss McCreery) was closely linebred to Cyrano, and bore a strong resemblance to him.

An untitled son of Cyrano, Broadrun Brownie, produced Blakeen Popover. Popover was the sire of the black Ch. Carillon Jongleur (sire of seven champions). Jongleur was the sire of the Best in Show winner Ch. Prankster Darius who was the sire of 14 champions.

CH. BLAKEEN CYRANO

Sire of 10 champions: Out of:

Ch. Lowmont Lord Jeremy   Barbet Josephine of Lowmont
Ch. Lowmont Lord Johanus

Ch. Verdant Vida   Mistress Grundy
Ch. Verdant Bon Vivant

Ch. Blakeen Mary Poppins
Eng., Swiss, French, German   Ch. Blakeen Mary Mont
  & Ital. Ch. Blakeen Agnes

Ch. Lord Cy of Lowmont   Laineux Noelle
Ch. Lowmont Lady Joan   Ch. Blakeen Ebony
Ch. Lowmont Lady Luck   Lowmont Lady Patricia
Ch. Wagonwheel Wicked Queen   Ch. Blakeen Routy-Two

            CH. BLAKEEN CYRANO (brn)
                Broadrun Brownie (brn)
                    Broadrun Popover
                        Ch. Carillon Jongleur (blk) 11
                            Ch. Prankster Darius (blk) 14

Ch. Prankster Darius, black Standard, by Ch. Carillon Jongleur ex Ch. Puttencove Sugar Plum. Best in Show winner, and sire of 14 champions. Bred and
owned by Prankster Kennels.

Ch. Kah's Kollector's Item (by Ch. Annsown Gay Knight of Arhill ex Ch. Puttencove Black Stella), dam of 10 champions at Monfret Kennels. Owned by Francis P. Fretwell, Monfret Kennels.

Am. & Can. Ch. Lady Joan of Lowmont (by Ch. Annsown Gay Knight of Arhill ex Lowmont Lady Clarissa), shown finishing her championship at the 1961 Poodle Club of America Specialty, handled by Howard Tyler. Last champion from Lowmont Kennel. Dam of 11 champions. Owned by Susan Radley Fraser, Bibelot Kennels.

54

Leading Standard Dams

O F the three varieties, the Standard Poodle has by far the largest number of bitches that qualify as Top Producers (dams of three or more champions each).

Standard bitches are noted for the large number of puppies per litter, and litters of ten or more are not uncommon. Breeders can thus select the best from a large number of puppies within each litter.

The responsibility that a breeder faces in bringing a big litter of large puppies into the world has itself been an important factor in improving the variety over the last ten years. Standard puppies grow rapidly, and need lots of room and attention. There has been less demand for Standards than Toys or Miniatures, so they have not been harmed by the commercialism present in the other varieties. As a result, breeders breed their very best bitches, and breed them to the best possible studs.

The Standard has been established as a variety for a long period of time. There has been less mixing of colors than in Miniatures and Toys, and thus less problem with mismarks.

This insistence on rigid selection, practiced over a few generations, has worked considerably to the betterment of the variety. A list of 149 Top Producing Standard bitches reveals that 96, or almost two-thirds, are themselves champions.

The leading Standard dam is the black Best in Show winner, Am. & Can. Ch. Wycliffe Jacqueline, U.D., with 21 champions. Among these are seven Top Producers, including the leading Standard sire, Am. & Can. Ch. Wycliffe Thomas (50 champions).

In runner-up position are the half-sisters by Ch. Annsown Gay Knight of Arhill, Am. & Can. Ch. Lady Joan of Lowmont (dam of 11 champions) and Ch. Kah's Kollector's Item (dam of 10 champions).

The two leading white Standard bitches are Ch. Princess du Labory of Salmagundi and German Ch. Nelly v.d. Schneeflocke of Blakeen, each with eight champions.

Ch. Rimskittle Rampant (by Ch. Prince Philip of Belle Glen ex Rimskittle Congratulation), black Standard female, Best in Show winner. Bred and owned by Mr. and Mrs. James E. Clark, handled by Mrs. Clark.

Eng. & Am. Ch. Martindell Alekai Kalania (by Ch. Alekai Kila ex Ch. Tambourine de la Fontaine), white Standard. Winner of eight Challenge Certificates in England. Owned by Miss Helen Martin, England.

Mrs. George Putnam with a promising young Puttencove.

55

Puttencove Kennels

THE Puttencove Kennels of Mrs. George Putnam is one of the most honored in America. I know of few strains that have so consistently passed on not only show type, but also great producing ability, from father to son and mother to daughter, generation after generation.

The Standards started at Puttencove with a brown bitch puppy, Blakeen Solange, by Ch. Harpendale Monty of Blakeen x Nunsoe Alter Idem of Blakeen. When the time came, Solange was bred to the great Ch. Blakeen Cyrano, and on May 15, 1936 produced Puttencove Candida—Mrs. Putnam's beloved "Candy." Candida was a lovely-headed, short-bodied, charming bitch and only a slight scar denied her a show career. She was the dam of five champion sons and founded the Puttencove Standards. Candida was bred twice to Ch. Carillon Joyeux producing Ch. Puttencove Peachstone, Ch. Puttencove Blaise and Puttencove Jemima. Candida was also bred to Ch. Carillon Rene to produce the Best in Show winner, Ch. Puttencove Reveille. From Candida's breeding to Ch. Kaffir of Piperscroft came Can. Ch. Puttencove Ivan, and the Best in Show winner, Ch. Puttencove Impetuous. Impetuous was the sire of 11 champions including the famous Ch. Carillon Colin of Puttencove.

Colin, as a handsome black seven-weeks-old puppy by Impetuous out of Ch. Carillon Colline, was offered to Mrs. Putnam by Blanche Saunders, the famous obedience expert and owner of Carillon Kennels. Miss Saunders was well aware of the puppy's quality, but she was busy with war work and knew that Mrs. Putnam would give him the opportunity he deserved. This was one puppy that lived up to every expectation and then some. In limited showing, Colin won five Bests in Show, but his lasting importance is based on his great siring ability. Colin marked a turning point in the black Standard variety. His influence was so great that the majority of black Standards in the ring today are direct descendants. Colin was an impressive dog with great intelligence. He sired a total of 21 champions including Ch. Puttencove Halla's Hugo (sire of six champions), Ch. Puttencove Serenade (dam of six champions) and Ch. Annsown Sir Gay (sire of 22 champions). Halla's Hugo sired Ch. Puttencove Sugar Plum who produced five Prankster champions. An untitled Colin son, Fanfaron Impressario, was the sire of five champions. Sir Gay was a Best in Show winner, and he sired a number of noted producing sons.

The black Ch. Carillon Rene (by Carillon Reveur ex Carillon Francoise), who had been purchased as a six months old puppy, was the head of an important sire line at Puttencove. Rene was the sire of four champions. Bred to Candida he produced Ch. Puttencove Reveille. Rene bred to Puttencove Jemima (ex Candida) gave Ch. Puttencove Grenadier. Grenadier sired four champions including Ch. Puttencove Midshipman (ex Puttencove Miss Impy who was by Ch. Puttencove Impetuous). Midshipman sired 11 champions including Ch. Puttencove Minuteman (x Puttencove Halla, also by Ch. Puttencove Impetuous). Minuteman was also the sire of 11 champions.

The black bitch Carillon Eve of Puttencove (full sister of Ch. Carillon Courage) was an important producer at Puttencove. Bred to the imported gray Ch. Griseley Labory of Piperscroft, she produced Puttencove Prudence and Puttencove Penelope. Prudence bred to Ch. Carillon Rene gave Ch. Puttencove Samantha (dam of three champions). Samantha bred to the great Colin gave the lovely Ch. Puttencove Serenade, who was the dam of six champions. Serenade's daughter, Ch. Puttencove Spring Song, was the dam of three champions at Monfret Kennels. Puttencove Penelope was bred to Ch. Puttencove Impetuous to produce the outstanding producer Puttencove Halla (dam of seven champions). Halla bred to Ch. Puttencove Midshipman produced Ch. Puttencove Minuteman (sire of 11 champions). Halla bred to Colin gave Ch. Puttencove Halla's Hugo (sire of seven champions).

On a judging trip to California in 1952, Mrs. Putnam purchased a white bitch puppy, Astron Lily of Puttencove (by Ch. Pillicoc Barrister ex Ch. Astron Silver Star). Lily was bred to Ch. Loabelo Jonny (grandson of Barrister) to produce the handsome white Ch. Puttencove Promise. Promise had a truly exciting career in the ring and his quality quickly carried him to the top. Promise was Best of Breed at the Poodle Club of America Specialty in 1957. He was Best in Show at Westminster in 1958. Promise was an equally great sire with 27 champions to his credit including Ch. Alekai Nohea (sire of six champions), Can. Ch. Calvados de la Fontaine (sire of five champions), Ch. Puttencove Kaui (dam of three Alekai champions) and Ch. Tambarine de la Fontaine (dam of three Alekai champions). Promise's son, Ch. Puttencove

Moonshine, was Best of Breed at the parent specialty in 1958 and 1959, and is the sire of four champions.

There has never been the necessity for commercial consideration at Puttencove. Mrs. Putnam has aimed to produce beautiful Poodles of sound temperament, generation after generation, for the joy of it. Mrs. Putnam is a past president of the Poodle Club of America, and an honored judge in the show ring. There have been more than 60 Standard champions bearing the Puttencove prefix.

Puttencove Candida

Ch. Puttencove Minute Man

Ch. Puttencove Serenade

Ch. Lowmont Madame d'Aiquillon, one of a famous litter from Ch. Sunstorm's Harvest by Ch. Puttencove Vim, CD, CDX, UD.

56

Lowmont Kennels

THE very young black puppy that afterwards became Ch. Blakeen Ebony was Miss McCreery's first Standard Poodle. As Ebony matured she turned on all her charm, as Poodle puppies can do, and won her owner's heart completely. Her breeder, Mrs. Hoyt, advised Miss McCreery to show her and she gained her title before she was fifteen months old. Ebony's first family, by Blakeen Hercule Poirot (Miss McCreery's sister's pet), contained Ch. Lowmont Lady Mary; and her second, by Ch. Blakeen Cyrano, produced Ch. Lowmont Lady Joan and Ch. Lowmont Lord Alexander. Ebony was by Ch. Griseley Labory of Piperscroft and Blakeen. The second foundation bitch was the gray Blakeen Jeanette by Ch. Ashridge Clair of Blakeen, Griseley's son. Barbet Josephine was also by Griseley, and Miss McCreery, after seeing the results of breeding these bitches to Ch. Blakeen Cyrano, decided that he was the ideal mate for them, and that the combination of the great Griseley Labory line with that of Cyrano was again ideal. There was nothing haphazard about this decision. It was the result of careful experiment and thought.

Cyrano, whom I saw at Blakeen as a young dog, still remains in my mind as my beau ideal of a Standard Poodle. To me, he had everything—a most exquisite, long lean head, with particularly dark oval eyes and that beautiful, soft Poodle expression. He was very compact and soundly put together, had perfect feet and legs, and his hindquarters were faultless. His personality was overwhelming and I fell in love with him on sight! He moved with light-footed grace and carried a heavy coat of light clear brown. Of all the lovely Poodles I saw at Blakeen (and there were a great many), Cyrano was the one I would have liked to own. But, of course, I had no realization of how great a dog he was. Nevertheless, I was astonished when Mrs. Hoyt told me she was going to let Miss McCreery have him, and added, "He is going to a great love and understanding," which is the greatest price of all to those of us that love our dogs—a loving home. Cyrano (brown) was one of the two outstanding brothers by the imported Ch. Nunsoe Darling David (brown) x Blakeen Vigee Le Brun. Ch. Blakeen Durante, after gaining his American championship, went to England to continue his winning career there. Cyrano was shown as a youngster in 1936–1937 but came into full maturity in 1938 when he had a brilliant show career before he went to Lowmont to reign supreme for so many years.

After the advent of Cyrano at Lowmont, it became the story of one great dog and his skillful handling by an intelligent breeder. As he proved to be a dog that could be successfully line-bred, he was woven in and out of the Lowmont strain. There have been practically no Lowmont champions that have not had behind them at least one, and usually two or three, crosses to Cyrano. And this proven method was used successfully by outside breeders as well.

Cyrano was a prepotent sire. He sired 10 champions, but this was only a start in a great breeding record. Cyrano's daughters and granddaughters were excellent producers. Linebreeding to Cyrano was a formula for excellent results. Cyrano's son, Ch. Lowmont Lord Jeremy, was the sire of Annabella of Lowmont who produced three champions at Lottal Kennels. Annabella bred to Cyrano's son, Ch. Verdant Bon Vivant, gave Ch. Amber of Lottal and Ch. Vicki of Lottal—each the dam of three champions. Cyrano bred to Laineux Noel produced Ch. Lord Cy of Lowmont and Clementine of Lowmont. Clementine was the dam of four champions, all by Ch. Carillon Colin of Puttencove. Their son, Ch. Black Douglas of Lowmont, was the sire of three champions. Cyrano's daughter, Puttencove Candida, was a great producer with five champions and headed a large and important family at Puttencove.

In 1947 Mr. George Frelinghuysen presented Lowmont with Ch. Sunstorm's Harvest and Sunstorm's Snuff who were out of Blakeen Carina, a Cyrano daughter, but by different sires. Snuff sired five champions including the brown Best in Show winner, Ch. Robin Hood (x Cartlane Marguerite, a Cyrano daughter).

Howard Tyler, Miss McCreery's handler and friend, considered the brown Ch. Sunstorm's Harvest one of the finest Poodles he had ever seen, but she did not care for the show ring. Harvest was bred to Ch. Puttencove Vim U.D., and had what Miss McCreery considers the best litter ever bred at Lowmont. It included Ch. Lowmont D'Artagnon (sire of nine champions), Ch. Lowmont Madame Cambalet (dam of four champions at Lottal), Ch. Lowmont

Ch. Sunstorm's Harvest (by Silver of Piperscroft of Sunstorm ex Blakeen Carina) owned by Lowmont Kennels & Mr. George Freylinghusen.

Madame de Chevreuse and Ch. Lowmont Madame d'Aiguillon. The blood-lines of Cyrano were further intensified with the breeding of Ch. Lowmont Madame d'Aiguillon to Ch. Robin Hood. This breeding produced four champions Ch. Lowmont Lady Cadette (dam of seven champions at Bel Tor), Ch. Lowmont Lady Fabiola (dam of three champions at Sterg-O), Ch. Lowmont Lady Candida and Ch. Lowmont Comte de Rochefort. Cyrano's daughter, Lowmont Happy Lady, was bred to Sunstorm's Snuff to produce Ch. Lowmont Lady Dorothy. Lady Dorothy bred to d'Artagnon produced three champions including Ch. Lowmont Monsieur Hercule Poirot. Hercule Poirot sired Ch. Bel Tor Hosanna who was the dam of nine champions.

Ch. Blakeen Cyrano's double grandson, Blakeen Popover, sired Ch. Carillon Jongleur, who sired 11 champions.

The last champion to finish under the Lowmont banner was Am. and Can. Ch. Lady Joan of Lowmont, who was by Ch. Annsown Gay Knight of Arhill x Lowmont Lady Clarissa. Lady Joan was whelped July 13, 1958. Lady Joan finished her title at the Poodle Club of America Specialty in 1961. Miss McCreery presented Lady Joan to Susan Radley Fraser in Canada where she became the dam of 11 champions including the great winner Eng. Am. and Can. Ch. Bibelot's Tall Dark and Handsome.

Miss McCreery loved her Poodles and there was but one consideration in her planning for them—the production of beautiful Standards. This she did with great skill, with results beyond anyone's most hopeful dreams. She was without question one of our greatest breeders.

Ch. Bel Tor Morceau Choisi, with
breeder-owner Mrs. J. A. Mason.

Ch. Bel Tor Gigadibs

Ch. Bel Tor Hosanna

57

Bel Tor Kennels

MRS. Mason once told me that the kennels, like Topsy, just grew and that it was hard to tell when the dogs stopped being just beloved pets and became a kennel. When it became a question of the three Masons moving out of their house to make room for the dogs, the first kennel building was erected.

The name Bel Tor was made up of the first few letters of the names of Mrs. Mason, her daughter and her son: Rebecca, Belinda and Tobias. It was originally *Beltore* but was afterwards divided and the last letter dropped and became as it is now—Bel Tor—and was registered in 1951.

The first litter of Bel Tor Poodles was whelped in March 1943 from Lowmont Lady Juliette, a daughter of Ch. Blakeen Cyrano, and sired by Sunstorm's Merry Messenger (Marechal of Piperscroft x Eng. Ch. Marlene of Piperscroft). A brown dog, Drambuie, who closely resembled his maternal grandsire, Ch. Blakeen Cyrano, was retained from this litter and later bred to a black bitch, Dubonnette (Ch. Intrepid of Misty Isles ex Antoinette), which Mrs. Mason had bought from Mrs. Olga Rogers. From this litter came Yvette Jeanne and Black Velvet. At that time Mrs. Mason had a prejudice against exhibiting her dogs and, unfortunately, none of these early dogs were shown.

In later years Mrs. Mason changed her mind about showing, and the kennel has vigorously campaigned both light and dark-colored Poodles. The policy of this kennel has been to retire its winners as soon as they have completed their championships, so few have been campaigned for specials. One reason for this is that there is always another good youngster ready to step in and follow in the footsteps of those that have gone before. Mrs. Mason has, I believe, done the Poodle fancy a very real service by showing her outstanding Standard Poodle puppies through to their titles as puppies and in puppy trim—a feat seldom, if ever, accomplished before. In my opinion, one of the chief drawbacks in our breed has been the fact that most of our judges have required immense coats for top winning and have automatically overlooked dogs not in show clip. I feel that Mrs. Mason, in breaking through this barrier, has done much for the breed. This matter of coat has been a positive obsession with a great many judges. The requirement of immense coats, often of incorrect texture, has made it impossible for even a sensational puppy to win, and Poodles must be held back, sometimes a year or more, in order to win, regardless of how good in type they may be. It has been a great disadvantage and discouragement to serious breeders who have suffered in this unjust placing of coat over type and soundness, which finds no justification in our printed standard. Providing a puppy is of champion quality and has a promising jacket of correct texture, he should never be penalized for lack of length of coat. Mrs. Mason's puppies have done us all great service in blazing the trail for type first—and it is to be hoped that other fine youngsters will follow in their footsteps.

The impressive records of Bel Tor Kennels are largely based on two litters whelped within a three month period. Mrs. Mason had acquired the brown bitch, Ch. Lowmont Lady Cadette (by Ch. Robin Hood ex Ch. Lowmont Madame d'Aiguillon) as a result of her admiration of the beautiful Madame d'Aiguillon and the black bitch, Ch. Bel Tor Hosanna, as a choice of litter puppy by her Ch. Lowmont Monsieur Hercule Poirot. Both of these bitches were line-bred to Ch. Blakeen Cyrano through the Lowmont breeding. After careful thought Mrs. Mason decided to breed both to the handsome Best in Show winner, Ch. Annsown Sir Gay. Lady Cadette's litter was whelped December 18, 1953 and contained five champions, all with the Bel Tor prefix: Morceau Choisi, M'Amie La Belle, Madrigal, Make Believe, and Main Chance. A repeat breeding later produced two more champions—Bel Tor Lothaire and Bel Tor Petite Madelon. Hosanna's litter was whelped on March 6, 1954 and also contained five champions, four with the Bel Tor prefix: Gigadibs, Gasconade, Gentle Julia, Black Sheep, and Ch. Annsown Gay Melodie. The success of these two litters attracted immediate attention to Sir Gay's ability as an outstanding sire.

From these two litters Mrs. Mason retained the two black stud dogs Ch. Bel Tor Gigadibs and Ch. Bel Tor Morceau Choisi, and by crossing them to each other's daughters and line-breeding in later generations, has produced a continuing succession of Bel Tor champions.

Ch. Bel Tor Gigadibs, who Mrs. Mason considered almost overdone in every respect, seemed to have that extra something to give to his get and sired 28 champions. A number of his daughters became top producers (dam of three or more champions). These include Ch. Bel Tor Oui Oui Mille Fois (four), Ch. Bel Tor Prenez Moi (four), Bel Tor Hussar Chant de Noel (seven), and Ch. Darkin Dubious (three).

Ch. Bel Tor Morceau Choisi sired a total of 18 champions, including Ch. Bel Tor McCreery (sire of 32) and Ch. Bel Tor Vintage Wine (sire of five). He also has four top producing daughters: Ch. Bel Tor Pink Cloud (four), Ch. Bel Tor Lady Mary (four), Ch. Bel Tor Brunehilde (nine), and Bel Tor Philippa (four).

Morceau Choisi's brown son, Ch. Bel Tor McCreery, who was considered to closely resemble Ch. Blakeen Cyrano, sired 32 champions, including Ch. Bel Tor St. Ay Better Mousetrap, a dark red brown, who sired 19 champions, including Ch. Bel Tor Chance Of A Lifetime (sire of five champions) and Ch. Bel Tor Sandalwood (dam of four champions).

Another noted stud at Bel Tor was the refined, stylish black, Bel Tor Salad Days. He was sired by Ch. Torchlight Jackanapes x Bel Tor Stolen Hour, who was a daughter of Gigadibs and granddaughter of Morceau Choisi. Salad Days was the sire of 19 champions.

Bel Tor has been fortunate in having a long list of excellent producing bitches. In addition to those already mentioned there are several mother-daughter combinations which deserve inclusion. Ch. Bel Tor Hosanna (dam of nine champions) was the dam of Ch. Bel Tor Head Of The Class (dam of four champions, three of which are Best in Show winners) by Ch. Bel Tor Guillaume de Machaut, a son of Morceau Choisi. Head of the Class produced the beautiful blue Best in Show winner, Ch. Bel Tor Come Hither, who is the dam of four champions. The brown bitch, Ch. Beltore Bright Star (three champions) was the dam in one litter of Ch. Bel Tor McCreery (32 champions) and Ch. Bel Tor Lady Mary (dam of four champions), both named in honor of Lowmont Kennel's owner, Mary McCreery. The black bitch, Ch. Bel Tor Beautiful Dreamer (seven champions), was the dam of Ch. Bel Tor Brunehilde (dam of nine champions) by Ch. Bel Tor Morceau Choisi, and Ch. Bel Tor Destined To Be (dam of three champions) by Bel Tor Gunsmoke.

Mrs. Mason has an incredible ability as a breeder. The five champion stud dogs—Gigadibs, Salad Days, Morceau Choisi, McCreery and Better Mousetrap—have produced a combined total of 116 champions. There have been more than 100 champions bearing the Bel Tor prefix—a remarkable record in the annals of dog breeding.

Lois Nurmi with her Best in Show winner, Ch. Paloma's Bon Vivant (by Ch. Blakeen Sorcerer's Apprentice ex Salmagundi's Caviar).

58

Forzando Kennels

Unlike the two great Eastern kennels of Puttencove and Lowmont, where numbers of dogs have been used to produce beautiful Standards for well over thirty years, this comparatively small West Coast kennel houses only a few adult Standards at a time.

With three children, the dogs she successfully shows for other people, and her own Standards, Mrs. Nurmi, owner of Forzando Kennels, leads a busy life. Nevertheless, she has succeeded in gathering together white Standards of the best bloodlines and has handled them with skill.

The two foundation dogs were wisely chosen and were purchased as puppies at about the same time, for Ch. Blakeen Sorcerer's Apprentice joined his noted sire, Ch. Pillicoc Barrister, on the Pacific Coast at an early age and was to prove himself not only a big winner but a most successful sire. (The dam of Sorcerer's Apprentice was the imported Vulcan Champagne Carmen of Blakeen.) Sorcerer's Apprentice finished his championship with some ease and with comparatively little opportunity, sired five champions.

Mrs. Nurmi acquired another puppy who became Ch. Nurmi's Pizzicato Polka, a bitch whose breeding is interesting. Her dam was Ch. Blakeen Swansdown, brought to the Coast by Mr. and Mrs. Adolph Gugle as a puppy. She was a lovely bitch who was retired the minute she gained her title but had only one litter, of which Polka was one. Both of Swansdown's parents, Ch. Blakeen White Light and Ch. Blakeen The Swan, were by Ch. Broadrun Cheerio, a son of the noted Ch. Lucas Du Briois of Blakeen, and Swansdown was mated to Ch. Blakeen Snowstorm, another son of Lucas, to produce Polka—an example of successful line breeding.

307

The second bitch bought by Mrs. Nurmi was the white-bred black bitch, Salmagundi's Caviar, who was brought to the Coast by Mr. James Clark when she was in whelp to Ch. Puttencove Halla's Hugo. She produced a fine litter, of which the big winner, Ch. Rimskittle Black Pirate, was one.

Caviar, bred to Ch. Blakeen's Sorcerer's Apprentice, produced Ch. Paloma's Bon Vivant and his sisters Ch. Windridge Beaucoup of Paloma and Paloma's Syncopation. Although on the small side, Bon Vivant was a beautiful dog, and he was a Best in Show winner at all-breed and specialty shows. Bon Vivant was one of the leading white Standard sires with 26 champions to his credit. Bred to his full sister, Paloma's Syncopation, he produced Ch. Forzando Bergamasque (sire of five champions) and the Best in Show winner, Ch. Forzando The Imp of Ivardon (dam of three champions). Bon Vivant bred to his half sister, Ch. Windridge Black Medallion (by Ch. Blakeen Sorcerer's Apprentice x a Caviar daughter) produced Ch. Forzando High Regard, Ch. Forzando Good Intentions and Ch. Forzando Such Conceit. Bon Vivant sired four champions out of Hillcastle's Angelica (by Ch. Pillicoc Barrister). Bon Vivant bred to Miss Muffet of Monterey (Carillon bred) produced Ch. Windridge Claire de Lune and the Best in Show winner Ch. Hallmark Harmony O'Windridge (sire of six champions). Bon Vivant bred to Ch. Davdon Captivation produced the Best in Show winner Ch. Alekai Koe, who is the dam of three champions. Bon Vivant's sister, Paloma's Syncopation, produced two additional champions to those above—Ch. Forzando Merry Christmas (by Ch. Paloma's Christopher) and Ch. Ivardon Alba (by Ch. Ensarr Glace).

In Caviar's litter by Halla's Hugo there was also the black Rimskittle Lace (dam of three champions) and two very nice silver bitches, Rimskittle Queen of Trumps and Rimskittle Damask. Queen of Trumps bred to Sorcerer's Apprentice produced Ch. Windridge Black Medallion (mentioned above as the dam of three champions).

Ch. Nurmi's Pizzicato Polka proved her worth as a producer by becoming the dam of Ch. Paloma's Maestro (by Apprentice), Ch. Paloma's Christopher (by Windridge Sebastian A Paloma), and Ch. Forzando Pedro El Rey (by Bon Vivant). Polka's litter sister, Lady Dawn of Brookhaven, was the dam of Ch. Forzando Caligulaa, also by Apprentice.

Mrs. Nurmi has had some difficulty in settling on a prefix. At first she used her own name, then later used Paloma, which the AKC refused to register in her name. She finally settled on Forzando, so there will be less confusion now.

59

Alekai Kennels

WHEN Mrs. Henry J. Kaiser of Honolulu, Hawaii decided to breed white Standards it was important to her that Alekai should represent the best possible. Alekai is a combination of her first name, Alyce, and Kaiser. Mrs. Kaiser wisely decided to found her kennel on the best white Standards then obtainable and she searched the country for the best bloodlines and individuals. From Puttencove Kennels she acquired Ch. Puttencove Kaui (by Ch. Puttencove Promise x Ch. Puttencove Moonglow). From Ivardon Kennels came Ch. Ivardon Winter (granddaughter of Ch. Blakeen Bali Ha'i) and Ivardon Kenilworth of Ensarr (grandson of Ch. Puttencove Promise and Ch. Ensarr Glace). From the de la Fontaine Kennels in Canada came Ch. Tambarine de la Fontaine (by Ch. Puttencove Promise x Can. Ch. Cillette de la Fontaine). From the Davdon Kennels came Ch. Davdon Captivation (by the Best in Show winner, Ch. Hillandale C'Est Vrais x his Best in Show daughter, Ch. Davdon Miss Demeanor) and Ch. Davdon Suma Cum Laude (a C'Est Vrais granddaughter). Several of these were selected prior to their show careers and finished their titles under the Alekai banner.

Mrs. Kaiser built a beautiful kennel, acclaimed as one of the finest in the world, overlooking Maunalua Bay. She then set up an extensive file of records so that breedings and individuals could be properly evaluated.

Beginning with the first champions bred in 1961, Alekai has compiled an impressive list of winners and producers. Ch. Davdon Summa Cum Laude was bred to Ch. Puttencove Promise to produce a litter of five champions: Ch. Alekai Pikake (Best in Show winner), Ch. Alekai Hololaka (Best in Show winner), Ch. Alekai Mai Kai (Best of Winners at the Poodle Club of America

Ch. Alekai Ahi

Specialty 1962), Ch. Alekai Kona, and the Group winner Ch. Alekai Nohea (sire of six champions). Summa Cum Laude is also the dam of Ch. Alekai Lohea (by Ch. Ivardon King of Hearts), bringing her total to six champions. Ch. Tambarine de la Fontaine (a Best in Show winner) is the dam of Ch. Alekai Maunalua and Ch. Alekai Romance by Alekai Roma, and of Ch. Alekai Kalania by Ch. Alekai Kila. Kalania went to England where she finished her title in just six shows, and became one of the few American Poodles to win an English championship. Ch. Puttencove Kaui is the dam of three champions by Ivardon Kenilworth of Ensarr: Ch. Alekai Lawa, Ch. Alekai White Luan and Ch. Alekai Kila (sire of six champions). Kaui is also the dam of the Group winner, Ch. Alekai Kolohe by Ch. Puttencove Mohican. Ch. Ivardon Winter is the dam of two Best in Show winners by Ch. Alekai Nohea—Ch. Alekai Pokoi (16 Bests in Show) and Ch. Alekai Kuipo. Pokoi bred to Ch. Alekai Ahi produced Ch. Alekai Bali who finished his title with a Group win from the puppy classes. Ch. Ivardon Winter is also the dam of Ch. Alekai Loke by Alekai Roma. Ch. Davdon Captivation was bred to Ch. Paloma's Bon Vivant to produce the best in show winner Ch. Alekai Koe. Captivation was bred to Ch. Alekai Kila to produce the beautiful Best in

Ch. Davdon Captivation

Ch. Alekai Kila

Ch. Alekai Marlaine

Show winner, Ch. Alekai Marlaine (Group First at Westminster 1967), Ch. Alekai Marlin, and Ch. Alekai Ahi (Best of Winners—Poodle Club of America Specialty 1965). Ahi is the sire of Ch. Alekai Bali (mentioned above), Ch. Alekai Lahi (x Ch. Alekai Hololaka) and the Best in Show winner Ch. Tamara of Stonebridge (x Ch. Alekai Maunalua). Ch. Alekai Koe was bred to her half brother, Ch. Alekai Marlin, (both x Ch. Davdon Captivation) to produce three champions in one litter: Ch. Alekai Kate of Komar, Ch. Kaptain Kidd of Komar and Ch. Gaiety Heights Kelli of Komar.

Mrs. Kaiser, with valuable assistance from her handler Wendell Sammet, helped to reestablish the white Standard to top honors in the show ring. Although this kennel has been disbanded, the beautiful Alekai Poodles are a tribute to her wisdom and efforts.

Ch. Alekai Pokoi

Ch. Alekai Nohea

Am. & Can. Ch. Wycliffe Thomas with his breeder-
owner, Mrs. Donald Lyle.

60

Wycliffe Kennels

ONE of the most important kennels in Standard Poodles in recent years has been the Wycliffe Kennels of Mrs. Donald Lyle in the Pacific Northwest. Starting with the purchase of a black bitch puppy, Carillon Michelle, from Blanche Saunders in 1952, Mrs. Lyle has carefully evolved the black Wycliffe line. Michelle was by Santo-Labory of Carillon x Ch. Carillon Jestina. She won her title in the U.S. and Canada, and also held Am. C.D.X. and Can. U.D.T. degrees. Michelle was the dam of nine champions including Ch. Wycliffe Hilary of Carillon, Can. Ch. Wycliffe Little Lulu and Am. and Can. Ch. Wycliffe Jacqueline U.D.T. Hilary bred to Ch. Carillon Dilemma gave Ch. Carillon Gossip and Carillon Glitter (dam of four champions). Little Lulu was the dam of Ch. Wycliffe Zara (dam of five champions).

Jacqueline is the leading producing bitch in the breed with 21 champions to her credit. Jacqueline was sent East to be bred to Ch. Annsown Gay Knight of Arhill. The resulting litter contained Ch. Wycliffe Thomas (sire of 50 champions), Ch. Wycliffe Timothy (sire of 13 champions), Can. Ch. Wycliffe Talk of the Town (dam of three champions) and Can. Ch. Wycliffe Theresa (dam of nine champions). All four of these are either Best in Show winners or are Best Canadian-bred in Show winners. The fifth and sixth members of this litter were Ch. Wycliffe Twinkling Tiara and Ch. Wycliffe Theodore. Jacqueline's previous litter had been sired by Ch. Carillon Dilemma (a son of Ch. Annsown Sir Gay, thus a half brother of Ch. Annsown Gay Knight of Arhill). This litter contained five champions including Ch. Wycliffe Nicola C.D.X. (dam of eight champions). Nicola's daughter,

Ch. Wycliffe Victoria of Acadia, is the dam of six champions. Jacqueline was first bred to Bel Tor Hugues Capet (also a Sir Gay son) to produce three champions including Am. and Can. Ch. Wycliffe Glamourous Gillian. Gillian's daughter, Ch. Wycliffe Monica is the dam of four champions. Jacqueline's last two litters were sired by her son, Ch. Wycliffe Timothy, and from these came a total of seven champions including Ch. Wycliffe Virgil (sire of 24 champions) and Ch. Wycliffe Veronica (dam of four champions). Virgil, a Best in Show winner, is the sire of Eng. Am. and Can. Ch. Bibelot's Tall Dark and Handsome, who was England's Dog of the Year for 1966. Tall Dark and Handsome is the sire of ten champions. Jacqueline only whelped five litters of 41 puppies by four different sires, and from these came a total of 21 champions and seven top producers—a record which may stand for some time to come.

Jacqueline's most famous son was the great black Am. and Can. Ch. Wycliffe Thomas, who was whelped April 1, 1959. Thomas was a big dog measuring $26\frac{1}{2}$ inches at the withers. He was noted for his soundness and superlative disposition. He won from coast to coast. Thomas was Best of Winners at the Poodle Club of America Specialty in 1960 at just 13 months of age, and completed his championship in two weeks. He later won many Varieties, Groups, and nine Bests in Show. Thomas is the leading Standard sire in the history of the breed with 50 champions to his credit and his get are still being shown. Thomas' offspring have been important winners from coast to coast and they are proving producers of note. His son who died young, Ch. Jacques Le Noir of Belle Glen, was the sire of seven champions. Another son who unfortunately also died young was the Best in Show winner, Ch. Wycliffe Ian (sire of nine champions). In the East two full brothers Ch. Prince Philip of Belle Glen and Ch. Black Rogue of Belle Glen (both x Ch. Bridget of Belle Glen) are top producers. Another son in Ohio, Ch. Wycliffe Leroy, is producing well. Thomas' daughters are also producing well: Ch. Wycliffe Victoria of Acadia (dam of six champions), Ch. De Russy Keepsake (dam of four champions), Ch. Wycliffe Zara (dam of five champions) and Hexton Kennels' Ch. Annie Belle Glen (dam of five champions in one litter). Thomas was bred to his daughter, Ch. Wycliffe Zara, to produce the Best in Show winner, Am. and Can. Ch. Wycliffe Kenneth, who is the sire of nine champions. Kenneth is being retained by Mrs. Lyle as Thomas' heir at Wycliffe.

A number of current kennels are founded on Wycliffe stock. These include Acadia, Annveron, De Russey, Wentworth, Ledgehill, Dalwynne, Koronet, Loribon, Black Knight, Coquan and Bushy Run.

Mrs. Lyle does not have a large kennel, nor does she breed many litters, but she does have an exceptional family which she has carefully preserved and improved. She can well be proud of the Wycliffe accomplishments.

Am. & Can.
Ch. Wycliffe Jacqueline, U.D.T.

Am. & Can.
Ch. Carillon Michelle, Can. U.D.T.

Am. & Can. Ch. Wycliffe Kenneth

Am. & Can. Ch. Wycliffe Virgil (by Am. & Can. Ch. Wycliffe Timothy ex Am. & Can. Ch. Wycliffe Jacqueline), black Standard, shown going Best of Variety at 1964 Westminster Kennel Club under judge Melbourne Downing, handled by owner Joan Schilke Wicklander. One of the leading sires of the breed.

Ch. DeRussy Lollypop (by Ch. Wycliffe Dudley ex Ch. DeRussy Bedazzle, C. D.), black Standard bitch, multiple Best in Show winner. Pictured going Best in Show at Silver Bay Kennel Club of San Diego 1969 under judge Stanley J. Halle, with Frank T. Sabella handling. Owned by Frank and Susan Dale.

Ch. Blakeen Luzon (by Broadrun Cheerio ex Blakeen Nelly) bred by Mrs. James Luke, owned by Mrs. Sherman Hoyt.

Ch. Alekai Conquistador (by Ch. Jolipal Fabulous Fellow ex Ch. Road-coach Leilani), black Standard male. Sire of champions. Owned by Mrs. Samuel duPont, Hexton Kennels.

Ch. Bel Tor Come Hither (by Ch. Bel Tor St. Ay Better Mousetrap ex Ch. Bel Tor Head of the Class), blue Standard bitch. Multiple Best in Show winner. Owned by Susan North, Darkin Kennels.

Ch. Prince Philip of Belle Glen pictured going Best of Breed at 1966 Poodle Club of America Specialty. Left to right: Mr. William Rogers, presenting trophy; Mrs. Milton Erlanger, judge; Richard Bauer, handler; and Mr. U. D. E. Walden, club president. Owned by Mr. and Mrs. Frank Smith, Jr.

Ch. Tory Hollow Tomahawk shown going Best of Variety at the 1959 Poodle Club of Massachusetts Specialty show under Mr. Walter Morris, with Wendell J. Sammet handling. Bred and owned by Mrs. William J. Baird, Tory Hollow Farm.

61

Outstanding Standard Sires

Anderl Line

CH. CARILLON COLIN OF PUTTENCOVE

Whelped August 21, 1943   Died 1957

Bred by Mrs. Whitehouse Walker and Miss Blanche Saunders
Owned by Puttencove Kennels

```
                              Ch. Griseley Labory of Piperscroft, C.D. (gr)
                    Ch. Kaffir of Piperscroft (blk)
                              Ch. Quality of Piperscroft (blk)
          Ch. Puttencove Impetuous (blk)
                              Ch. Blakeen Cyrano (brn)
                    Puttencove Candida (brn)
                              Blakeen Solange (brn)

CH. CARILLON COLIN OF PUTTENCOVE (blk)

                              Ch. Stillington Claus O'Carillon (blk)
                    Ch. Carillon Courage, C.D.X. (blk)
                              Carillon Tragedie (blk)
          Ch. Carillon Colline (blk)
                              Ch. Nymphaea Jason (brn)
                    Ch. Carillon Celeste (blk)
                              Carillon Pivoine (blk)
```

CH. CARILLON COLIN OF PUTTENCOVE

Sire of 21 champions:	Out of:
Ch. Black Douglas of Lowmont	
Ch. Lady Virginia of Lowmont	Clementine of Puttencove
Ch. Lowmont Lady Sally	
Ch. Puttencove Young Clementine	
Ch. Puttencove Halla's Hugo	
Ch. Puttencove Huntress	Puttencove Halla
Ch. Puttencove Hester	
Ch. Puttencove Hermione	
Ch. Puttencove Serenade	
Ch. Puttencove Songstress	Ch. Puttencove Samantha
Ch. Puttencove Sabra	
Ch. Annsown Sir Gay	Annsown San Souci
Ch. Annsown Pixie	
Ch. Fanfaron Drage	Blakeen Snow Bird
Ch. Fanfaron Grand Marnier	
Ch. Avron's Chere	Carillon Sereine
Ch. Chloe's Jetee	Carillon Chloe
Ch. Madame Pompadour II	Puttencove Macaroon
Ch. Roadcoach Raconteur	Roadcoach Dear Clementine
Ch. Salmagundi's Golden Shadow	Salmagundi Angel Face
Ch. Verdant Yvette	Ch. Verdant Vida

Ch. Puttencove Halla's Hugo

CH. ANNSOWN SIR GAY

Whelped March 14, 1949   Died 1956

Bred and owned by Mr. and Mrs. Charles E. Wagmann

```
                            Ch. Kaffir of Piperscroft (blk)
               Ch. Puttencove Impetuous (blk)
                            Puttencove Candida (brn)
         Ch. Carillon Colin of Puttencove (blk)
                            Ch. Carillon Courage, C.D. (blk)
               Ch. Carillon Colline (blk)
                            Ch. Carillon Celeste (blk)

CH. ANNSOWN SIR GAY (blk)

                            Ch. Intrepid of Misty Isles (blk)
               Surrey Snafu (blk)
                            L'Audace Sans Glen (blk)
         Annsown Sans Souci (blk)
                            Ch. Blakeen Zombie
               Blakeen Spooky (blk)
                            Ch. Barbet Baiser
```

CH. ANNSOWN SIR GAY

Sire of 22 champions: Out of:

Ch. Bel Tor Morceau Choisi
Ch. Bel Tor Lothaire
Ch. Bel Tor Madrigal
Ch. Bel Tor Main Chance   Ch. Lowmont Lady Cadette
Ch. Bel Tor Make Believe
Ch. Bel Tor M'Aime La Belle
Ch. Bel Tor Petite Madelon

Ch. Bel Tor Gigadibs
Ch. Bel Tor Gasconade
Ch. Bel Tor Black Sheep   Ch. Bel Tor Hosanna
Ch. Bel Tor Gentle Julia
Ch. Annsown Gay Melodie

Ch. Sterg-O Gigolo
Ch. Sterg-O Jericho   Ch. Lowmont Lady Fabiola
Ch. Sterg-O Mambo

Ch. Carillon Dilemma, U.D.   Robin Hill of Carillon
Ch. Carillon Dart

Ch. Annsown Gay Knight of Arhill   Clairedge Cinderella
Ch. Arhill Clairedge The Clown

Ch. Tory Hollow Gay Token   Tory Hollow Caprice
Ch. Jamarden's Victor Hugo   Domino's Victoria
Can. Ch. Petitcote Crepe Suzette   Ch. Petitcote Bubbling Over

Ch. Annsown Gay Knight of Arhill

AM. & CAN. CH. WYCLIFFE THOMAS

Whelped April 1, 1959   Died August 13, 1967

Bred and owned by Mrs. Jean M. Lyle

```
                              Ch. Carillon Colin of Puttencove (blk)
                 Ch. Annsown Sir Gay (blk)
                              Annsown San Souci (blk)
        Ch. Annsown Gay Knight of Arhill (blk)
                              Carillon Conde (blk)
                 Clairedge Cinderella, C.D. (blk)
                              Juliette of Clairedge (gr)


AM. & CAN. CH. WYCLIFFE THOMAS (blk)

                              Petitcote Baron Chico (crm)
                 Int. Ch. Petitcote Domino, C.D. (blk)
                              Carillon Jabotiere (blk)
        Int. Ch. Wycliffe Jacqueline, U.D. (blk)
                              Santo-Labory of Carillon (blk)
                 Int. Ch. Carillon Michelle, U.D.T. (blk)
                              Ch. Carillon Jestina (blk)
```

AM. & CAN. CH. WYCLIFFE THOMAS

Sire of 50 champions: Out of:

Ch. Acadia Barbara Beloved
Ch. Acadia Black Bart
Ch. Acadia Bold Barnabas
Ch. Acadia Boulette   Am. & Can. Ch. Wycliffe Nicola, C.D.X.
Ch. Acadia Elegant Eric
Ch. Wycliffe Victoria of Acadia
Can. Ch. Wycliffe Brett

Ch. Annie of Belle Glen
Ch. Black Rogue of Belle Glen
Ch. Lady Margaret of Belle Glen   Ch. Bridget of Belle Glen
Ch. Prince Philip of Belle Glen
Ch. Wycliffe Gabriel O'Belle Glen

Ch. Dalwynne Darcy
Ch. Dalwynne Lasleigh
Ch. Dalwynne Malinda   Ch. Wycliffe Monica
Ch. Dalwynne Larissa

Ch. Dalwynne Scindi   Ch. Dalwynne Larissa
Ch. Dalwynne Scion

Am. & Can. Ch. Wycliffe Kenneth
Ch. Wycliffe Karyna
Can. Ch. Wycliffe Kathryn   Am. & Can. Ch. Wycliffe Zara
Can. Ch. Wycliffe Whitney

Ch. Acadia Dorinda
Ch. Wycliffe Xtra Animated   Ch. Acadia Boulet

Ch. Mistinguette's Monique
Ch. Mistinguette's Tommy   Ch. Pudeldorf Mistinguette

Ch. Monfret Modred
Ch. Monfret Morticia   Ch. Kah's Collector's Item

Ch. Monfret Music Maid
Ch. Monfret Music Maestro   Monfret Melody

Ch. Wycliffe Xtra Lucky Corbe
Ch. Wycliffe Xtra Lustre   Ch. Acadia Christa The Cover Girl

Am. & Can. Ch. Wycliffe Zara
Ch. Wycliffe Zoe   Can. Ch. Wycliffe Little Lulu, C.D.

Am. & Can. Ch. Wycliffe Ian
Ch. Wycliffe Cerce   Yolanda of Wycliffe
Can. Ch. Wycliffe Calypso

Ch. Loribon Canadian Caper
Ch. Hansonya Nine Mile Arisha   Ch. Bonne Bergere of Brigadoon

Ch. De Russy Keepsake
Ch. De Russy Karacul   Ch. De Russy Bedazzle

AM. & CAN. CH. WYCLIFFE THOMAS (continued)

Ch. Wycliffe Leroy
Can. Ch. Wycliffe Launcelot   Wycliffe Xtra Fancy

Ch. Wycliffe Quick March
Can. Ch. Wycliffe Quaestor   Ch. Wycliffe Victoria of Acadia

Can. Ch. Wycliffe Unona, U.D.T.   Wycliffe Melissa, C.D.
Can. Ch. Wycliffe Unona's Frederick   Can. Ch. Unona's Barberyn
Ch. Jacques Le Noir of Belle Glen   Si Bonne of Belle Glen
Ch. Pixdown Primadonna   Ch. Donna of Westford Ho
Ch. Wycliffe Homer   Wycliffe Winning Ways

Ch. Jacques Le Noir of Belle Glen shown going Best Puppy in
Show at 1961 Poodle Club of America Specialty under the late
Col. Ernest E. Ferguson, with Richard Bauer handling.

Ch. Black Rogue of Belle Glen

Ch. Prince Philip of Belle Glen

Am. & Can. Ch. Wycliffe Leroy

Am. & Can. Ch. Wycliffe Ian

AM. & CAN. CH. BEL TOR McCREERY

Whelped January 3, 1955   Died July 8, 1966

Bred and owned by Bel Tor Kennels

```
                        Ch. Carillon Colin of Puttencove (blk)
            Ch. Annsown Sir Gay (blk)
                        Annsown San Souci (blk)
        Ch. Bel Tor Morceau Choisi (blk)
                        Ch. Robin Hood (brn)
            Ch. Bel Tor Lady Cadette (brn)
                        Ch. Lowmont Madame d'Aiguillon (brn)

AM. & CAN. CH. BEL TOR McCREERY (brn)

                        Carillon Michel (blk)
            Lowmont Lord Dion (blk)
                        Ch. Lowmont Lady Joan (blk)
        Ch. Beltore Bright Star (brn)
                        Drambuie (brn)
            Yvette Jeanne (blk)
                        Dubonette (blk)
```

AM. & CAN. CH. BEL TOR McCREERY

Sire of 31 champions: Out of:

Ch. Bel Tor Hussar Belle du Bal
Ch. Bel Tor Hussar Busby
Ch. Bel Tor Hussar Jubilee   Bel Tor True Love of Woodlawn
Ch. Bel Tor Hussar Tambourineur
Ch. Bel Tor Pink Lemonade

Ch. Bel Tor Blackberry Wine
Ch. Bel Tor Georgia Brown   Ch. Bel Tor Oui Oui Mille Fois
Ch. Bel Tor Knave of Hearts
Ch. Bel Tor Sweet Tart

Ch. Bel Tor Caramel Souffle
Ch. Bel Tor Butternut   Ch. Bel Tor Sandlewood
Ch. Bel Tor Flying Colors

Ch. Bel Tor Rosewood
Ch. Bel Tor Black Helen
Ch. Bel Tor Blushing Bride   Ch. Bel Tor Pink Cloud
Ch. Bel Tor Bonfire
Ch. Bel Tor In The Pink

Ch. Darkin Full of Sound and Fury
Ch. Darkin Measure For Measure   Ch. Bel Tor Come Hither
Ch. Darkin Perchance To Dream

Ch. Molly Brown's Misty Cognac
Ch. Molly Brown's Moonshine   Ch. Nancyn's Molly Brown
Ch. Molly Brown's Slivovitz

Ch. Bel Tor Bombazine   Kayes Lady Milan
Ch. Kayes Rodney's Brown Magic

Ch. Bel Tor Genial Host   Ch. Bel Tor Prenez Moi
Ch. Bel Tor Good Faith   ＊

Ch. Bel Tor Brown Fern   Ch. Bel Tor Flight of Fancy
Ch. Bel Tor Hickory Stick

Ch. Bel Tor St Aye Better Mousetrap   Canorwall Of Thee I Sing
Ch. Rondylo Here's Damon   Ch. Bel Tor Here's How

Ch. Bel Tor St Aye Better Mousetrap

AM. & CAN. CH. PUTTENCOVE PROMISE

Whelped January 20, 1955   Deceased

Bred and owned by Puttencove Kennels

```
                        Ch. Pillicoc Barrister (wh)
            Ch. Blakeen Bali Ha'i (wh)
                        Blakeen Morning Star (wh)
        Ch. Loabelo Jonny (wh)
                        Nunsoe The Duke (wh)
            Vulcan Champagne Carmen of Blakeen (wh)
                        Vulcan Champagne Capella (wh)

AM. & CAN. CH. PUTTENCOVE PROMISE (wh)

                        Pillicoc Courier (wh)
            Ch. Pillicoc Barrister (wh)
                        Blakeen Surrey Romance (wh)
        Astron Lily of Puttencove (wh)
                        Ch. Pillicoc Pegasus (wh)
            Ch. Astron Silver Star (si)
                        Von's Jezebel (blk)
```

330

AM. & CAN. CH. PUTTENCOVE PROMISE

Sire of 27 champions: Out of:

Ch. Alekai Pikake
Ch. Alekai Hololaka
Ch. Alekai Nohea   Ch. Davdon Suma Cum Laude
Ch. Alekai Kona
Ch. Alekai Mai Kai

Ch. Puttencove Alii
Ch. Puttencove Lani
Ch. Puttencove Kaui   Ch. Puttencove Moonglow
Ch. Puttencove Noelle
Ch. Puttencove Moonshine

Ch. Puttencove Gay de la Fontaine
Ch. D'Artagnan de la Fontaine
Ch. Sincerely de la Fontaine   Can. Ch. Cillette de la Fontaine
Ch. Tambarine de la Fontaine
Can. Ch. Amo de la Fontaine
Can. Ch. Calvados de la Fontaine

Ch. Ivardon Queen Anne
Ch. Ivardon Victorian   Ch. Forzando The Imp of Ivardon
Ch. Ivardon Sheraton

Ch. Stonewood Barrister   Anastasia of Stonewood
Ch. Cream Puff Promise

Ch. Lafayette of Kenilworth   Puttencove Desdemona
Ch. Chantilly Legacy   Ch. Puttencove Pact of Chantilly
Ch. Rolindo Callie's Carry On   Devandale April Day
Ch. Nagy Pegasus de Bo Mi   Ch. Nagy Angelique Zephyr
Ch. Puttencove Snow White   Phemister's Scaramouche
Ch. Franmar's Snow Storm   Ch. Pen-Y-Bryn Shoelace

Ch. Puttencove Moonshine

CH. PALOMA'S BON VIVANT

Whelped August 6, 1952

Bred and owned by Mr. and Mrs. R. H. Nurmi

```
                              Pillicoc Courier (wh)
                 Ch. Pillicoc Barrister (wh)
                              Blakeen Surrey Romance (wh)
       Ch. Blakeen Sorcerer's Apprentice (wh)
                              Nunsoe The Duke (wh)
                 Vulcan Champagne Carmen of Blakeen (wh)
                              Vulcan Champagne Capella (wh)

CH. PALOMA'S BON VIVANT (wh)

                              Ch. Lucite of Salmagundi (wh)
                 Salmagundi's Domino (blk)
                              Pillicoc Confident (blk)
       Salmagundi's Caviar (blk)
                              Ch. Lucite of Salmagundi (wh)
                 Ch. Salmagundi's White Queen (wh)
                              Ch. Pillicoc Pearl (wh)
```

CH. PALOMA'S BON VIVANT

Sire of 26 champions: Out of:

Ch. Foremost Earl of Hardy High	
Ch. Miss Tinquette	
Ch. Sheri's Winter Lark	Ch. Palmares Risette
Ch. Rusvel's Priceless Platter	
Can. Ch. Lili Marlene	
Ch. Glory Lark	
Ch. Glory Napoleon	Hillcastle's Angelica
Ch. Glory Lilyon	
Ch. Forzando Pandora of Glory	
Ch. Forzando High Regard	
Ch. Forzando Such Conceit	Ch. Windridge Black Medallion
Ch. Forzando Good Intentions	
Ch. Forzando Bergamasque	Paloma's Syncopation
Ch. Forzando The Imp of Ivardon	
Ch. Fifi of Rafter-O	Ch. Carmel's Coquette
Ch. Jacques of Rafter-O	
Ch. Hallmark Harmony O'Windridge	Miss Muffet of Monterey
Ch. Windridge Claire de Lune	
Ch. Salutaire Stagestruck	Valentine Gigi
Ch. The Brightest Dazzling Star, C.D.	
Ch. DeLanas Siboney v. Nibelheim	Ch. Zsa Zsa v. Nibelheim
Ch. DeLanas Tico Tico v. Nibelheim	
Ch. Alekai Koe	Ch. Davdon Captivation
Ch. Chante's Magic Moment	Cardon's Jete D'Amour, C.D.
Ch. Forzando Pedro El Rey	Ch. Nurmi's Pizzicato Polka
Ch. Forzando Feminine Fancy	Forzando Lady Love

Ch. Blakeen Sorcerer's Apprentice, shown with breeder-owner Lois Nurmi.

Retrieving Poodles of the Greenspring Poodle Club: Stonewood Heidi, bred, owned, and trained by Charles LeBoutillier, Jr.; Wye Town Canis Major, owned and trained by Mrs. Dorman Covington; and Sugar and Spice, owned by Miss Ruth Hyde.

Shown at the Greenspring Poodle Club Retriever Demonstration are: Mrs. Gordon Fisher, Jr., with Wye Town Canis Minor, Mrs. Tyler Wrightson with Pom, Mrs. Martha Covington, trainer, with Wye Town Canis Major, Mrs. William Lewis with her Poodi-Man-Dark Victory, CD, and Mrs. Charles Le Boutellier with his Stonewood Gold Standard, UDT.

62

Poodles as Retrievers

I have always maintained that a cut and dried routine such as an obedience test, however well performed, is a proof of tractability rather than intelligence. In my opinion a dog shows his intelligence by successfully solving an unrehearsed emergency situation without prompting or human supervision. In hunting many situations arise and the dog's intelligence grows by leaps and bounds to meet them. He develops resourcefulness and a lightning quick understanding. All his mental and physical faculties are stretched to the utmost. He becomes alert, and alive in a manner that is sometimes uncanny.

In all the world there is nothing more fascinating, to those that love them, than to watch the growth and development of a Poodle's mind. There are few closer bonds than that between the hunter and his clever dog. The Poodle is meant to be man's companion. His one desire in life is to share all of his master's activities. Retrieving is his ancient and honorable profession. Today he takes to it like a duck to water, if given half a chance. There are many proofs of this former ability in early paintings, engravings and descriptions in old sporting books, and in illustrations reproduced in this book. As Miss Brunker says in her description of the ideal Poodle, "He is game, too, and many keepers have been forced to confess that a Poodle may put a trained gun dog to shame."

To those of us that love them, any activity that brings out the truth about them is good news. The smallest Poodle is an honest, self-respecting little dog, highly intelligent, deeply devoted, and with a dignity few other dogs possess. So it is all the more distressing that they should be

335

Stonewood Gold Standard, "Stevie," presents his bird to his master, Mr. Charles Le Boutellier. Stevie is by Ch. Blakeen Cafe Parfait, CDX, one of the first Poodles in recent times to be trained for retrieving.

"Pom," owned by Mrs. Tyler Wrightson, finds his bird.

subjected to the silly whims and caprices of vapid owners—decked with jeweled collars, dressed in silly costumes—even dyed to match the silly dresses of silly women. It is heartening to see them coming back to the useful work for which they were born.

A small group of people in Maryland, members of the Greenspring Poodle Club, have earnestly set about with great success to prove that as retrievers, Poodles have what it takes. Living in the center of duck and goose hunting country, these people are determined that their Poodles should have professional training and every opportunity to develop into first-class hunting dogs. The prime movers in the activity are Mr. and Mrs. Gordon Fisher and Mr. and Mrs. Charles le Boutellier, who have bred, owned, and trained their Poodles for retrieving very successfully.

The puppies are played with and trained from early puppyhood, and are companions of the children in the families. Most of them are obedience trained, since it seems to be the general consensus that this lays a firmer foundation for future work as retrievers. But this depends on the individual dog.

Nobody that knows and understands Poodles would ever question either their IQ's or their teachability. What was questioned was whether Poodles would have the physical stamina to endure the rugged weather conditions such as hunting demands. Could they take long hours in icy water and mud in the coldest weather? The only way to answer this question was to try it and see. The dogs came through with flying colors, undismayed by difficulties. They could take it and did with gusto! As Mr. Henry Davis wrote in *Sports Afield* regarding an exhibition by Poodles, "They were steady under the gun, the dogs exhibited fine handling response, excellent scenting ability, a good turn of speed and a highly encouraging enthusiasm for the tasks they were asked to perform." Says Charles le Boutellier of the older Poodles that are trained retrievers, "Their tremendous development of brain power, resourcefulness, assurance, and empirical knowledge is a revelation."

The ancient theory that Poodles working in the water needed a heavy coat to protect their lungs—which has been responsible for the Poodle's clip for hundreds of years—has been exploded. These dogs are kept in the "lamb or retriever clip" with about two inches of hair all over—and face, feet, and tail clipped short. For them it works just as well and is far easier to care for. Although the Poodle's coat is somewhat water resistant, the dog can shake a short clip dry quicker than a long one.

The Greenspring Poodle Club has retrieving classes which meet regularly under the able direction of Mrs. Martha Covington.

What kind of dogs are trained? The best show stock. Mrs. Sherman Hoyt was a pioneer in this as in so many other Poodle activities. Her Ch. Blakeen

337

Ch. Cinnamon Cyrano of Boli, CDX, brings in his duck
first time out, without any previous retriever training.

Mrs. Covington's Wye Town Canis Major bringing in his duck.

Cafe Parfait, CDX, was trained by her as a retriever and afterward found a home as the foundation dog for Mrs. Fisher. This lovely Poodle was a son of the famous Int. Ch. Nunsoe Duc de la Terrace of Blakeen, who was best in show, all breeds, a number of times—indicating his lovely type as well as his brains.

The question I asked was, "How great a part does heredity play in a Poodle's retrieving ability?" Although many of the Poodles that have been trained descend from Ch. Blakeen Cafe Parfait, the answer seems to be "not very much." The Poodle's natural swimming and retrieving ability seem to be strong enough to start with—inherent in the breed as a whole. Naturally, some puppies have more of it than others, but it is strongly entrenched in the breed.

The canine star of the Greenspring group of hunting Poodles is perhaps Mr. le Boutellier's Stonewood Gold Standard, UDT. His really remarkable personality and brains and the style and dash of his work stand out as exceptional. He is followed by his sons, Mrs. Fisher's Wye Town Canis Minor and Mrs. Covington's Wye Town Canis Major.

To prove the Poodle's natural ability for retrieving, I will cite another example. Mr. Robert Richardson's brown Standard, Cinnamon Cyrano of Boli, was an obedience winner, but he retrieved his first duck without previous training—and has since become a first-class hunting dog.

To date, all modern experiments have been made with Standard sized Poodles, but there is no reason the larger Miniatures could not be trained to retrieve smaller game. During the war I had quite a family of Muscovy ducks that had a pen with a pond, completely surrounded by a six-foot fence. My Miniature Ch. Sherwood Louis Philippe, who was the most enterprising dog on four feet, was fascinated by them. Nothing any of us could do could keep him out of the duck pen. He would climb in, swim around the pond, capture a duck and appear proudly before me, inconveniently wet and holding an indignant Muscovy almost as big as he was! He presented it hunting dog fashion. How he managed to scale the high fence with such a burden we never found out. No amount of scolding cured him. He never bruised or hurt them—except their feelings—and never could be convinced that they were not there for his enjoyment in retrieving them! Of course, such a dog could have been easily trained for serious retrieving, and there must be others like him.

The group of breeders in Maryland are doing Poodles a great service. They are all sportsmen in the best sense of the word—intent on developing the brains and retrieving ability of their Poodles for the sheer joy of it.

Corded Poodle, Achilles

63

The Corded Poodle

CORDED poodles, so popular in the early nineties, are now almost unheard-of. Although a few still exist abroad, I know of none in America. At one time they were so numerous in England that a separate classification was asked for them but wisely not granted. There has been much argument pro and con in regard to the texture of the coat that will successfully cord, and there are many noted breeders past and present on both sides. Some say any coat rolled between the fingers and greased will cord but others say that it must be the type of coat that falls into long strands naturally. Also, those that have handled the corded Poodles say that it is a matter of heredity. This latter theory seems to me to be likely and I believe, too, that the coat should cord naturally.

The cords consist of new hair at the bottom near the skin and undoubtedly of old hair carefully rolled and greased to keep it from breaking. The cords are described as being "about the thickness of a crow quill." In "The American Dog," W. R. Furness (1891) writes fully of the corded Poodle, which he says is of German origin. "The coat should cord all over the body except on eyebrows, mustache and imperial which should be straight, even and without wave, and of a glossier texture than the rest of the coat. The cords on the ears should reach far down the shoulders and so mingle with those of the neck as to render the ears almost undistinguishable." The ears of Lyris, imported into England in the early '90s, were said to measure 37 inches when held out straight from the head and measured from tip to tip. "On the head," says Mr. Furness, "the cords should fall away from the center, leaving a well defined crown, and should show no

341

tendency to stand erect like those of a water spaniel." The same authority says, "The entire coat, from the base of the skull to the root of the tail should part evenly down the back, showing a clearly defined parting, and should touch the ground, completely hiding the forelegs and feet, and this combined with the cords from the throat and chest, give the dog the appearance of wearing petticoats."

The coats on many of the corded dogs were immensely long and swept for several feet on the ground. However, this was in some cases somewhat modified with a reasonable length of coat in front and the dog clipped in ordinary show clip behind.

Corded Poodles went out of fashion for a number of reasons. One was that the weight and inconvenience of such immense coats seriously hampered the Poodle's activity and health. Another was that as the coat could not be combed nor properly washed it was often full of insects, and always dirty and greasy, which made the unfortunate dog a very malodorous creature.

Very few corded Poodles remain anywhere and they have become rarities and curiosities rather than serious competitors in the show ring.

General Lannes decorating the great "Moustache".

64

Anecdotes on the Poodle

NAPOLEONIC WARS

POODLES played a valiant part in the hearts of the French soldiers of this period and fought side by side with them in many a battle.

The Emperor Napoleon himself dictated the details at St. Helena of a touching incident after the battle of Marengo. The Emperor, making the rounds of the battlefield at night, came upon two friends killed in the battle, one of his Grenadiers and his faithful Poodle, whose last conscious act had been to lick his master's face. Said the Emperor, "It was in the beautiful clear moonlight, in the profoundest solitude of the night; never had anything on any of my battlefields caused me a like emotion."

Moustache, Morfino, Thoutou, Sancho, Mazuta, Barbuche and other Poodles are forever enshrined as national heroes in the hearts of the French.

Moustache, decorated for bravery in battle by General Lannes (1860), was the idol of the soldiers, who made him a military coat and cap. He is said to have been very docile and to have learned with an astonishing faculty, little short of incredible. An amusing story is told of him by one of his soldier friends. It concerns a ham, cooked, no doubt as only a Frenchman could do it, and placed on the table for the General's dinner with Moustache sniffing with appreciation. But when the General sat down to dinner the ham had disappeared. Naturally, suspicion fell upon Moustache. But he, pulling at the trouser of his friend, led him to a near-by tent where the real culprit was discovered with the half-eaten ham beside him.

Morfino was the pet of a young Italian officer who fought in the campaign against Russia. He was separated from his master in the confusion at Berezina and believed to be lost, but rejoined his master, having faithfully followed the trail of the army for many thousands of miles and arriving in a pitiful state of weakness and starvation.

POODLES IN THE ARMIES

Thoutou was the pet of a regiment of Zouaves in Africa. His sire was another regimental dog who was killed in action and sadly buried by the Zouaves. That night they were awakened by an uproar and rushed out to find all the dogs of the regiment, led by Thoutou, fighting off a band of pariahs who were trying to dig up the body of their comrade. Thoutou, upon the return of the regiment to Constantinople, rested from the fatigues of battle in oriental ease, "petted by the civilians, beloved by the natives and esteemed by the soldiers."

When the Zouaves were hastily ordered to the aid of Italy against the Austrians, word went out that no dogs were to be allowed aboard the transport. The broken-hearted soldiers hit upon the idea of smuggling their favorites inside the regimental drums. But alas, a final salvo was ordered by their colonel upon embarking, and the terrified dogs within set up such an uproar, one of them even bursting out of his prison, that they had to be left behind. Only Thoutou understood and bore the horrible experience in silence and so was safely smuggled aboard the ship which arrived in due time safely at Genoa. Once in Italy, Thoutou, more beloved of the soldiers than ever, quickly distinguished himself in many ways. He captured a number of enemy spies.

Barbuche, another army Poodle, was one of three inseparable friends that fought in the Italian campaign. He was the pet of Petit Jean, a waif who had been lost, and of old Sergeant Fougasse, who took them both under his protection. Child and dog grew up under military discipline and became the pets of the entire regiment. In time Petit Jean became a drummer boy and perished on the battlefield and Barbuche lost a front leg, cut off while he was defending his dying little master. Fougasse, mad with grief, rallied his men and routed the enemy. Years later Fougasse, fallen upon bad times, was earning his living with a Punch and Judy act and by the tricks of faithful Barbuche on the roadside, when an old woman who was watching, burst into tears saying she recognized the doll Punch and that it had belonged to her lost boy. Fougasse then told her of the life and death of Petit Jean.

Sancho was found on the battlefield of Salamanca, guarding the body of his dead master (a French lieutenant), by Lord Worchester, who brought him home to England. Sancho is said to have been sweet and docile with his English friends but sad and apparently grieving for his French master. There exists a print of him showing him to have been a handsome, large white dog.

344

POODLES' SENSE OF SMELL

The Poodle has a very keen nose, a fact which no doubt came from his early use as a hunting dog and accounts for his ability as a hunter of truffles. There are many stories illustrating this ability.

Marquis, Alexander Pope's Poodle, is credited with finding his valuable watch presented to him by the Queen of England, and lost on the hunting field, long after other searchers had given up.

Two visitors walking on the promenade at Vaux were robbed of wallet and watch. The gentleman called a policeman who had with him his dog, Canichon. The officer ordered the Poodle to "hunt" after having him sniff the gentleman's pocket. The Poodle went through the crowd and jumped upon a well-dressed man, growling. The man was searched and three stolen watches recovered, among them that of the visitor. Again telling Canichon to "hunt," the policeman followed him to a door at which the dog scratched and growled. Forcing the door, the officer found a young priest sitting at a table. From his sleeve tumbled a stolen snuff box and in his pockets were several stolen purses, including that of the visitor. The policeman told the visitors that they had been looking for some time for the thieves but had not been able to find them, no doubt because of the clever disguises. But for Canichon they would never have been found.

Dumont, walking with his Poodle and a friend on the Boulevard St. Antione, struck up a wager and hid a six livre piece in the dust of the road, declaring that the dog would find it. After they had gone a little farther he ordered the dog to find what he had lost. The Poodle went obediently back but found a traveler pocketing the coin. He followed the traveler to an inn where he was fed and petted, but the Poodle watched his new friend and no sooner did he pull off his trousers than the dog seized them and raced home, followed by the irate traveler. However, when it was all explained to him, he marveled at the Poodle's cleverness and faithfulness in carrying out a command.

AUTHORS AND THEIR POODLES

From the days of Alexander Pope on down the years, Poodles have been the favorite companions of authors, perhaps because of their uncanny understanding of moods, their adaptability and quiet content near those they love.

Pope's Poodle, Marquis, has been mentioned elsewhere.

The author's mother, who lived abroad at the time of the Franco-Prussian War, well remembered the Poodles of the well-known Georges Sand. Her carriage was a "Spider Phaeton" and she drove two champagne-colored ponies. The seat behind, instead of having the customary little groom in chamois pants, green coat and shiny hat with a cockade, was occupied by two big champagne-colored Poodles with huge green bows on their heads. While the carriage was in motion the dogs sat proudly with their long ears blowing in the wind. But when it stopped they both jumped down and ran to the ponies' heads, holding the reins until their mistress was ready to start off again. Then they climbed back on their perch and sat haughtily until the next stop. It can be imagined with what delight this equipage was welcomed by the children of the town, of which my mother was one.

In modern days the Poodle's firmest friend was Alexander Woolcott, whose dog Harpo (named after Harpo Marx, and a "creator of gayety in others") and a later friend, "Pip," were well known to all his friends and radio fans. Mr. Woolcott also had a great many Poodle friends belonging to others, among them Mrs. Hoyt's beautiful white Standard Ch. Blakeen Eiger, for whom he had a special affection and understanding.

Booth Tarkington's Figaro, a black Standard, is another well-known American dog very often photographed with his master. He was well educated and did a number of tricks to the great amusement of Mr. Tarkington's friends. Some of the most delightful descriptions of Poodles are to be found in Tarkington's books. Among them is that of "Gamin" in "Gentle Julia," who was described as having "a bang like a black chrysanthemum, eyes like twinkling garnets, and a clown's heart so golden that he sometimes reminded me of the Jongleur of Notre Dame."

Gertrude Stein was another author whose white Poodle was well known and often photographed with his mistress. Mignon Eberhardt, so dear to the hearts of mystery fans, had a chocolate brown miniature called Ginger, whom she describes as owning her.

And there are many others.

POODLES AND ROYALTY

In the latter part of the eighteenth century and the beginning of the nineteenth, Poodles were the popular pets of the aristocrats of France and England. In castles and chateaux, salons and villas, they were the valued companions of the titled and royal folk of that period.

The Duke of Argyll's Poodle's portrait is still in the family collection. The dog was so devoted to his master that, left behind in London, he appeared at the gates of Inveray Castle, Scotland, having traveled 470 miles to find his beloved master.

An early English print shows the Prince Regent at his dressing table attended by his valet, while his Poodle is watching his toilet gravely. A sadder scene is shown in a French print of the French King, Louis Philippe, and his Queen fleeing in the snow with their faithful Poodle following them into exile.

346

Prince Rupert, a dog lover like all the Stuarts, is said to have had a Poodle that was at his side during the war with Cromwell.

The ill-fated Prince Imperial of France owned a Poodle who was his inseparable companion. The dog is described as being "very black, rather large, his eyes soft and his character charming."

Today the Poodle finds a place at court with the Royal Family of Sweden.

TRAINED POODLES

From the time when "The Marquis de Gailerdain" and "Madame de Poncette" danced the minuet for England's Queen Anne at Bath in the eighteenth century, until the present day when all trained dog acts contain at least one or two little white Poodles, the Poodle has been the performing dog par excellence.

Many noted troops of trained Poodles have existed, among them, that of Monsieur Corvi (1865), mentioned in the French book on Poodles, *Caniche*.

The author well remembers as a child in Paris (1891), the trained Poodles at the Nouveau Cirque. They were all white dogs but not all of them were small. Jojo and Toto were very large white Standards, clipped in a most fantastic fashion and sporting very long tails with no less than six snowy pompons on them. The smaller dogs put on different acts. Ballroom scenes, in which the dogs were clad in elaborate dress clothes and bowed politely and danced gravely round and round, were a feature. But dearer to childish hearts were the spirited battle scenes where Poodles in red coats nobly defended their fort, attacked by Poodles in green coats. Miniature cannons were fired and it was all very exciting. The defenders always won. My favorite was the fire act where a building burst into flames and lady Poodles in nighties threw out their children (very plural and of obviously rag construction) and were rescued by gallant Poodle firemen in red coats, with a small efficient fire engine. The ladies were very wet when carried down the ladders to safety but they were so happy to be rescued that nobody minded. The little dogs ran off the stage in a very happy way and seemed to enjoy their acts, so that the children in the audience felt happy with them. One of the features of the old theater was that the show ring sank slowly at the end of the show and slowly filled with water and all the performing dogs and horses and some humans plunged in amid much splashing and barking, to the infinite delight of the children. I think the manager must have had a real insight into the childish mind.

Helen Hayes and her childhood pet.

65

The Poodle of Helen Hayes, America's Most Beloved Actress

THERE was much excitement on board the ocean liner, the *Champlain*, on that September day in 1939, as it loaded its cargo and passengers at Southampton, England. The English crowds on the docks seemed as nervous and excited as the American passengers on board the vessel, and with good cause. This was one of the last ships to leave England, carrying passengers back home to America to escape the perils of the war in Europe.

Just before the final signal for departure was given, an English lady dashed madly up the gangplank, carrying in her arms a black Poodle. She had no time to waste. Looking frantically around the crowd of passengers, she caught sight of an attractive young person standing near the rail. She had no idea who this passenger was, but she must have sensed some sort of kindred spirit in the little figure that stood watching her and her dog with such interest, for she rushed up to her and began talking nervously.

"Please, my dear, pardon this seeming rudeness, but they have given orders to kill all the dogs. Would you take Turvy back to America with you —and take good care of him?"

Now out of all the hundreds of people on board that boat the English lady could not have found a more cordial or more gracious person than this young American—and she loved dogs! She gladly accepted the Poodle and handed the owner her card. The name on the card was Helen Hayes.

The final signal, "All visitors off!" was heard. The English lady rushed down the gangplank, not trusting herself to look back at her beloved pet. The big steamer moved slowly out of the harbor, bearing several hundred nervous people who had been caught in a foreign country at the beginning

349

Eng., Am., and Can. Ch. Firebrave Pimpernel (by Firebrave Alphonse ex Ch. Firebrave Nicolette) breeder, Mrs. Munro, Firebrave Kennels, England, owner, Herder Kennels, Canada.

of the war, but none was so nervous or so frightened as a certain little refugee dog, who was being taken across the ocean to escape possible death at home.

Turvy had no idea what a lucky dog he was. He had no way of knowing that his new mistress was America's most beloved actress. He only knew that he felt very miserable when the boat rocked and rolled, causing him both fright and seasickness. For the first few days he ate almost nothing and slept very little, but after being nursed carefully by his loving new mistress, he began taking an interest in the life about him.

The thing that puzzled him most was the blackouts on the boat. How could he understand that there was danger of submarines and that the lives of all on board would be in peril if the boat were seen?

Finally, after ten long days at sea, the *Champlain* docked safely in New York Harbor—and Turvy had his first glimpse of America, his future home. Soon he and his mistress arrived in Nyack, New York, where he was introduced to his new family.

66

Ballad for Poodles

BY MARY VAN DER VEER

*Dedicated to "les caniches gaie" everywhere
and most especially to
my Desdi.*

The Poodle comes from long ago to grace the present day;
Beside his master through the years, he has served in every way.
His showmanship is unsurpassed, it's gained him world renown.
With pom-poms gay and nimble wit, he played the circus clown.
He jumped through hoops and read the cards and danced on skillful paws;
The audience was his delight, he thrilled to their applause.
He did his tricks in royal court or in the open mart—
He noticed not the clothes of a man, since he could read his heart.

He served as ladies' boudoir pet, obliging every whim;
He slept on satin, sniffed at cream, while silk adorned his trim.
And many a fervent, whispered wish has sought his thoughtful ears,
And many a Poodle coat's been wet by royal, secret tears.
For he bore upon his earnest brow, his mistress' cares and woes
And cheered her with his loyal eyes and play-bows at her toes.

As sporting dog he brought the fowl that dropped before the gun,
For his nose is keen and he loves the sport and the pride of a good job done.
His quick eye marked each fallen bird, his great heart followed through
To send him surely, strongly in, each time with zest anew.
Daunted not by coldest lake nor a long dark-water swim,
Nor duck that fell to sheltering reeds, it could not hide from him.
His great coat streaming from his plunge, his pom-pom up behind,
With dark eyes proud and gentle jaw, he'd offer up his find.

He's worked with men at varied tasks, the gipsies taught him one—
To hunt for truffles beneath the beech was nightly forest fun.
O it was all a game to him and he was happiest
To seek before his master's stride, true comrades of the quest.

His talents led him every way and from the law in part!
For his thick coat proved a valued nest to smugglers and their art.
The canine played his part here well: a uniform meant retreat!
And gendarmes got no second glimpse as he sought the crowded street.
Then—quick!—across the border and the guardsmen never knew
Of rarest laces wrapped beneath, nor jewels like sparkling dew.

Not so risque were all his jobs—he's done his turn with sheep
In shadow-cast Swiss valleys and where mountain sides grow steep.
And he knows the feel of traces, yes, he's even pulled a cart—
Adaptability supreme fits him for any part.

Now his pom-pom trim has been the aim of many jeering jest,
For there are those who do not know each part is for the best.
Clipped thus four hundred years ago—(for he was ever vain!)—
Beneath awnings on the market square, beside the River Seine.
His chic coiffure has lasted from that time so long ago
To the modern canine beauty shops—far cry from alfresco!
And through the years he's worn his coat in many different styles,
Commanding ones and modest ones and those provoking smiles.

O, he's had his bit of national fame as hero dog of France,
When he bore the royal banner above his staunchest Poodle prance;
They were marching through the battle and the standard bearer fell—
It was his Poodle saved the colours, stepping proud through all that hell.

Today the Poodle's history is but romance left behind.
It is sad that hunters pass him by, he'd like to show his kind,
And no more truffles does he seek, nor march to war with men,
Nor dance on stage to pleased applause to "do his tricks again!"
Instead he's posed on the end of a string and gaited and posed some more—
He, the most versatile canine of all, must find it a bit of a bore!

Ch. Priscilla of Gaystream (silver standard bitch) owned by Mr. and Mrs. Charles R. Miles, Eslar Kennels.

The obedience ring is a little more fun with "sit" and "come" and "heel,"
Though he hastens to fetch a bit of wood with a pride he does not feel—
For he'd rather race on the living shore with the mud beneath his toes
And fight the cold grey waters for the game that thrills his nose.

Yes, he's truly worked at every task, but notice in each one—
It's always for the people, whom he loves, these deeds he's done.
And that trait comes through in him today, from countless centuries
    strong—
He is the true companion to whomever he may belong.

—MARY VAN DER VEER

Ch. Broughton Golden Count 'M, (apricot Toy male) by Broughton Tui Tui ex Broughton The Little Dowager, breeder-owner, Broughton Kennels.

Ch. Ensarr Glace (by Ch. Lucite of Salmagundi ex Ch. Pillicoc Pearl), white Standard. Note beautiful head and expression. Glace was a Best in Show winner, and sire of champions. Owned by Mrs. W. French Githens, Ensarr Poodles.

67

Poodle Ailments, Prevention and Treatment

A list and description of the maladies that may beset a dog would lead the reader to believe that dog-keeping is a hopelessly difficult and expensive avocation, whereas in truth a dog bred from sound, healthy parents, well fed and otherwise decently cared for, is unlikely to be sick. Most of the canine ills enumerated in the volumes on canine medicine seldom occur. With most of them I have had no experience whatever, despite that I have owned and bred many hundreds of dogs.

Our problem is to keep our dogs well, rather than to cure them after they are sick.

As a breed, Poodles are singularly healthy and normal and subject to few ailments. In my many years of breeding Miniatures, for instance, I have never had a single surgical operation upon a dog or any of the ills that come with whelping in most other breeds. Nor have I found Poodles to be subject to the many skin troubles which so often beset other dogs.

It is true, of course, that a Poodle may pick up mange mites or a fungus infection, like any other dog, and must then be treated accordingly; but the general "hot spots" and eczemas that so often plague other dogs are not often parts of Poodle troubles.

Skin infections are difficult for amateurs to diagnose. If mange, fungus, herpes, or other skin irritations appear, it is best to have a microscopic examination by a veterinarian to make sure of the exact cause, which usually can be easily remedied, once it is known what the trouble is. Many dog owners bark up the wrong tree and apply mange remedies for irritations that are not caused by mange mites at all.

355

Occasionally Poodles have bits of dry skin in their coats, especially when they are casting the dead hair and with it the dead skin. This dryness yields to a simple application of a little warm olive oil or cocoanut oil, or, in most cases, when the coat is brushed out the scruff will disappear without further treatment.

But if Poodles do not commonly have skin troubles, their ears are another matter. I have found Poodles very prone to so-called cankers of the ears. Most of these are caused by allowing water to get into the ears when bathing the dog and failing thoroughly to dry them afterwards. But the trouble is not always so simple and may range from actual mange mites and harvest mites to infection caused by summer foxtails, fungus infections, and even streptococcic infections, sequelae of distemper or other illnesses. All ear trouble is very stubborn; and unlimited patience, unremitting daily care, and great gentleness are required for a complete cure. Any liquid used in the ear should be warmed to the temperature of the dog's body, and the ears should be thoroughly dried out with a swab of cotton afterward, before the application of either powder or salve. When the ear canal is badly caked with brown deposit, it should be irrigated with warm peroxide of hydrogen, allowing the solution to remain in the ear for fifteen minutes, bubbling up and loosening the hard-packed matter, which is then easily removed. After thoroughly drying and cleaning the ear, I dust into the ear boracic acid powder.

Some ear troubles do not readily respond to dry treatment, however, and the use of some one of the various salves or lotions designed for the purpose is then indicated. If continued regular treatment with simple remedies and complete cleanliness does not heal the ear, a veterinarian should be consulted. By careful examination, he will be able to tell what form of ear trouble the Poodle is suffering from and suggest the correct treatment. It is obvious that a fungus infection requires a different medication from that used for harvest mites or ear mange. There is no need to prolong the dog's suffering longer than necessary. Again I want to stress the fact that any treatment of the ear must be undertaken with extreme gentleness and must be unremitting.

Another rather common condition, which does not come under the head of actual illness, is the tendency of almost all Poodles in puppyhood and of some adults to lose flesh and to appear emaciated. Such very active dogs run off flesh very readily and quickly. Some of their loss of flesh may be due to surplus nervous energy, some of it to mal-absorption of their food, or to their not eating enough food to provide fuel for their activity. For thinness resulting from using excess energy, I have found that a nap of several hours immediately after being let out following the midday meal will sometimes result in gain of weight. For mal-assimilation, some form of medicine which will help digest their food is valuable. And for lack of appetite, a tonic is required. Of course, all thin dogs should be examined for worms and checked for a bilious tendency as well. For thinness, whatever its cause, vitamin B_1, given in large doses, is of the utmost value when used consistently over a considerable period.

Some dogs are allergic to certain foods, so if such dogs are not right in weight, try changing the diet until you discover what does and what does not agree with them, always remembering that meat in some form is essential. Some dogs will digest eggs very well; others do not. Some thrive on a small amount of fat, butter, bacon, or fish oil; others cannot tolerate these foods. You must find out by trial and error just what your individual Poodle needs. Cottage cheese is an excellent food, relished and digested by most dogs.

Of course, quiet and calmness at mealtime is essential. A dog compelled to eat with a hubbub of noisy human activity or other interfering dogs is made very nervous, sometimes cross, and often does not thrive as it should. Many wild animals retire to their lairs to eat; and dogs can still benefit from this ancestral habit of taking their food in seclusion.

Distemper in Poodles is a very serious matter, more serious than in many other breeds. Every precaution should be taken to prevent their contracting this canine scourge. They should be immunized very thoroughly against it. Temporary shots of serum up to three months, then a course of permanent shots of vaccine, followed by refresher shots before journeys, first shows and possible exposure, will usually protect a dog against distemper. If this prophylaxis is not absolute, it will reduce the severity of the disease. This immunization should be entrusted to a veterinarian, who should choose the time and method. And dogs should be kept away from known sources of infection at least until fully grown.

Distemper with Poodles tends to take two of its most dangerous forms: the gastro-intestinal form, and that form which affects the nervous system. At the first indication of lack of appetite, dopiness, shivering or cold symptoms, consult your veterinarian at once after taking the dog's temperature per ano. Should this run over 101°, the dog's normal temperature, you may be in for trouble.

It is better to care for the distemper patient at home with the dog in his familiar quarters, if they are warm and secluded, if the owner can spare the time for the constant nursing that distemper requires, and if telephone connection with the attending veterinarian is available. The dog's bed should be in a warm room, free from drafts, raised from the floor, and separate from that of its sick companions, if there are any others. Quiet and freedom from all excitement is indicated.

The diet is all-important, and if the dog can be kept eating regularly

Am. & Can. Ch. Onyx Alec of Miramar (by Ch. Tydel's Black Magic ex Sheldon's Black Angel), black Miniature. Best in Show winner and sire of champions. Owned by June Wery, Poodles Miramar.

Eng. Ch. Braebeck Jonella of Montfleuri (by Firebrave Spiro of Braebeck ex Braebeck Kema of Piperscroft), black Miniature. Full sister to Eng. & Am. Ch. Braebeck Toni of Montfleuri.

the battle is half won. The food should be light, easily digested and without excessive bulk—scraped beef in small and frequent meals, easily assimilated cereals, Pablum or other dry, precooked cereals that are prepared for babies. The various symptoms must be treated as they appear, and the veterinarian should be consulted at every crisis. The dog's temperature taken at frequent and regular intervals is a valid indication of how the case is going.

Although the prophylaxis may or may not confer complete immunity upon a dog, it frequently spells the difference between success and failure, between life and death. Few dogs immunized against distemper contract the disease at all, and fewer of them die of it. Many presumably immunized dogs have distemper in an extremely mild form, with two or three days of lassitude and indisposition, which may escape the notice of all but the most observant owner.

But no matter how light the case has been, it must be remembered that the dog's heart is often badly weakened by distemper. Little or no exercise should be allowed during convalescence; above all, none of a violent kind, as dogs apparently recovered from distemper have been known to keel over and die from exertion. Nor should the dog be permitted excessive excitement or be exposed to chill or wet for at least three months.

Another serious aftermath of this dreadful plague may be a glandular imbalance or a morbid metabolism. This is more serious than usually supposed. Every effort must be made to replace those minerals and vitamins destroyed by the disease and to increase the dog's power to assimilate them. The glandular disturbance may be so great as to impair reproduction, both in stud dogs and brood bitches, for as long as a year after recovery from distemper. The endocrine system must be gradually restored to normal functioning with the use of vitamins, especially B_1, C, and E, and by such treatment with hormones as the veterinarian may prescribe. The glandular balance may be reestablished with correct treatment, but much valuable time may be lost.

In treating ailing Poodles it should always be remembered that they are extremely sensitive to their owner's thoughts and moods. They need reassurance, to know you think they are not in danger. You should make every effort to be cheerfully affectionate and to encourage them. Never give the dog the idea that you are anxious over his condition. Assume that he needs just a little rest and relaxation. Poodles have fighting hearts and a will to live, especially where their devotion to their owner is involved. Many a really sick Poodle has pulled himself from the very jaws of death by the sheer will to live and not leave the person whom he loves. That is why Poodles most need their owner when they are ill and do better for him than for strangers, no matter how kind and gentle the strangers may be.

Fleas, lice, and ticks upon the dog are not difficult to destroy. A bath will serve such a purpose. It is not always so easy to prevent reinfestation. It is certainly safe, however, to spray DDT in solution upon the bed and upon the floors and walls of the dog's quarters. Better than DDT for direct application to the dog I have found to be a preparation known as chlordane. It appears to be harmless even on the youngest of puppies and has no deleterious effect upon the growth, color or texture of the coat. I can vouch that it destroys insects almost instantly.

Insects are vectors of various canine diseases and their presence on and around the dog may result in more than mere annoyance and irritation. This does not imply that every flea means a tapeworm or that every fly is a carrier of distemper virus. However, insects may be hazards as well as pests to a dog. They are rather easily eradicated and prevented, and they should not be tolerated.

There are some half-dozen kinds of internal parasites that infest dogs, and many owners administer vermifuges to their dogs at regular intervals whether the worms they are called upon to expel are present in the dog's intestine or not. Vermifuges are irritants and should be used only when there is adequate reason to believe them necessary. Adult dogs may harbor worms for a considerable period without apparent harm. A dog known to have worms should be relieved of them, but too much solicitude may be as harmful as neglect.

It may be assumed that puppies by weaning time are infested with lumbercoid worms, since few puppies escape such infestation. They may be purged of them with almost any one of the proprietary anthelmintics prepared especially for puppies, directions for the administration of which are given in or on the package in which they are marketed. Seldom mentioned in such directions, however, is the need to have the puppy's alimentary canal empty at the time the vermifuge is given to him. Food and water should be withheld from the puppy for at least twelve hours before he is wormed. This is at least conducive to the success of the treatment.

After a puppy has been cleansed of his worms, he may require no further treatment for them during a long and happy life. If it is suspected that a dog harbors worms of any kind, it is wiser to submit a sample of his feces to a veterinarian for microscopic examination than to dose the animal upon what may be a false assumption. If the examination of the feces reveals the infestation of the dog with worms, he may be treated by the amateur at home with a vermifuge designed to expel the particular kind of worms he is known to harbor, or he may be entrusted for that treatment to the veterinarian, who is equipped for and experienced in such a purge. The latter is the safer course.

The humane owner of a dog known to be infested with worms will be disposed to rid it of them promptly and completely, but without the precipitance and the violence of medication that may harm the dog. A dog's worms are no warrant for the owner's panic.

Mild conjunctivitis and other irritations of the eye can usually be cured with a few days of treatments, night and morning, with opthalmic yellow oxide of mercury of 1 percent or 2 percent or with opthalmic sulphanilimide ointment of 5 percent. Often the use of these remedies may be alternated with better results. A small amount of the ointments should be squeezed from the small tube directly upon the eyeball. Even when no irritation is apparent, it is well to apply a bit of one of these collyriums to the dog's eyes once or twice a week to cleanse them of dust and prevent infection. More serious infections or injuries to a dog's eyes are matters for the attention of the veterinarian.

Poodles are little different from other dogs in their diseases and the remedies for them. However, Poodles bred from healthy parents are seldom ill. There are two mistakes owners of Poodles are prone to make. One is to be always running to the veterinarian at the most minute and often imaginary sign of the dog's indisposition; the other is neglect of real and grave illness in the hope or assumption that the Poodle will recover without medical attention. Of the two errors, the former is the most frequent as it is the least harmful. Poodle owners are, as a lot, intelligent and most of them reasonably affluent. They value their dogs, are alert for their indispositions, and are able to afford veterinary services. This can, as I have intimated, be overdone. The healthy Poodle, immunized against distemper, well fed and reasonably cared for, is not likely to be ill, and nervous anxiety about his health is as harmful to the owner as to the dog.

The veterinarian is, however, an ace-in-the-hole in time of real Poodle trouble. It is frivolous to bother him with minor illnesses than can as well or better be treated at home; but in the event a Poodle's malady is serious or threatens to become serious, it is best to consult the veterinarian without delay. Do not procrastinate. Having consulted him, accept his counsel and follow his instructions, exactly.

Eng. Ch. Black Tulip of Burdiesel and her son, London Pride of Burdiesel, black English Miniatures, owned by Chris Siedler, Burdiesel Kennels, England.

Am. Can. & Mex. Ch. Mariman Silver Beau (by Panorama Hideho ex La Gai Silver Belle), silver Toy. Best in Show winner and sire of champions. Owned by Mrs. Kenneth Law.

68

Home Training of Poodles

_____

THERE are on the market so many adequate books devoted in their entirety to training dogs in general for obedience that it would be supererogatory to treat of that subject here in the limited space at my disposal. It is enough to say that Poodles are notorious mimics and it is only needful to convey to them the idea of what it is desired that they shall do and they may be depended upon to accept the instruction. However, a few hints and cautions about the home training of Poodles, and especially of Poodle puppies, may supplement the information about the training of other kinds of dogs.

Before the teaching of the Poodle is begun at all, it is necessary to win his full affection and confidence. These are well worth the preliminary time invested. The Poodle must never be permitted to fear his trainer's wrath or severity. Poodles have breed traits of character in common, in addition to which they have individual personalities which the trainer must take into account and sometimes make allowances for. It is these quirks of mentality and temperament that make Poodles so interesting and their training at once a problem and a pleasure. Each one must be considered separately and his cooperation courted.

As a lot, Poodles are extremely sensitive and have a sense of justice that no trainer can override. They will comply with anything asked of them, but they refuse to be browbeaten or driven. Some of them are hard-headed and even stubborn for trainers of whom they are suspicious; but once they have thoroughly learned a lesson they will never forget it. Poodles tend to be set in their ways, so that care must be taken to teach them exactly what they are expected to do in exactly the way they are expected to do it for the rest of their days. Any modification of a response is more difficult to inculcate than the original response.

The trainer must never betray the loss of his temper or permit the dog to suspect his irritation. He must speak in a firm, emphatic tone of voice, but never an unkind or petulant tone. The same word or gesture of command must be employed without variation for a given response, and it must be repeated over and over again until the lesson is learned and perfectly mastered. When the Poodle at length perceives the command and responds to it correctly, his obedience should be rewarded with tidbits of food and lavish praise, after which the command is repeated and after the correct response the reward also should be repeated.

No Poodle should ever be punished for its failure to understand what is wanted of it. The routine should be gone over patiently time after time until he comprehends what is expected of him. However, once the trainer is sure that the dog understands, the pupil must feel the teacher's wrath when he fails to obey a command. Punishment may take the form of scolding and grave expression of disapproval or even a spanking (not too hard) with a rolled newspaper. Punishment must be prompt and absolutely just, or it will do more harm than good. A Poodle should never be really whipped for any reason; a real whipping may ruin his temperament and disposition. But when one is absolutely sure a Poodle understands the meaning of a command, he should never be permitted to get away with disobedience. If it takes a week, the trainer must keep right at the task until the dog has made the correct response. The minute the dog obeys, he should be petted and praised and he should be given a respite from his work. The trainer's tact, gentleness, and patience are first requisites in the education of a Poodle.

Dogs, and especially young dogs, should not be tired with long, drawn out lessons. Ten or fifteen minutes a day are in general enough, provided the lessons are regular. They may be more frequent than daily, but in any event, they should not be long and considerable intervals should be given the dog between them.

One of the first things to teach a puppy is that "No!" means "No! Stop what you are doing at once!" When a puppy takes a bedroom slipper to chew upon, it should be taken from him gently with "No!" in a firm voice. When he starts to misbehave in the house, he should be told "No!" and taken outside immediately. With dogs, as with children, a positive rather than a negative attitude succeeds best, and along with the "No!" some alternative activity should be substituted for the one forbidden. When the slipper is taken away from him, he may be given an old shoe for his own or a safe toy to play with. When he is caught in the act of soiling the house, he should be shown where he may safely relieve himself. He must not, above all, be nagged at all day long. With some harmless and approved activity, he will not find so much mischief to get into.

The first thing a house pet must learn is house manners and cleanliness. However, to try to housebreak a tiny puppy is as futile as it is cruel, for like a small human baby, he is unable to control his sphincters. Little puppies should have their own pen or room with the floor covered with newspapers, and they should not be permitted to roam around, wetting on rugs and carpets, because if this is permitted to them in their infancy it will be difficult to break them of the habit after they are larger.

House training should begin when the puppy is four or five months old. When it is undertaken, one person must devote his time to the job, which may sometimes be accomplished in as short a time as five days, but which usually requires some three weeks or a month. With patience and above all with regularity, any puppy can be perfectly housebroken. He must be taken outside to relieve himself regularly, every two hours. If the following facts are remembered, it will save a great deal of trouble. All puppies want to relieve themselves when they wake from sleep, after eating, after violent play, and after vigorous grooming. If a puppy is restless, he should be taken outside immediately. He will soon learn to go to the door and whine or otherwise show a desire to be taken outside, if the same door is used consistently to take him out.

It is my policy during the house training age of a puppy to confine him at night (and often during parts of the day) in a pleasant, warm sleeping box, with a door which can be firmly closed. The puppy is put to bed in such a box after his last run at night—as late at night as is convenient—and let out as early as may be in the morning. He is reluctant to soil the bed in which he is closely confined, and he soon learns to control his sphincters and to retain the excreta. The use of such a sleeping box has another purpose also; it teaches the Poodle to remain quietly shut up so that he can be left for short periods during the day safely out of mischief. In later life, a dog so trained will accept confinement in a crate as a matter of course, if one wishes to travel with him or to ship him. Naturally, no puppy should be confined for long periods and one should always be taken out-of-doors to relieve himself before he is put in his box and immediately upon being released from it.

One of the most important things about housebreaking a puppy is to take him to the same spot each time he is taken out of the house for relief and to make sure he does what he is taken out for. He should never just be turned out and forgotten. It is wiser to stay with the puppy and make sure that he has emptied his bladder or his bowels. Puppies, like children, are inattentive little beings, and very often go out and play only to come

365

in and soil the floor of the house. But if it is insisted upon that they relieve themselves outdoors before they are readmitted to the house, this does not occur.

When a puppy relieves himself out-of-doors, he should be lavishly praised and told, "That is a good boy. So-and-so is such a good boy." Soon he will learn what is meant when he is told, "Come on and be a good boy." When the Poodle puppy comes to know what he is taken outside for, half the battle is won, for the Poodle's desire is to comply with human wishes. The trainer must not relax, however, until the puppy responds each and every time he is taken out and the trainer must be right there to make sure of what the puppy does.

If the puppy misbehaves in the house and can be caught in the very act (no puppy remembers what he did fifteen minutes ago), he should be taken to the soiled spot and forced to listen to the riot act. In the course of such a lecture, the floor may be violently struck with a rolled newspaper for several minutes. Then the dog should be taken out-of-doors immediately to the area where he is accustomed to relieve himself. It is seldom necessary to strike the dog, since he will respond to the noise of the paper and the scolding words as well.

No puppy can be expected to retain his excreta for long intervals. If a puppy is not taken out every two hours, and oftener if necessary, he soon loses heart, gets confused, and misbehaves. Every two hours should be the rule until the dog is completely grown up, after which every three hours, with at least one and better two long walks each day, will suffice. Dirty dogs are the results of the lack of consideration for them by their owners and ignorance of the basic requirements of cleanliness. The abuse of house-broken dogs, who are expected to endure long, weary hours without relief, is more common than one likes to believe. No matter how well trained a dog may be, he should never be imposed upon with such thoughtless cruelty.

Spots on the rug or floor which the dog has soiled should be so thoroughly cleaned that no odor remains, and they may be later sprinkled with cayenne pepper. This tends to prevent the repetition of the offense, since dogs are prone to relieve themselves in the same place time after time.

Housebreaking a dog is a simple process, all that is necessary being watchfulness, consideration, and patient regularity.

There are other lessons to be learned. If it is not desired that a Poodle shall get on such furniture as he may wish, he should be given an old chair for himself, a covered new one, or a basket well off the drafts of the floor. He should be taught that this is his (Poodles have a keen sense of possession) and a refuge where he may go with his ball and his other cherished playthings. The trainer should be firm about the Poodle's getting on other pieces of furniture. Again, "No!" firmly spoken, is all that is needed. If he does not obey, he should be taken off the forbidden spot, carried to his own bed, petted, given his plaything, and told to "Stay." If he again gets out, he must be held in the place where he is wanted and told to "Stay!"

All dogs should be taught to sit or lie quietly on command. This is brought about by putting the dog in his bed and telling him to "Stay there." Every time he starts to leave, he should be put back and held there until he knows what is meant. He should not be forced to "stay" too long, but should be released with an "All right!" after approximately five minutes. A Poodle will soon learn what is expected of him.

To teach a dog to lie down, pressure should be placed on the hips with the right hand and the dog's front legs be pulled forward with the left hand. He should be held gently in position and the word "Down" used. This should be repeated several times each day. To teach a dog to sit, one should use gentle pressure on the hips along with the command "Sit." The front legs should not be touched, but the hand should be kept on the neck until the dog understands what is wanted of him. Then the "All right!" command will allow the dog to get away.

No effort should be made to teach a dog two things at once. He should master one lesson before he starts on another. The routine should be firm and the procedure, including the commands, should always be identical. Commands should not be shouted. The speech should be distinct and emphatic, but the manner reassuring. The dog should feel perfectly safe and confident while at his lessons. He wants nothing so much as to please his master.

Dogs must be made to understand the word "Come" or that the calling of their names means "Come." As a rule, merely calling them and rewarding them with a tidbit or loving praise when they respond is enough. If a dog is headstrong about this, a long cord attached to the collar enables the trainer to reel him in at the command "Come." I have never found it necessary to do this; and I have few greater pleasures than the sight of my Poodles rushing happily and tumbling over one another to get to me when I call them. Each one strives to be first to arrive at my side for an affectionate caress.

Car manners are important for the dogs which ride with us, and I know of nothing more annoying than a dog that refuses to stay put in an automobile, but rather jumps back and forth, up and down, seeking to be the center of attention, every minute. Much as I love dogs, I have ridden with some dogs that completely exhausted me after a few miles of travel. Dogs like to see the passing show through the windows of the car, and it is unkind to force them to stay in a place from which they cannot see out. A place in a car should be allotted to a dog and the dog should be taught to stay in it. Every time he jumps down from his place, he should be put back and told to "Stay," or "Sit," or "Down," always using the same word for a specific command. He must be made to understand that "No!" means "No!" He will soon learn, and master and dog will have many pleasant hours together, since all dogs love to ride in an automobile.

I am no believer in allowing dogs to be off the leash in traffic, since I have seen many pitiful accidents from the practice, even with dogs that were presumably well trained. However, the command "Stop!" on the lead before crossing the street is a useful one. If the trainer says "Stop!" and pulls the dog to a complete halt, he will soon learn the command and it will be unnecessary to pull him up short.

Many persons teach their dogs to "heel," that is to stay at the level of their hip, but I have mainly to do with show dogs and find that the inclination to "heel" in the show ring is not conducive to a dog's appearing at his best. Hence I do not teach my dogs to "heel" and never use the command.

I find that so-called obedience training is not best for show dogs and it adds to their confusion in the ring. Therefore, I do not try to make obedience dogs of dogs I intend to use for exhibition. A show dog should be taught show manners, but a dog trained for obedience should be kept for that purpose alone.

A few short, simple commands uttered in a firm voice—"No," "Down," "Sit," "Stay," "Come," "All right," "Good dog"—are about all a puppy needs to know to begin with and they can be employed in many situations. Of course, everybody wants his dog to learn his way of doing; and, once the rudiments are learned, the rest follows simply and easily. Dogs that are our daily companions learn to understand not only our moods but our unspoken thoughts. All dogs should be talked to, just as one would speak to another person, conversationally and considerately. One is astonished at how much and how readily they understand. The bond between a Poodle and the person who loves it and whom it loves can grow into a vast comfort and joy.

These few suggestions will enable the amateur to begin the training of his Poodle. Thereafter, it is recommended that the reader obtain the following books:

The Complete Novice Obedience Course
The Complete Open Obedience Course
The Complete Utility Obedience Course

—all by Blanche Saunders and published by Howell Book House, 845 Third Avenue, New York, N.Y. 10022.

Miss Blanche Saunders with her famous black Standard Poodle, Ch. Carillon Jester, U.D.T., Int. C. D. Jester was the star of two Obedience demonstrations at Yankee Stadium, before crowds of 75,000, and was featured on television and in many Obedience films.

Eng. Ch. Oakington Puckshill Ambersunblush (by Puckshill Ambersuncrush ex Puckshill Ambersprite), apricot Toy bitch. Best in Show all-breeds, Crufts, England 1966. Bred by Mrs. Myles Dobson. Owned by Mrs. Paul Perry, Tio Pepi Kennels, England.

Ch. Frenches Golden Jewel, Toy from the Kennels of Mrs. Price Jones, England. *Photo by B. Thurse, England.*

69

Color Breeding

BLACK

BLACK is the basic, dominant color in Poodles, as in other breeds that carry the same range of color. When mated with any of the other colors, it acts as a pure dominant. And as a rule it also carries the greatest perfection of type.

A black Poodle's coat should be absolutely dense and inky, and the skin should have a distinct bluish cast. To keep it this way, or to clear it if it is shaded, is relatively simple. The magic formula is simply to breed black to black and never allow the admixture of any other color. But outside European countries where it is obligatory, this is very seldom done consistently. Yet, without question it is the only way to get and keep inky black, practically unfading coats.

Only one cross is safe—that of black's own dilution, brown—which, if sparingly used, will not affect the purity of color. But, of course, such brown crosses must be used very sparingly and not too close together. Some breeders believe that although this cross does not affect the coat color, it does lighten the color of the eyes. The fact that brown does not affect the purity of black coats is a recognized fact, and even in countries where the mixing of colors is banned, such a mixture is permitted.

Many black strains, such as my own Sherwood Hall, black-bred for many generations, carry a brown gene which causes browns to appear every now and then in an otherwise black litter. Such browns carry very dark eyes and pigmentation.

Silver and blue crosses in a black strain are fatal for soundness of color and most difficult to breed out. They leave a most unpleasant grayish shading in the coat and are crosses that never should be used.

It is not definitely known whether eye color is part of the same gene for color, or whether it follows a pattern of its own. In countries where black must be bred only to black, the eyes are very dark, almost black, and in my own Sherwood strain I achieved the same result. But nothing has been proven scientifically. Be that as it may, eye color, like any other point, can be fixed by selection. There is no doubt that light eyes have grave need of correction in the majority of our American blacks and also in many of our recent English importations. A dark, velvety, oval eye plays an important part in the beautiful Poodle expression we all desire in our dogs. It is too valuable an asset to overlook or to lose carelessly. And in no other color does a light eye stand out as unpleasantly as in a black Poodle.

WHITE

White is simply an absence of any color whatever and is a recessive. So a white dog mated to another white dog, no matter how much color there may be behind them on both sides, will always produce an all-white litter. And it is this fact that has made it possible to improve the faulty head type in white Miniatures in recent years. As an example, the paper white Ch. Snow Boy of Fircot, by Harwee of Mannerhead, a black from an exceptionally good-headed strain from Solitaire of Piperscroft, a gray bitch, when mated to pure white bitches produced white puppies with the type of head of their black grandsire. Ch. Snow Boy therefore became one of the greatest sires of whites of all time.

White, like the other recessives, may be buried in a colored strain for many generations, and when two dogs both carrying a white gene are mated together, a white puppy is a possibility regardless of what color they themselves may be.

White has in the past been freely used as a dilutant in the creation of silver Standards from blacks, and also to produce apricots from browns. But although it apparently works better with blacks to produce silvers than it does to dilute brown, it is the trickiest of crosses. A certain amount of mismarked offspring always appear, varying in degree. Perhaps the few clear-colored dogs are worth the waste and pain of destroying the worthless dogs that result—perhaps not. That would, I think, depend upon the type and quality of the individual dogs.

How difficult it is to get good, sound, solid colors by crossing white with colors is amply shown by the struggles of Toy breeders. Working with purebred white Toys and solid-colored Miniatures, the mismarked Poodles that appear are legion. The scope and variety of mismarkings are tremendous as compared with mere handfuls of really sound colored Toys.

372

BROWN

Brown is a recessive or dilution of black and closely related to it, although the color globules are different in shape. And if black is unharmed by a brown cross, brown is greatly benefited by a black cross to keep the color and pigmentation dark.

Like all recessives, brown bred to brown breeds true. For instance, my Ch. Sherwood The Chocolate Dandy, the only brown to appear in many generations in a black-bred strain, when mated to a brown bitch invariably threw an entire litter of browns. Whereas, bred to a black carrying a brown gene, the browns, if any, were in the minority. Of course, to produce even one brown puppy, both black parents must carry a brown gene.

On the Continent only the darkest shades of brown are recognized, such as the deepest shades of chocolate. But in England and with us, all the various shades are allowed, and there is no color that has as many charming color variations. These range from almost black chocolate—and by the way, all brown puppies, no matter what shade they are going to be in later life, are born very dark. The beautiful reddish chestnut brown is brilliant, and there is a shade which is almost liver colored. I had a bitch that was a dark walnut color like old furniture, and there are cinnamon browns both light and dark. There may be pale brown of cafe-au-lait and parchment shades, and of course the various shades of gold from rich old gold to pale champagne. The pinkish apricots and creams are all browns further diluted, with cream as the furthest dilution of all at the end of the line.

The worst and commonest defect in browns is their marked tendency towards light eyes, pale yellow at their worst, with light pinkish eye-rims, lips, and noses. This robs them of true Poodle outlook and expression and gives them either a bold or a vapid expression.

The eyes of all browns, dark or light, should be several shades darker than their coats and just as dark as it is possible to get them. Dark eyes are always surrounded by dark eye-rims, and the lips and nose are the same dark shade. One or two black crosses help to keep the eyes and pigmentation dark. A really dark-eyed brown is invaluable for the breeding of browns.

In the lighter dilute shades, it is possible to get actual black eyes and correct pigmentation, which adds a hundred percent to the attractiveness of these charming colors.

SILVER AND BLUE

Blue and silver are, of course, the best-known dilutants of black, and as they are recessive they will breed true. At their best they are beautiful dogs, but none of the other colors are as difficult to get correct in color, properly modeled in head, and sound of structure. Even now they are not the equals of the blacks in Poodle type.

The correct blue is a light, clear, unshaded blue, about the color of a light, not dark, blue Persian cat. And when it is correct and carries black eyes and nose, it can be very lovely. However, this shade is extremely rare, and a dark, dismal steel, or even merely unsound black, has very often been considered ideal, which is, of course, very far from being the case.

Silver, which is the furthest dilution of black, should, in my opinion, be as near pale platinum as possible and with few shadings. However, light shadings of a darker color, while not desired, are not too much of a drawback.

There is no more popular color than silver or none as greatly misunderstood. Gun metal, taupe with a brownish tinge, a sort of dirty pewter, and an all-over dreary, dark gray are very common, and, to my mind, neither silver, blue, nor black, and are very depressing.

The statement made by Mrs. Campbell Inglis that the famous Miniature bitch "Leila" and her famous grandson Eng. Ch. Flashlight of Mannerhead were both silvers with a distinct and beautiful lavender tinge, I believe is most interesting.

Silver puppies, like the apricots that come from silver breeding, are nearly always born jet-black and then gradually turn lighter at the roots of their hair. Very occasionally a puppy is born pure silver, but not often. The black disappears, sometimes rapidly and sometimes with annoying slowness. Most fanciers cut the puppy hair down to the light color "to clear" the color.

Silver and blue may be bred to each other and will invariably produce silvers and blues. No other cross is permissible, though cat breeders sometimes use a cross of cream to lighten the blue. However, in my experience, you may get anything except paler silver in such a cross. Nothing ruins the light, clear color more quickly or more effectively than a cross of black, except perhaps a brown infusion. Nothing is gained by such a mixture and much is lost.

In Miniatures, silvers have existed from the very foundation of English breeding and for this reason have also been present in Toys. But until very recently silver Standards were extremely rare. A number of kennels have been experimenting with some success in diluting blacks with white blood to produce silvers. Although a great number of mismarked Poodles have resulted, a few pale silvers have appeared as well. Now there are enough of them so that they can be bred to each other and so avoid, to a great extent, the mismarkings that occurred in the original cross.

374

Silcresta Silver Smoke, Miniature Poodle, with the Toy, Eng. Ch. Silcresta Silver Sprat.

Three generations of Silver Miniature champions: Eng. Ch. Silcresta Silver Swank (foreground) with his dam Eng. Ch. Silcresta Beechover Silver Slipper (right), and his daughter Eng. Ch. Silcresta Silver Siren.

Ch. Meisen Golden Gamin (by Little Sir Echo of Meisen ex Aprishan of Bouchard), apricot Miniature male. Specialty Best in Show and Group winner. Sire of several Champions.

Ch. Pixiecroft Sunbeam (by Ch. Meisen Golden Gamin ex Merriel of Pixiecroft), apricot Miniature bitch, America's greatest winning apricot Poodle. Bred by Mark Crawford and Ted Doucette, Pixiecroft Kennels. Owned by Mrs. Gardner Cassatt, Beaufresne Poodles.

Ch. Beaufresne The Gilded Lily (by Ch. Summercourt Square Dancer of Fircot ex Ch. Pixiecroft Sunbeam), apricot Miniature bitch. Specialty and all-breed Best in Show winner. (Pictured as a puppy.) Bred and owned by Mrs. Gardner Cassatt, Beaufresne Poodles.

APRICOTS

Apricot is still the rarest of the colors in all three varieties of Poodles, the most difficult to get, and the hardest to care for as it tends to fade in the sun. It is, at its best, extremely beautiful, and because of this and the rarity of the color, everybody wants to have an apricot Poodle. Many breeders are trying all sorts of combinations to produce this color, usually most unsuccessfully. It is not understood, for the most part.

In both creams and apricots there exist two types—the dogs that have light eyes and brownish or lighter eye-rims, lips, and noses; and the dogs that have black eyes, eye-rims, lips, and noses. Much latitude has, in the past, been allowed in the matter of eye color and pigmentation, when this color was rarer than it is at present. But the most expert English breeders of both past and present agree with me that since light eyes spoil the beautiful Poodle expression so sadly, even in the rarest light colors they are to be condemned.

Apricot is a term which, like brown, covers a somewhat wide field of color, ranging from all the shades of gold, from pale to dark orange, and so on to the true apricot, with a pinkish tinge exactly like the inside of an actual ripe apricot.

At present, apricots fall into three different classes. First, those that appear in cream lines. These are born rather a deep, clear color like what in England is called "a ginger cat." These puppies tend to fade later to cream, and may or may not return to their original color as they reach full maturity. Second, apricots that come of basically colored lines of brown, silver, and possibly some black blood. These are, like the silvers, born black and gradually turn lighter, and do not tend to fade unless exposed to too strong direct sunlight, which no apricot can tolerate. Third, apricots that come from a strongly line-bred family of this color. These do not fade as readily as the cream-bred apricots, but are still, of course, comparatively rare.

True apricot is just what it says—the exact color of the inside of a ripe apricot, pinkish in tone and soundly colored right down to the skin. The ears, especially in young dogs, are usually somewhat darker but of the same shade, and should not, in my opinion be faulted unless they are an off-color or different shade. Within the scope of this rare color there are several shades, including the sensationally beautiful clear orange coloring, and various shades of gold from deep old-gold to lighter tints. Also, the pinkish apricot may vary from light to dark in tone. Nearly all apricot litters contain at least one cream, which is natural since cream is just one step down the scale in color and so closely connected. Many creams of apricot breeding

377

will produce deep-colored apricots if bred correctly to another deep-colored apricot.

Like all recessives, apricot should be bred to apricot with as many apricot ancestors as possible. For instance, I have several litters that have two apricot parents, four apricot grandparents, six apricot great-grandparents, six apricot great-great-grandparents, and six apricot great-great-great-grand-parents. Of course, this is extremely unusual in a rare color but a certain amount of line breeding to color is necessary to preserve apricot and to keep the color clear and unshaded.

Apricot puppies are born a clear unshaded apricot, some lighter than others and with or without brown toenails. They are usually darker at birth than they are when mature. There are also apricots which are born either black or brindle and clear the way silvers do. They have one great disadvantage—the colored hair almost never clears completely on their ears. My experience indicates that such puppies do not occur when both parents are apricot but only when one of them is a different color.

In my decade of breeding apricots I found a number of problems. First of all, in this rarest of the color types, head type, particularly, has often been sacrificed for the sake of color. The average apricot tends to have, like the early whites, the ancestral head—thick skull, short foreface, round eyes, and small, flying ears. Second, those with too much brown blood have very light eyes and pinkish-brown eye-rims, lips, and noses. This is not faulted in our Standard but it is most unattractive and has kept the apricots from the popularity they so richly deserve. Third, the correct color is difficult to hold and with too much white or cream blood tends to fade.

The apricot color has been known for more than 50 years in Poodles. The first Poodle to be registered as apricot was Whippendell Abricotinette, who was whelped October 11, 1912. Abricotinette, a Miniature, was bred by Millie Brunker of the famous Whippendell Poodles. Miss Brunker was partial to the rarer colors and did considerable experimenting in color breeding. Her blue Moufflon Bleu, who was of great use in the creation of the silver Miniature, was the grandsire of Abricotinette. Unfortunately Abricotinette was killed before she could be used to establish a line of this color.

The next apricots of note did not make their appearance until the advent of Ch. Venda's Sunkista of Blakeen (January 17, 1935) and her daughter Ch. Venda's Winter Sunshine of Blakeen. Sunkista was by the famous blue Venda's Blue Masterpiece out of a brown. Her daughter, Sunshine, was by Petit Morceau of Piperscroft, who was a black with a brown and an apricot gene. Morceau also sired the apricot Ch. Venda's Gold Bell (whose dam was a white). Perhaps due to the lack of the right apricot male for these bitches, this line has not continued as an unbroken apricot line. Winter Sunshine was bred to Ch. Venda's The Black Imp of Catawba and she produced the lovely brown Ch. Blakeen Eldorado. The apricot gene was hidden by the black and the brown genes, but it did reappear in later years when given the opportunity. Ch. Meisen Golden Gaiete is a latter day descendant of Sunkista and Winter Sunshine.

The mink breeders have done enormous research at great expense in an effort to produce new and rare colors. They have even hired trained geneticists in their quest. Poodle breeders with the basic colors of black, brown and white plus the dilution factors in varying degrees have created, mostly haphazardly, a tremendous range of Poodle colors. Unfortunately great harm has been done to the blacks and browns, and breeders in all three varieties are concerned with the blacks and browns fading in later years. Even worse than this is the tremendous number of mismarked Poodles which continue to appear each year. Now that certain apricot lines have been created, the introduction or mixing of other colors with apricots is unnecessary and harmful.

Hilda Meisenzahl's Meisen strain is the most successful in this country and she is emphatic in stating that apricots should only be bred to apricots, and that by doubling the apricot genes the color will deepen. Her accomplishments are outlined in the story of the Meisen Kennel earlier in this volume.

The apricot Miniatures and Toys in England for the most part are descended from a deep apricot dog named Aureolin of Toytown. Aureolin was by the cream Whippendell Petit Eclair (Whippendell Duvet ex Nunsoe Sixpence) out of an apricot Bechamel of Toytown (Paul of Toytown ex Whippendell Bambinette). English breeders interested in apricots bred to Aureolin and this is perhaps the strongest continuing apricot line in existence today. The apricots of Venda's, Frenches, Fircot, Puckshill and Greatcoats all trace back to Aureolin not once but many times. In this country the Sherwoods, the Broughtons and the Millbrooks all descend from Aureolin through the Aureolin-Frenches line. Capt. and Mrs. James Brough's Broughton Kennels have been pioneers in the breeding of apricots, both in Toys and Miniatures. Their Ch. Broughton Golden Count 'M is a lovely little apricot Toy. Three English apricot Toy champions, Eng. Ch. Frenches Golden Jewel (five c.c.'s), Eng. Ch. Rhosbridge Golden Shred (11 c.c.'s) and Eng. Ch. Oakington Puckshill Ambersunblush (Best in Show at Crufts) all go back directly in tail male line to Aureolin.

Successful apricot breeders agree that apricots should be kept pure. The introduction of any other color presents problems. Breeding to blacks usually results in the apricot being covered completely. Breeding to browns introduces the danger of unattractive brown noses and points. Breeding to pure whites poses the problem of white chests and toe markings or even a dark apricot line down the back on a cream dog. Much is lost and little gained. Mrs. Dobson, Ambersunblush's breeder, suggests, "Start with a good apricot bred apricot bitch, the purer the line the better. If you can stick to this colour they will get deeper through each generation. All white should be eliminated." Miss Meisenzahl and Mrs. Dobson have been most generous in sharing their own experiences. Their advice should be most helpful to those interested in this beautiful color.

Earlier I made the statement that apricots with too much white-bred white ancestry behind them tend to fade. A dog like Mrs. Hoyt's famous Ch. Snow Boy of Fircot, with a famous black sire (Harwee of Mannerhead, sire of two champions) and a gray dam, is vastly different from a white-bred white of German or French origin with nothing behind it but white dogs for many generations, or the original white-bred white Toy Poodles. It was this introduction of colored blood, black and its dilutant silver, which accounts for the splendid Poodle type of the Fircot Miniatures and others bred like them, which includes the majority of our modern white winners. Blacks and dilute black that have carried the true type from the beginning were generations ahead in sheer type from the early whites, and, for that matter, even those purebred whites of French and German breeding today. It is from the colors behind them that the best modern whites derive their beautiful lean heads, oval eyes, long ear leathers and general all-over excellence of type. White or the complete absence of color is recessive and, like all recessives, breeds true when mated to dogs of the same recessive color. This fact made Ch. Snow Boy, mated to white bitches, the greatest white sire of his day. Now, individual whites from colored breeding like the Fircots do less harm in the breeding of apricots than pure white ones. However, white-bred whites tend to lighten the color and give it a fading tendency, as breeders of light colored Toys with a long line of white-bred Toys behind them know to their sorrow.

And what of creams? Creams, unlike whites, do not lack pigmentation and are genetically far different from whites, being the furthest dilution of brown, just a step below apricot in the color scale and closely related to it. Creams always appear in apricot strains. And with the advent of so many very beautiful cream dogs, this color is beginning to be more appreciated and understood. One thing has not been clearly stated or understood until quite lately. This is that creams may fade to such an extent that they appear to be ice white. This, I'm sorry to say, has been helped by the dislike of the color on the part of many breeders and handlers of the past who would look at a beautiful cream dog and say, "Oh well, it can be bleached white," which has always irritated me, since I've always thought cream a lovely soft color in its own right. But without any artificial aid some creams fade of themselves.

Professor Whitney's examination of white hair from a number of white breeds revealed the presence of minute color globules in some of the hairs

Ch. Blakeen Van Aseltine, owned by Howard Tyler.

of apparently pure white dogs. Commander Hinton, in his column in the English *Our Dogs,* tells of considerable work done by British breeders on this subject. This shows that many white Poodles that look white are in reality faded creams and not genetically pure white at all. He believes, after a great many years of breeding whites exclusively, that the puppy that is whelped cream and later turns white is simply a faded cream. My own experience bears this out. Therefore, since I think cream is a beautiful color, I try my best in my breeding operations to produce creams that are deep and rich of color and not a washed-out hue. By the same token, I want my whites to be a glistening, snowy white like something off a wedding cake. I also class any puppies whelped cream as creams, regardless of how white they appear later in life.

The two terms "white" and "cream" should not be used loosely and incorrectly as they so often are. It can be seen that they are absolutely different colors, though both recessive—one the total absence of color, the other the furthest dilution of brown.

Professor Whitney's summary and conclusion after the examination of hair samples of a number of white breeds, including white Poodles, stated, "The Poodles with icy white coats belong to the black hair type, those with warmer tones in their white coats belong to the yellow hair type. Corrobo-

Ch. Istar de la Nuit and Ch. Pavil-lon Baldassare, photographed in France in 1954 when they were being exhibited there, owned and handled by Frank T. Sabella.

rated by microscopic examinations and breeding reports." The black haired type have dark eyes and black eye-rims, lips, and noses. Those of the yellow type have light eyes, and brown eye-rims, lips, and noses in the case of apricots and creams. All creams and apricots with dark eyes, eye-rims, lips, and noses, have a predominance of black haired inheritance. Thus, scientific data confirms the experience of practical breeders. It is, of course, obvious that white dogs of colored breeding that carry even a tiny amount of color even in a few hairs of their coat are not genetically white, and undoubtedly carry cream and probably apricot genes as well.

I hope the foregoing will clarify the situation as far as apricot breeding is concerned and show clearly that white, white-bred whites are harmful in apricot breeding, although whites of colored ancestry may not be; and that creams are not just impure, incorrect whites but a color in their own right and closely related to apricot.

MISMARKED POODLES

Perhaps this is as good a place as any to discuss a serious menace to the Poodle breed and one which apparently occurs not only from the mixing of white with the other solid colors but also from the use of too much silver blood in a black strain.

The so-called "mismarks" seem to show a definite pattern, either the complete "Airedale" markings or a broken pattern with the color on only some of the parts in which tan is found on the Airedale instead of on all of them. Blacks or browns may carry this design in any of the dilute colors, such as brown, tan, cream or any of the many shades of brown, or the markings may be silver or blue or even white. The off-color runs along the inside of the legs, back and front, across the chest, along the side of the face, under the tail, under the chin, and on the paws.

Scientifically, I believe, the mismarking is caused by an incomplete masking of the dilute color by a dominant one. In any event the result is a parti-color, and the Poodle should be a solid color. The theory is that the puppy will in time change to the color of the markings, but this does not as a rule prove to be the case. Selling such a puppy as a pet does not end the matter, for if it is bred it will likely produce other parti-colors like itself. The pattern is hereditary, and even solid colored dogs from a mismarked strain will produce mismarked puppies. This mismarking may skip a generation, or even two, only to recur. This is so recognized that many breeders in England, where mismarkings are more common than with us, refuse to mate mismarked bitches to their good studs or even a bitch of solid color known to have mismarked ancestry. Of course, such a strain should never be used for breeding, and any dog or bitch known to carry this inheritance should never be bred.

Experiments should be left in the hands of those who wisely limit the color-cross to one mating and who understand just what they are trying to do. White should not be bred to any other color except white. Of all the colors, it is the worst offender in producing mismarked solids.

SUMMARY OF COLOR BREEDING

To sum up briefly the known facts concerning the various colors:

Black is heavily dominant over all the other colors and will overlay them in a Mendelian pattern. Mismarks come when the overlay is not complete. Black also carries the banner for true Poodle type.

White is recessive, and bred to another white or cream will produce only whites or creams.

Brown is a recessive. Brown bred to brown will produce only brown.

Apricot is a recessive. Apricot bred to apricot will produce apricot or perhaps some cream if this color appears close up in the background.

Pure silver to silver will produce only silver. However, two hybrid silvers may also produce whites, creams, or silver-beiges, if those genes are present.

Hybrid blacks may carry any number of colors recessively. These colors can only be determined by breeding, since the dog in appearance will be black.

The safest rule in color breeding is to breed like color to like color.

In founding strains of the dilute colors, not only should the mating be to the same color, but also, a certain amount of line breeding is recommended.

BIBLIOGRAPHY

ALL OWNERS of pure-bred dogs will benefit themselves and their dogs by enriching their knowledge of breeds and of canine care, training, breeding, psychology and other important aspects of dog management. The following list of books covers further reading recommended by judges, veterinarians, breeders, trainers and other authorities. Books may be obtained at the finer book stores and pet shops, or through Howell Book House Inc., publishers, New York, N.Y.

Breed Books

AFGHAN HOUND, Complete — *Miller & Gilbert*
AIREDALE, Complete — *Edwards*
ALASKAN MALAMUTE, Complete — *Riddle & Seely*
BASSET HOUND, Complete — *Braun*
BEAGLE, Complete — *Noted Authorities*
BOSTON TERRIER, Complete
  Denlinger and Braunstein
BOXER, Complete — *Denlinger*
BRITTANY SPANIEL, Complete — *Riddle*
BULLDOG, New Complete — *Hanes*
BULL TERRIER, New Complete — *Eberhard*
CAIRN TERRIER, Complete — *Marvin*
CHIHUAHUA, Complete — *Noted Authorities*
COLLIE, Complete — *Official Publication of the*
  Collie Club of America
DACHSHUND, The New — *Meistrell*
DOBERMAN PINSCHER, Complete
  Noted Authorities
ENGLISH SETTER, New Complete — *Tuck & Howell*
ENGLISH SPRINGER SPANIEL, New
  Goodall & Gasow
FOX TERRIER, New Complete — *Silvernail*
GERMAN SHEPHERD DOG, Complete — *Bennett*
GERMAN SHORTHAIRED POINTER, New — *Maxwell*
GOLDEN RETRIEVER, Complete — *Fischer*
GREAT DANE, New Complete — *Noted Authorities*
IRISH SETTER, New — *Thompson*
IRISH WOLFHOUND, Complete — *Starbuck*
KEESHOND, Complete — *Peterson*
LABRADOR RETRIEVER, Complete — *Warwick*
MINIATURE SCHNAUZER, Complete — *Eskrigge*
NEWFOUNDLAND, New Complete — *Chern*
NORWEGIAN ELKHOUND, New Complete — *Wallo*
OLD ENGLISH SHEEPDOG, Complete — *Mandeville*
PEKINGESE, Quigley Book of — *Quigley*
POMERANIAN, New Complete — *Ricketts*
POODLE, New Complete — *Hopkins & Irick*
POODLES IN PARTICULAR — *Rogers*
POODLE CLIPPING AND GROOMING BOOK,
  Complete — *Kalstone*
PUG, Complete — *Trullinger*
ST. BERNARD, New Complete
  Noted Authorities, rev. Raulston
SAMOYED, Complete — *Ward*
SCHIPPERKE, Offical Book of — *Root, Martin, Kent*
SCOTTISH TERRIER, Complete — *Marvin*
SHETLAND SHEEPDOG, New — *Riddle*
SHIH TZU, The (English) — *Dadds*
TERRIERS, The Book of All — *Marvin*
TOY DOGS, Kalstone Guide to Grooming All
  Kalstone
TOY DOGS, All About — *Ricketts*
WEST HIGHLAND WHITE TERRIER,
  Complete — *Marvin*
YORKSHIRE TERRIER, Complete
  Gordon & Bennett

Care and Training

DOG OBEDIENCE, Complete Book of
  Saunders
NOVICE, OPEN AND UTILITY COURSES — *Saunders*
DOG CARE AND TRAINING, Howell
  Book of — *Howell, Denlinger, Merrick*
DOG CARE AND TRAINING FOR BOYS
  AND GIRLS — *Saunders*
DOG TRAINING FOR KIDS — *Benjamin*
DOG TRAINING, Koehler Method of
  Koehler
GO FIND! Training Your Dog to Track
  Davis
GUARD DOG TRAINING, Koehler Method of
  Koehler
OPEN OBEDIENCE FOR RING, HOME
  AND FIELD, Koehler Method of — *Koehler*
SPANIELS FOR SPORT (English) — *Radcliffe*
STORY OF DOG OBEDIENCE — *Saunders*
SUCCESSFUL DOG TRAINING, The
  Pearsall Guide to — *Pearsall*
TRAINING THE RETRIEVER — *Kersley*
TRAINING YOUR DOG TO WIN
  OBEDIENCE TITLES — *Morsell*

Breeding

ART OF BREEDING BETTER DOGS, New
  Onstott
HOW TO BREED DOGS — *Whitney*
HOW PUPPIES ARE BORN — *Prine*
INHERITANCE OF COAT COLOR
  IN DOGS — *Little*

General

COMPLETE DOG BOOK, The
  Official Pub. of American Kennel Club
DOG IN ACTION, The — *Lyon*
DOG BEHAVIOR, New Knowledge of
  Pfaffenberger
DOG JUDGING, Nicholas Guide To
  Nicholas
DOG NUTRITION, Collins Guide to
  Collins
DOG OWNER'S HANDBOOK, The New
  Hajas & Sarkany
DOG PSYCHOLOGY — *Whitney*
DOG STANDARDS ILLUSTRATED
DOGSTEPS, Illustrated Gait at a
  Glance — *Elliott*
ENCYCLOPEDIA OF DOGS, International
  Dangerfield, Howell & Riddle
JUNIOR SHOWMANSHIP HANDBOOK
  Brown & Mason
SUCCESSFUL DOG SHOWING, Forsyth Guide to
  Forsyth
TRIM, GROOM AND SHOW YOUR DOG,
  How to — *Saunders*
WHY DOES YOUR DOG DO THAT?
  Bergman
OUR PUPPY'S BABY BOOK (blue or pink)